THE
OXYRHYNCHUS PAPYRI
VOLUME XLVI

THE
OXYRHYNCHUS PAPYRI

VOLUME XLVI

EDITED WITH TRANSLATIONS AND NOTES BY

J. R. REA

Graeco-Roman Memoirs, No. 65

———

PUBLISHED FOR

THE BRITISH ACADEMY

BY THE

EGYPT EXPLORATION SOCIETY

3 DOUGHTY MEWS, LONDON, WC1N 2PG

1978

PRINTED IN GREAT BRITAIN
AT THE UNIVERSITY PRESS, OXFORD, BY VIVIAN RIDLER
PRINTER TO THE UNIVERSITY

AND PUBLISHED FOR

THE BRITISH ACADEMY
BY THE EGYPT EXPLORATION SOCIETY
3 DOUGHTY MEWS, LONDON, WC1N 2PG

ISSN 0306–9222
ISBN 0 85698 076 5

PREFACE

EXCEPT for the sub-literary Greek–Latin Glossary (**3315**), all the items in this volume are documentary. They have been chosen for a variety of reasons. Perhaps the greatest general interest will be roused by **3285**, which is a Greek version, written down in the second half of the second century A.D., of a legal text known hitherto from a Demotic papyrus of the third century B.C. Its implications for legal and historical studies will need further investigation. The persistent ill fame of the emperor Elagabalus is illustrated in **3298–9**, texts of the late third century. Several items concern the prosopography of Roman officials in Egypt and the chronology of their terms of office; for example, there is a new prefect of *c*. A.D. 300–1 in **3301–3**, a new first-century epistrategus in **3273**, and a new head of the *idios logos* in **3274–5**, of the reign of Trajan. Many of the remaining documents concern officials and institutions involved in the local administration of Oxyrhynchus.

All the items have been edited by Dr. Rea, who also compiled the indexes. He would like to thank the other General Editors and Dr. Coles for their constantly available aid and comfort, Professor G. R. Hughes and Dr. W. J. Tait for specialist Egyptological advice on **3285**, and Professor O. Neugebauer for expert advice on astronomical matters in **3298–9**. The technical and scholarly work of the Oxford University Press and its readers has also made its usual invaluable contribution to the volume and is very gratefully acknowledged.

P. J. PARSONS
J. R. REA
E. G. TURNER
General Editors
Graeco-Roman Memoirs

August 1977

CONTENTS

TABLE OF PAPYRI

I. DOCUMENTS OF THE ROMAN PERIOD

All dates are A.D.

II. DOCUMENTS OF THE BYZANTINE PERIOD

III. PRIVATE LETTERS

IV. SUB-LITERARY TEXT

LIST OF PLATES

NUMBERS AND PLATES

NOTE ON THE METHOD OF PUBLICATION
AND ABBREVIATIONS

THE method of publication follows that adopted in Part XLV. As there, the dots indicating letters unread and, within square brackets, the estimated number of letters lost are printed slightly below the line. The texts are printed in modern form, with accents and punctuation, the lectional signs occurring in the papyri being noted in the *apparatus criticus*, where also faults of orthography, etc., are corrected. Iota adscript is printed where written, otherwise iota subscript is used. Square brackets [ ] indicate a lacuna, round brackets ( ) the resolution of a symbol or abbreviation, angular brackets ⟨ ⟩ a mistaken omission in the original, braces { } a superfluous letter or letters, double square brackets ⟦ ⟧ a deletion, the signs ‘ ’ an insertion above the line. Dots within brackets represent the estimated number of letters lost or deleted, dots outside brackets mutilated or otherwise illegible letters. Dots under letters indicate that the reading is doubtful. Lastly, heavy arabic numerals refer to Oxyrhynchus papyri printed in this and preceding volumes, ordinary numerals to lines, small roman numerals to columns.

The use of arrows (→, ↓) to indicate the direction of the fibres in relation to the writing has been abandoned for reasons put forward in a paper given to the XVth International Congress of Papyrology (Brussels, 29 August–3 September, 1977) by E. G. Turner. In this volume most texts appear to accord with normal practice in being written parallel with the fibres on sheets of papyrus cut from the manufacturer's roll. Any departures from this practice which have been detected are described in the introductions to the relevant items.

The abbreviations used are in the main identical with those in E. G. Turner, *Greek Papyri: an Introduction* (1968). Some titles published too late to be included in that list, e.g. P. Petaus, P. Yale, are abbreviated according to the one given in *BASP* 11 (1974) 1–35. It is hoped that any new ones will be self-explanatory.

NOTE ON INVENTORY NUMBERS

THE inventory numbers in general follow a set pattern, of the form 20 3B.37/D(3)a. Here '20' is the number of the present cardboard box; '3B' refers to Grenfell and Hunt's third campaign at Oxyrhynchus; '37' is the series number given within that year to the metal packing box; 'D' indicates a layer of papyri inside that box. A few inventory numbers have the form A. B.3.2/A(6); these refer to a separate series of boxes.

ADDITIONS AND CORRECTIONS TO PAPYRI
PUBLISHED BY THE
EGYPT EXPLORATION SOCIETY

I **87** (= W. *Chr.* 446) 14–15. For [ὑ]πολόγωϲ ὀμνύω read [ὁ]μολογῶ ὀμνύϲ. See **3308** 8 n.

170 (descr.) Text fully edited in *BASP* 13 (1976) 17–19.

IV **722** See *ZPE* 20 (1976), 58–60, for an interpretation.

27. For Ἀχ[ιλλεῖ read Ἡρ[ακλᾷ. Ibid. 59.

30. For οὐδ' ἐπιϵ[read οὐδὲ μέ[ρουϲ. Ibid. 59.

VI **891** 1–2. For ['Εφ' ὑ]πάτων Οὐαλερίῳν Κων-

[ϲ]τᾳρτ[ίο]ν κᾳὶ Μαξιμιᾳ[νοῦ

read [ἐπὶ ὑ]πάτων τῷν κυρίων ἡμῷ[ν

[Κων]ϲτᾳρτί[ο]ν κᾳὶ Μᾳξιμιᾳνοῦ.

7. For διαϲ‚‚( ) read διαϲη(μοτάτου). See **3297** 1 n.

912 40. For [Ϲεβα(ϲτοῦ) Φαμε]νὼθ ᾳ read and restore, probably, [Ϲεβαϲτοῦ] Θὼθ ᾳ. Cf. J. F. Gilliam, 'The Death of Alexander Severus' in *CÉ* 31 (1956) 149–51, esp. 151; X. Loriot, 'La date du P. Reinach 91' in *ZPE* 11 (1973) 147–55, esp. 148 n. 7, 150.

A photograph shows that the trace after the break is rather high, much more suited to theta than to nu. The resulting date, 1 Maximinus, Thoth 1, is impossible, but it is quite easy to accept that this lease for the year 2 Maximinus, A.D. 235/6, was drafted at the end of 1 Maximinus, effectively summer A.D. 235, to refer to 'the incoming 2nd year' (line 8) and with a date clause referring to 1 Maximinus, and that the fair copy was actually made on the first day of 2 Maximinus, the scribe following his exemplar unthinkingly and adding the day's date without making the consequential changes. If that is right, the date was 30 August, A.D. 235 and ought to have been expressed as 2 Maximinus, Thoth 1.

VII **1014.** Identified as Achilles Tatius in *ZPE* 22 (1976) 14–17.

VIII **1083**[1]. See Ch. Theodoridis, 'Zwei neue Wörter für Aischylos und der P . Oxy. 1083, fr. 1', in *ZPE* 20 (1976) 47–53.

1083[1] 2. See *ZPE* 24 (1977) 254.

XII **1452** 51. For οἷϲ read αἷϲ. See **3279** 18 n.

On the interpretation of ὑπ(ερ)(ετέϲιν) see ibid.

1475 36. For Παρθικοῦ read probably Περϲικοῦ. See *Collectanea Papyrologica: texts published in honor of H. C. Youtie*, ed. Ann E. Hanson, II (= PTA 20), No. 68, 36–8 n. (p. 468).

1515 14. For Ϲκυβᾶτοϲ read Ϲκύβαλοϲ. See **3289** 2 n.

XIV **1627** 27. For [. . . .]ν read perhaps [ἀξιω]θ(είϲ). See *BASP* 13 (1976) 82.

XX **2256**[6], **2256**[8]. See C. Corbato, 'Una ripresa eschilea nella *Pace* di Aristofane' in *Studi Triestini di Antichità in onore di Luigia Achillea Stella* (Trieste, 1975) 323–35.

XXII 2310. See C. Gallavotti, 'I giambi di P. Oxy. 2310 attribuiti ad Archiloco', in *Philologus* 119 (1975) 153–62.

2338. See *ZPE* 18 (1975) 199–204 for various corrections.

2345. Various corrections in *BASP* 13 (1976) 187–8 and n. 28, 189–90.

XXIV 2418 1. For].τικῷ read ϲχολ]αϲτικῷ. See *ZPE* 24 (1977) 199–200.

2422 38. For Πιϲομποῦϲ read Ποϲομποῦϲ (checked from the original); cf. XLIII 3122 5 and n. On the basis of this misreading Professor Youtie has suggested restoring Π[ι]ϲον- ποῦϲ in P. Mich. X. 602. 9–10, see *ZPE* 21 (1976) 216. This too should be corrected to Π[ο]ϲονποῦϲ. J. R. Rea.

XXVII 2476. To the bibliography on the games at Panopolis add now A. Bernand, *Pan du désert*, No. 82 (pp. 233–41).

XXXI 2536. See M. Treu, 'Theons Pindarkommentar (Pap. Oxy. 2536)', in *Serta Turyniana* (Urbana, 1974), 62–85.

2551 verso i 20. For Ἀντωνῖνοϲ] ὁ ἕτεροϲ read Ἀντωνῖνο]ϲ μικρόϲ. See 3299 2 n.

XXXVI 2782. See K. Treu, 'Liturgische Traditionen in Ägypten (zu P. Oxy. 2782)', in *Studia Coptica* (Berlin, 1974), 43–66.

XXXVIII 2843 25. For εἴδουϲ read μέρουϲ. See *ZPE* 20 (1976) 58–60, which also treats the inter- pretation of this and the parallel documents.

2849. For a comment on the background see *ZPE* 22 (1976) 44–6.

XL See E. G. Turner, *Oxyrhynchus and Rome*, in *HSCP* 79 (1975) 1–24, esp. 16–24. Cf. *ZPE* 24 (1977) 265–71, esp. 269–70; a new inscription, assigned to the middle of the second century A.D., from Tlos in Lycia, refers to 1,100 ϲιτομετρούμενο, ἄνδρεϲ. The *numerus clausus* suggests an organization similar to that in Oxyrhynchus.

XLI 2954. See J. Herrmann, *Zum Edikt des ... Heliodoros*, in *ZRG* 92 (1975) 260–6.

2985, 2986. Cf. perhaps *ZPE* 24 (1977) 129–32. The Michigan papyrus published there (inv. 347) may well concern the same Theon and Chaeremon. J. C. Shelton.

XLII 3012 1–10. New supplements suggested in *ZPE* 22 (1976) 17–18.

3016. On *xenocritae* see *Festschrift für E. Soidl*, ed. H. Hübner *et al.* (Köln, 1975) 15–24.

3018 1–5. Various suggestions in *BASP* 13 (1976) 170–1.

XLIII 3094. This letter is addressed, 'To Eutyches who distributes branches (θαλλοδοτοῦντι) under the gateway of the Serapeum by the great image'. Attention has been drawn by a reference in *Collectanea Papyrologica: texts published in honor of H. C. Youtie*, ed. Ann E. Hanson, I (= PTA 19) 321–2, n. 25, to the publication by T. Kraus in *Jahrb. d. Deutschen Arch. Inst.* 75 (1960) 88–99 of the head and foot (Abb. 1 and 2) of an over-life-size statue of Sarapis alleged to come from Oxyrhynchus.

It would be absurd to claim that the fragmentary statue and the μεγάλη εἰκών must be the same, but the comparison is undoubtedly interesting. J. R. Rea.

3099 7 n. The hypothesis that the Oxyrhynchite gerusia was founded *c.* A.D. 225 is now disproved by P. Wisc. II 56, a document of A.D. 209.

3119. See *ZPE* 24 (1977) 187–96 for arguments tending to date the document to the persecution of Valerian in A.D. 259/60.

3122 5 n. To the references for the village of Ποϲομποῦϲ add P. Mich. X. 602. 9–10 and XXIV **2422** 38. See above under XXIV **2422** 38.

XLIV **3151.** Remarks on various sections by various authors are to be found in *ZPE* 22 (1976) 34, 35–6, 40.

XLV **3241.** See *ZPE* 20 (1976) 58–60.

P. Ant. II 67. See A. Wouters, 'P. Ant. 2. 67: a compendium of Herodian's περὶ καθολικῆϲ προϲῳδίαϲ, Book V' in *Orientalia Lovaniensia Periodica* 6–7 (1975–6) = *Miscellanea in honorem Josephi Vergote*, 601–13.

P. Ant. III 144. Identified as Aelius Aristides, *Panathenaicus*. See *CÉ* 50 (1975) 197–201.

P. Hibeh II 179. See R. Kannicht, 'Euripidea in P. Hib. 2. 179', in *ZPE* 21 (1976) 117–33, and J. Diggle, 'P. Hibeh 179 and the *Heracles* of Euripides', in *ZPE* 24 (1977) 291–4.

P. Tebt. I. Numerous items described in this volume are now published in full in P. Tebt. IV, see concordance ibid. pp. xii–xiii.

  36. 9–10. For εἰϲ τὴν [τετρα]¹⁰/κα⟨ι⟩ει{ϲ}κοϲτήν read ειϲτην[.....]¹⁰/κα εἰϲ Κοϲτῆν. See *CÉ* 50 (1975) 267–8.

  93. 57–9. Revised with commentary in *CÉ* 50 (1975) 263–7.

P. Tebt. II 335. 17. For μεμ[ιϲθωμένον] read and restore probably πεπ[ραμένον]. *CÉ* 50 (1975) 207.

  501 descr. Edition in *Acme* 29 (1976) 141–4.

  682. Identified as Xenophon, *Oec.* 18, 9. See *CÉ* 49 (1974) 354–5.

I. DOCUMENTS OF THE ROMAN PERIOD

3267–3270. LEASES OF FISHING RIGHTS

Leases of fishing rights are rare. The only other certain example is P. Wisc. I 6, see the improved text in *ZPE* 12 (1973) 262–4. The fragmentary P. Strasb. 569 may be another. In P. Mich. V 274, 317, and 322a and in P. Giss. Univ. Bibl. I 12 fishing rights are associated with the properties leased. Compare also P. Oxf. 12.

For state control of fishing and the regulations see R. Taubenschlag, *Law²*, 664–6.

Three of these four papyri are of interest also for the words χάρυβδις and χαρυβδεύειν. The first means a sheet of water, perhaps a pool of rough water at the foot of some lock-gates, see **3267** 5 n. The use of it as a common noun meaning a whirlpool is recorded in *LSJ*. The verb is entirely new and evidently signifies to fish in such a piece of water, perhaps by a particular method, see **3269** 4–5, **3270** 11 n.

3267

34 4B.76/C(1–5)c   7 × 10 cm.   *c.* A.D. 37–41

The back is blank.

```
                    .        .        .       .
              ...............]νενο.[.]....
              ...............] τοπαρχίας
              .............].......φηϲι τῷ
              ...........]τωι ἔτει Γαΐου Καίϲαροϲ
  5           Ϲεβαϲτοῦ Γερμ]ανικοῦ χάρυβδιν ἐφ' ᾧ
              ...........]ϲ ἐργατείαϲ καὶ τῆϲ
              ...........]ϲ πάϲηϲ ἑκάτερον
              μεταδο]ῦναι καὶ παντὸϲ τοῦ πε-
              ριγινομέ]νου ἰχθύοϲ ἔχειν ἑκά-
  10          τερον α]ὐτῶν κατὰ τὸ ἥμιϲυ. ὁ δὲ
              μεμιϲθωμέ]νοϲ παρέξεται ἁλεῖϲ
              ......]...κειϲ. μηδενὶ δὲ τῶν
              ὁμολογ]ούντων ἐξόντοϲ πα-
              ραβαίνειν] τι τῶν ὁμολ[ογηθέν-
  15          των ........].[.].[..........
                    .       .       .       .       .
```

11 l. ἁλιεῖϲ

B

'(X agrees to lease to Y?) the pool (near the village of A of the B?) toparchy (which he says he bought in?) the . . . *n*th year of Gaius Caesar Augustus Germanicus, on condition that each of them shares the supply of fishing-tackle(?) and all . . . and that each takes a half share of all fish coming in. The lessee will supply fishermen (in sufficient numbers?). None of the agreeing parties shall have power to contravene any of the agreed conditions . . .'

1–3 This passage remains rather intractable. The traces suggest ἐν οἷ[c] ἔχει [περὶ (κώμην) τῆς (ποιᾶc)] τοπαρχίας (ποιοῖc?) ἐδάφηcι (= ἐδάφεcι), but this is hard to reconcile with the date in the dative and the isolated position of χάρυβδιν (5), and the presumed misspelling is also not encouraging. Possibly χάρυβδιν is the end of a relative clause which began with ἥν, defining the position of the pool and the date of its construction or acquisition. If φηcί is to be recognized, it is not preceded by ὡc or an infinitive ending.

4 Restore probably διελθόντι or ἐνεcτῶτι and the number of the regnal year. Regnal years of Gaius run from one to five. Only δευτέρῳ is excluded by the trace. The dative case makes it appear that this is some antecedent date and not the year for which the lease was agreed, but if it is right to take τω at the end of 3 as the article belonging to ἔτει only the current year or the one immediately preceding are at all likely to be referred to and this would confine the document to the reign of Gaius.

5 χάρυβδιν. In 3269 and 3270 the procedure denoted by the verb χαρυβδεύειν is practised in the vicinity of some locks. It looks as if the χάρυβδιc might be the pool of rough water at the foot of the locks.

In P. Ryl. II 123 iii 11 Χάρυβδιν is interpreted as a village name, see index (p. 450) and WB III Abschn. 16a s.v., but the detailed description of it by toparchy, village, and κλῆροc, indicates that it is a common noun as here.

See also *Collectanea Papyrologica* (*Texts published in honor of H. C. Youtie*, ed. Ann E. Hanson) Part II (= PTA 20) No. 68. One clause of this land lease of A.D. 266 runs (17–22):—ἐπὶ τῷ ἡμᾶc τοὺc μεμιcθω-μένο[υc] ἔχειν ἄνευ φ⟨ό⟩ρου πρὸc cυνβροχιcμὸν τῆc λινοκαλάμηc ἣν ἔχειc περὶ τὴν αὐτὴν Ἀντιπέρα Πέλα πληcίον λάκκου Διογενίδοc λίμνην οὖcαν ἐντὸc χαρύβδεωc Παcινείκου ἀπὸ μηνὸc Παχών, 'on condition that we, the lessees, are to have, rent-free, for the retting of the flax, the reservoir which you possess near the same Antipera Pela, close to the cistern of Diogenis, and which is within(?) the pool of Pasinicus, from the month of Pachon'. It is not at all clear what sort of sheet of water the λίμνη was, nor is it possible to be sure whether it formed part of the χάρυβδιc or not, since ἐντόc frequently means 'on this side of'.

6 ἐργατείαc. In X 1450 6 ἐργατεία seems to have a concrete sense, 'tools or workmen', says the note. Here, if it is not abstract, it should mean 'tackle', since the fishermen are to be supplied by the lessee (11). Restore, perhaps, something like τῆc ἁλιευτικῆ]c ἐργατείαc καὶ τῆc | 7 [ἄλληc ἐπιμελεία]c πάcηc.

9 ἰχθύοc. For the collective sense cf. XIX 2234 16.

11 ἁλεῖc. For the contraction cf. J. H. Moulton, *Grammar of N.T. Greek* ii 89–90; for -ειc acc. pl. cf. Mayser i 270–1.

12]. . .κειc. The traces seem to be—1: foot curved to left. 2: part of the left-hand side of a round letter. 3: part of a long descender, ι or ρ. The word is not πελέκειc, cf. P. Cair. Zen. IV 59783. 11, 16 πελέκειc ἁλιευτικοί.

E. G. Turner has suggested αὐ]τάρκειc, 'sufficient', P. J. Parsons τοὺc ἐπ]ιεικεῖc, 'able, capable'. Both words would suit the meagre traces, but this sense of ἐπιεικήc (see *LSJ* s.v. ii, 2) is not certainly attested in the papyri. For αὐτάρκηc cf. P. Lond. III 948 (p. 220). 11 παρεχόμενοc ὁ κυβερνήτηc τοὺc αὐτάρκειc ναύταc. For the order ἁλιεῖc τοὺc αὐτάρκειc, strange at first sight, cf. E. Mayser, *Grammatik d. gr. Papyri* ii 2 § 64 (pp. 57–8).

3268

46 5B.48/D(4–8)b   7 × 11 cm.   Second century

The back is blank.

Διονυcίῳ καὶ τοῖc cὺν
αὐτῷ ἐπιτηρηταῖc ἰ-
χθύοc πόλεωc νομοῦ
Ὀξυρυγχείτου
5   παρὰ Cαραπᾶ Ἀθηναί[ου
τοῦ Cαραπίωνοc. ἑκου-
cίωc ἐπιδέχομαι τὴν
ἄγραν τοῦ ἐκβηcομένου
ἰχθύοc διώρυχοc Θεμό-
10 θεωc cὺν ὑποχέαc
καὶ θύραc ἀφέcεωc Φοβόου
φόρου cυ.[.....] δραχμῶν
..]ακοcίῳ[ν καὶ κε]ραμίου
12–15 letters]οc[...

· · · · ·

2–3 ἰ|χθυοc   10–11 l. cὺν ὑποχεῦcι καὶ θύραιc

'To Dionysius and his fellow supervisors of fish for the city and nome of Oxyrhynchus, from Sarapas son of Athenaeus grandson of Sarapion. Of my own free will I undertake the fishing for the fish forth-coming from the canal of Themothis(?) together with the fish-traps(?) and doors of the sluice at Phoboou at the rent . . . of 200(?) drachmas and a jar . . .'

2 On ἐπιτηρηταί see F. Oertel, *Liturgie*, 237–46, N. Lewis, *Inventory of Compulsory Services*, s.v.

3 πόλεωc νομοῦ. Cf. BGU IV 1062 (= W. *Chr.* 276). 3–4, as corrected in BL I 93 from W. Schubart, *Papyri Graecae Berolinenses*, 36.

4 At the end a long horizontal acts as a filler sign.

9–10 Θεμό|¹⁰θεωc. The name is new. The last two letters in 9 might possibly by λῳ.

10 ὑποχέαc. Cf. 3269 2 n.

12 cυ.[.....]. This recalls τὸν cυνφωνηθέντα φόρον in 3269 10 but a phi should have left some trace and space tells against cυμφωνηθέντοc, which in any case would seem to require the article. Other possibilities, suggested by E. G. Turner and P. J. Parsons, might be cυνόλ(ου), cύνπ(αντι), and cυν-αγ(ομένου), but no exact parallel for any of these has yet been found. Before δραχμῶν we might expect ἀργυρίου, perhaps abbreviated to αργ⁻.

13 Space favours [δι]ακοcίῳ[ν, but [τρι]ακοcίῳ[ν may be possible. The ligature to kappa excludes δραχμῷ|¹³[ν ε]ἴκοcι.

κεραμίου. Cf. P. Wisc. I 6. 13–14, 20–22, where the jars contain fish products, θριccία and γαρηρά.

3269

28 4B.57/L(1–3)a   8×9 cm.   Third century

The back is blank.

·   ·   ·   ·   ·

```
......] ἄγραν ἰχθύ[ων 6–8 letters ἀνα-]
βάϲεωϲ τοῦ ἐνεϲτῶτοϲ α (ἔτουϲ)″ ἀπό τε ὑπο-
χέων πρὸϲ ταῖϲ περὶ Πέλα θύραιϲ Τα(ν)-
ύρεωϲ καλουμέναιϲ ἐπὶ τῷ ϲὲ καὶ χα-
5    ρυβδεύειν κατὰ τὸ τέταρτον μέ-
ροϲ ἐν ταῖϲ αὐταῖϲ θύραιϲ πρὸϲ τὸ ἔ-
χειν τοὺϲ μεμιϲθωκόταϲ τὰ λοι-
πὰ τέταρτα τρία παρέχονταϲ λί-
να καὶ ϲκάφαϲ καὶ ἁλιέαϲ ὧν πάντω(ν)
10   τὸν ϲυνφωνηθέντα φόρον αὐτόθι
ἀπεϲχήκαμεν διὰ χειρὸϲ ἐκ πλήρουϲ
πρὸϲ τὸ τὴν ἄγραν αὐτὸν ποιήϲαϲθαι
ἀ]κωλύτωϲ ἐφ' ὃν προϲήκι χρόνο(ν)
...]...ιαϲ οὔϲηϲ τῷ [Ζ]ωίλῳ δια
15   ........] ποιήϲαϲθαι .....τ'ταιϲ
```

·   ·   ·   ·   ·

2 αϛ″   3 τᾱ   9 παντῶ   13 l. προϲήκει; χρονο̄

'(We agree that we have leased to you?) the right to fish . . . (during?) the Nile flood of the present first year from the fish-traps(?) by the sluice-gates at Pela called the gates of Tanyris on condition that you also(?) fish the pool(?) with a fourth share (in the catch) in the same sluice gates so that the lessors shall have the remaining three shares on providing nets (lines?) and boats and fishermen, for all which things we have received on the spot the agreed rent in cash in full so that he may do the fishing without hindrance for the appropriate term, with a proportionate share reserved(?) to Zoilus . . . to do(?) . . . .'

1 ἄγραν ἰχθύ[ων. Cf. **3270** 9, P. Wisc. I 6. 3–4; or ἰχθύ[οϲ cf. **3268** 8–9. One of the items leased in P. Giss. Univ. Bibl. 12 is θήρα ἰχθύαϲ and the same phrase occurs in official reports and accounts, P. Hamb. 6, P. Osl. III 89–91, PSI III 160, VII 735. After ἰχθύων in this position **3270** has ὑδάτων τῆϲ οὔϲηϲ ἀναβάϲεωϲ. Here we might have had either ὑδάτων or τῆϲ οὔϲηϲ.

2 ἀπό τε ὑπ̣οχέων. Cf. **3268** 10. The translation 'fish-traps' is a mere guess. The word ὑποχεύϲ is known only from *CGL* iii 368. 6, where it is a gloss on Latin *trulla*, cited in the section *de aureis*, and so evidently from Juvenal, *Sat.* iii 108. *Trulla* is a vessel of some sort, perhaps a ladle or scoop. A much better attested word is ὑποχή, denoting some kind of fishing-net.

The τε is difficult. Perhaps it goes with καὶ χαρυβδεύειν even though the verb is in a subordinate construction. As a reading it is unavoidable.

3 Pela is a village in the western toparchy, cf. e.g. X **1285** 81. From the name of Antipera Pela in the same toparchy (XIV **1659** 42, cf. XXVII **2473** 16, XIV **1637** 33) we know that both villages stood by a considerable body of water, probably the ancient equivalent of the Bahr Yusuf. This agrees

with the fact that Oxyrhynchus itself, which had two quarters called North Quay and South Quay (Βορρᾶ Κρηπῖδος, Νότου Κ.) was either in the western toparchy or adjoined it on its south side (XII 1475 22 n., XII 1421 3 n.).

Τα(ν)ύρεως. Cf. 3270 10, 12. New as a place-name, it is cited dubiously as a woman's name in NB.

8–9 λίνα. Translate probably 'nets' rather than 'lines'. The Oxyrhynchites are supposed to have abstained from eating fish caught on hooks because of the danger of the hook having touched a sacred fish, Plut. *De Iside et Os.* 7, Aelian, *H.A.* x 46. In fact fish-hooks have turned up in the boxes of Oxyrhynchus papyri, but though they seem to be made of some sort of bronze, to judge from the verdigris on them, there is no guarantee that they are contemporary with the papyri.

In XIX 2234 14 λίνων almost certainly refers to nets. Fishing with lines and bait during that mass poaching expedition is hardly conceivable.

12 αὐτόν. The construction has changed since the subjective ϲε in 4; cf. τῷ [Z]ωίλῳ, 14.

14 [...]...ίαϲ. Perhaps restore [ἀνα]λογίαϲ, with reference to the profit-sharing mentioned above, cf. *ZPE* 3 (1968) 3–5 = H. C. Youtie, *Scriptiunculae* ii 947–9; ἐξουϲίαϲ seems not to fit the traces.

15 .....τ'ταιϲ. This looks like a diastole between two mutes, as occurs commonly in third-century texts. Possibly, however, it is a sign of abbreviation, with ταιϲ following separately. A relevant word would be θρίττα, cf. 3268 13 n., but although the first letter might well be theta the intervening traces seem to be too extensive for θρίτταιϲ or even θρείτταιϲ; nor does this word suggest any easy restoration of the text.

3270

18 2B.73/D(d)   15×25·5 cm.   14 September–15 October, A.D. 309

ὑπατ[είαϲ τ]ῶν δεϲποτῶν ἡμῶν Οὐαλερίου Λικιννιανοῦ
Λικιν[ν]ίου Ϲεβαϲτοῦ καὶ Φλαυίου Οὐαλερίου Κωνϲταντίνου
υἱ[ο]ῦ βαϲιλέων.   (vac.)
Αὐρηλίῳ Ϲαραπίωνι Ἀφύγχιοϲ ἀπὸ τῆϲ λαμ(πρᾶϲ) καὶ λαμ(προτάτηϲ) Ὀξυ-
5 ρυγχιτῶν πόλεωϲ καὶ τοῖϲ κοινωνοῖϲ μιϲθωταῖϲ
εἰχθυηρᾶϲ πόλεωϲ Ὀξυρυγχίτου   (vac.)
παρὰ Αὐρηλίου Λουκίου Λουκίου ἀπὸ τῆϲ αὐτῆϲ πόλε[ω]ϲ
καὶ τ]ῶν κοινω[ν]ῶν. ἑκουϲίωϲ ἐπιδεχόμεθα μ[ιϲ]θώϲαϲ-
θαι ἄγραν εἰχθύων ὑδάτων τῆϲ οὔϲηϲ ἀναβάϲεωϲ
10 θυρῶν Τανύρεωϲ καὶ Ματρίνου ὥϲτε ἡμᾶϲ χα[ρ]υβδε[ύ-
ειν διὰ τῶν θυρῶν ἢ καὶ ἄλλουϲ ἀγρεύειν τ[..]...[
καὶ τελέϲομεν ὑπὲρ φόρων τῶν θυρῶν Τα[νύρεωϲ
καὶ Ματρίνου ἡμῖν τοῖϲ μιϲθωταῖϲ ἀργυρίο[υ τάλαντα
δεκατέϲϲερα καὶ δραχμὰϲ τριϲχιλίαϲ παρ[έχοντεϲ
15 ἡμῖν ἁλιέ⟦υϲ⟧'αϲ' καὶ λίνα .[........].του[c. 10 letters
ἀπολαμβαν..[..]..ερου....ω.[...].[c. 12 letters
τῶν περιγινομένων εἰχθύων. βεβ[αιουμένηϲ

1 ϋπατ[ειαϲ   3 ϋἱ[ο]υ   4 αφυγ'χιοϲ, λαμϟ, λαμϟ   5 ρυγ'χιτων   6 l. ἰχθυηρᾶϲ; οξυρυγ'χιτου   9 l. ἰχθύων; ϋδατων   10 τανυρεωϲ   12 ϋπερ   13 l. ὑμῖν   15 l. ὑμῖν   17 l. ἰχθύων

δὲ ἡ[μῖ]ν τῆ[ς] ἐπιδοχῆς π[οι]ησόμεθα τὴν ἄγρ[αν ἀκωλύ-

τω[ς καὶ ἀπο]δώς[ο]μεν τὸν [φ]όρον με[τ]ὰ τὴν [ἄγραν.

20   κυρία ἡ [ἐπιδοχὴ καὶ ἐ]περωτη[θ]εὶς ὡμο[λόγησα.

(ἀλλὰ καὶ [.......]ε ἡμᾶς ἐν ταῖς θύραις [Ματρίνου (καὶ?)

ἐν τοῖς ἀπηλι[ωτι]κοῖς μέρεσι περειχώ[ματος

Cενεμσεὲ καὶ [λιβι]κοῖς μέρεσι τῶν αὐτῶν θ[υρῶν

Ματρίνου. ἐπὶ τῶν δεσποτῶν ἡμῶν Γα[λερίου Οὐαλερίου

25   Μαξιμιανοῦ καὶ Οὐαλερίου Λικιννιανοῦ Λι[κιννίου

τῶν ἀνικήτων Cεβαστῶν καὶ τῶν δ[ε]σπ[οτῶν ἡμῶν

Μαξιμίνου καὶ Κωνσταντίνο[υ] τῶν ἐπιφαν[εστάτων

Καισάρων υἱῶν τῶν βας[ιλ]έων [..].[

Ὀκτωβρ[

———

30 (m. 2)   Αὐρηλιο[

        καὶ α..[

      Back (m. 3) ἐχθ(έσεως?) (ταλ.) α

            ἔσχ(αμεν?) (ταλ.) ι ⟨(δρ.)⟩ ʹΒ

22 l. περιχώματος   28 ὕιων   32 εχθ ⌐   33 εσχ⸌ ⌐

'In the consulship of our masters Valerius Licinianus Licinius, Augustus, and Flavius Valerius Constantinus, son of the emperors.'

'To Aurelius Sarapion son of Aphynchis from the glorious and most glorious city of the Oxyrhynchites and to his partners, contractors of the fishing concession of the city (and) of the Oxyrhynchite nome, from Aurelius Lucius son of Lucius from the same city, and his partners.'

'Of our own volition we offer to lease the right to fish in the waters of the present Nile flood at the lock-gates of Tanyris and Matrinus on condition that we fish the pool(?) through the lock-gates and also fish by other methods(?), and we shall pay for rents of the lock-gates of Tanyris and Matrinus to you the contractors fourteen talents and three thousand drachmas of silver, supplying for you fishermen and nets . . . of the fish that come to hand. If our offer is confirmed we shall carry out the fishing without hindrance, and we shall deliver the rent after the fishing-season(?). This offer is valid and in answer to the formal question I gave my assent. (And we are also to . . . in the lock-gates of Matrinus (and?) in the eastern sections of the embankment of Senemsee and the western sections of the same gates of Matrinus.)'

'In the reign of our masters Galerius Valerius Maximianus and Valerius Licinianus Licinius, the unconquered Augusti, and our masters Maximinus and Constantinus, the most noble Caesars, sons of the emperors, . . . October.'

(2nd hand) 'I, Aurelius . . . and . . .'

Back. 'Arrears, 1 (?) talent. Received, 10 talents 2,000 drachmas.'

6 πόλεως Ὀξυρυγχίτου. Cf. **3268** 3 πόλεως νομοῦ Ὀξυρυγχείτου. It presumably means 'city (and) nome of Oxyrhynchus'.

10 Τανύρεως. Cf. **3269** 3.

11 τ[..]...[. The very meagre traces will allow τ[ρό]πο̣υ[ς. If the word were certain it would confirm that χαρυβδεύειν signifies a definite method of fishing. Since a charybdis is a place, τ[ό]πο̣υ[ς migh

be attractive and could be accepted as a reading, but this good English construction, 'to hunt the woods, to fish the stream', etc., seems improbable in Greek.

14–15 παρ[έχοντες] ἡμῖν (= ὑμῖν cf. 13). This restoration seems best. In **3269** it is for the lessors to provide men and tackle. In **3267**, however, the lessee supplies them.

15–16 It is possible that the pattern was κ[αὶ ......].του[ϲ (boats of some sort?; cf. **3269** 8–9) ὥϲτε ἕκαϲτον] | ἀπολαμβάνει[ν] τὸ ἐροῦν (= αἱροῦν) αὐτῷ μ[έρο]ϲ [(ποϲτὸν) πάντων] | τῶν περιγινομένων εἰχθύων.

18–19 [ἀκωλύ]|τωϲ. Cf. **3269** 13.

19 μετὰ τὴν [ἄγραν. Cf. P. Wisc. I 6. 18–19 [ἐπὶ] τῇ ἄγρᾳ (cf. *LSJ* s.v. ἐπί B II 2). In other types of lease one finds μετὰ τὸν χρόνον. This rather suggests that ἄγρα is used to mean the fishing season, and the mention of the Nile flood (9) reinforces the suggestion.

20 The scribe writes in the plural throughout except in the 'stipulation' clause. The singular is the standard formula, cf. D. Simon, *Studien z. Praxis d. Stipulationsklauseln*, 46, but possibly Lucius was the only representative of his party at the concluding of the contract.

21–4 This clause was either left out of the body of the contract by mistake or was added as an afterthought. The opening bracket should probably have been matched by a closing one after Ματρίνου in 24.

21 [........]ε. The last letter is roughly made, but seems much more like ε than ν. Probably we should restore an aorist infinitive, e.g. [χαρυβδεῦϲ]ε (= χαρυβδεῦϲαι), depending on a verb of agreement understood.

[Ματρίνου] is restored on the basis of τῶν αὐτῶν θ[υρῶν] Ματρίνου (23–4).

22–3 περειχώ[ματοϲ] Ϲενεμϲεέ. This is a new embankment name.

24 The space available for Γα[λερίου Οὐαλερίου is rather short; possibly the second *nomen* was accidentally omitted because of the homoeoteleuton.

24–8 Here a dating clause expressed in terms of regnal years is expected, cf. XXXI **2585** 1–2 n. Instead we have a clause that looks as if it is imitated from dates by magistrates or provincial governors. No other example is known to me. It is impossible to say whether or not the regnal year numbers were given in the damaged portion. They would be 18 (Galerius), 6 (Maximinus), 4 (Constantine), 2 (Licinius) = A.D. 309/10.

29 Ὀκτωβρ[. This limits the date to the period XVIII Kal. Oct.–Id. Oct. (14 September–15 October), A.D. 309. See WB III Abschn. 7 s.vv εἰδοί, καλάνδαι, νῶναι, for various ways in which it might have been expressed.|

30–1 Restore probably something like Αὐρήλιο[ϲ Λούκιος καὶ οἱ κοινωνοὶ μεμιϲθώμεθα τὴν ἄγραν] καὶ ἀπο[δώϲομεν τὸν φόρον ὡς πρόκειται.

32–3 The endorsement in 32 is close to the top edge and slightly left of the middle; that in 33 is about 2 cm. below and further to the left. If I understand them correctly, the lower entry was written first, when a representative of the lessors made a note that, of the rent of 14 talents 3,000 drachmas, 10 talents 2,000 drachmas had been received.

The higher one is a note of arrears. One might expect the sum to be the difference between the total rent and the sum mentioned in the lower endorsement, which would be 4 talents 1,000 drachmas, but there is only one figure after the talent symbol. Presumably, therefore, these notations were made on separate occasions, as their placings indeed suggest. As well as the payment of 10 talents 2,000 drachmas, noted down, at least one other instalment was paid—some blotted remains of ink near the top edge on the right might possibly be part of the record of it. The higher entry is the sum outstanding after the second or a subsequent instalment had been paid.

33 ἐϲχ(αμεν?). The form restored supposes that the damaged abbreviation sign is the L-shaped wedge that is a vestigial alpha. However, it may be simply an oblique stroke, in which case perhaps ἔϲχ(ομεν) should be preferred.

3271. Petition to a Prefect

39 3B.78/J(1–3)c   7·5 × 8·5 cm.   *c.* A.D. 47–54

Only the top survives of this petition to Cn. Vergilius Capito, prefect of Egypt A.D. 47–52. It is interesting because the petitioner is apparently the mother of two Roman citizens and householder of a house in the Gamma district of Alexandria, and because it contains a word that has not yet appeared in the dictionaries.

The back is blank.

> Γναίωι Οὐεργιλίωι Καπίτωνι δι(ὰ) δύο υἱ(ῶν)
> Κλαυδίων Ποτάμωνος καὶ Ἀπολλ( )
>   παρὰ ᾿Ιϲιδώρας τῆς Ἀπολλωνίο(υ) .[
> δε κατὰ δὲ τεκνοθεϲίαν Διονυϲίο(υ)
> 5   ῾τοῦ καὶ ... ωνίου᾿ Ἀλεξανδρ ... ϲταθμούχου
>   οἰκίας τῆς οὔϲης ἐν τῷ γ̄
>   ...]......[

1 ϙ̣, υἱ°   2 απολ^λ   3 απολλωνι̅   4 διονυϲι̅

'To Gnaeus Vergilius Capito by agency of (her) two sons Claudius Potamon and Claudius Apoll(onius?) from Isidora daughter of Apollonius but, by adoption, of Dionysius alias ...onius, Alexandrian, householder of a house in the Gamma district ...'

1 Capito's term as prefect lasted from some time before 25 January, A.D. 48 till at least 24 April, A.D. 52, see *ZPE* 17 (1975) 272. The first date rests on the usual view that in *CIL* iii 6024 the iteration figures for *trib. pot.* (VII) and *imp.* (XV) are correct, so placing the inscription earlier than the eighth assumption of *trib. pot.*, and that the figure for the consulship should be corrected from V (A.D. 51–4) to IV (A.D. 47–50).

Capito's successor was in office certainly by 29 March, A.D. 54, possibly earlier in that year, see *ZPE* 17 (1975) 273. His predecessor was in office in Claudius' seventh term of *trib. pot.*, 25 January, A.D. 47–24 January, A.D. 48. Therefore the years in which this document may fall run from A.D. 47 to A.D. 54.

υἱ(ῶν). Presumably Isidora's sons had acquired the Roman citizenship recently, some time in the reign of Claudius. The phrasing is awkward, because it is not clear at first whose sons they are. It was perhaps a matter of precedence that, as Roman citizens, they should be mentioned before their mother.

2 Ἀπολλ( ). For possible names see NB and D. Foraboschi, *Onomasticon*. Most likely, of course, is Ἀπολλ(ωνίου), particularly as this is his maternal grandfather's name, see 3.

3–4 At the end of 3 the traces are very cramped. At the beginning of 4 the letters δε are placed to the left of the normal alignment, but this is slightly obscured by the fact that the interlineation in 5 also begins in ecthesis. It has not proved possible to identify here any antithesis to κατά ... τεκνοθεϲίαν, such as φύϲει.

It may be that the traces at the end of 3 were the letters ου, written too closely to satisfy the writer and so cancelled and replaced by the raised omicron; δε may be an erroneous repetition of δέ, but it is difficult to see why it should be outside the normal left-hand alignment.

4 τεκνοθεϲίαν. This word is not in LSJ or Suppl., but see P. Col. Zen. I 58. 9, a reference given in S. Daris, *Spoglio Lessicale* under the erroneous lemma τεκνόθεϲιϲ, which was invented in the index of P. Col. Zen. I.

5 ...ωνίου. Perhaps Ἀρθωνίου or Ἀμμωνίου. Other possibilities are given in F. Dornseiff–B. Hansen, *Rückläufiges Wb. d. gr. Eigennamen*, 239–40; none seem more attractive than the two already mentioned.

Ἀλεξανδρ.... It looks very much as if Ἀλεξανδρέως was written first and altered, presumably to a feminine form intended to refer to Isidora. Ἀλεξανδρίς is attested, but rarely, see P. M. Fraser, *Ptolemaic Alexandria* ii 116 n. 24, also Ἀλεξανδρῖτις, cf. *CIG* 3142. 40. Neither of these is recognizable here. I am inclined to think that Ἀλεξανδρίνης can be read, though I cannot find this form used of persons elsewhere. Her sons are Romans, so that one would be disposed to think that she herself was of the full citizen class of Alexandria, but that does not automatically follow. In any case the term here is both doubtfully read and of doubtful interpretation.

If, in spite of my view, the word was altered to, and not from, Ἀλεξανδρέως, it and the following expression will apply to Isidora's adoptive father.

cταθμούχου. Cf. F. Preisigke, *Fachwörter*, 158. The word usually applies to the owner of premises let to tenants.

6 τῆς οὔςης ἐν τῷ γ̄. For the division of Alexandria into five *grammata*, alpha to epsilon, see P. M. Fraser, *Ptolemaic Alexandria* i 34–5. If γ̄ is rightly read, this is the first documentary reference to the Gamma district, cf. *ibid.* 35. Only *a* is a possible alternative, but it seems much more likely that the left-hand part of this letter is a curved and sloping upright than that it is part of the loop of alpha. For the whole phrase cf. BGU IV 1115. 16–17 οἴκῳ ἐν cυνοικίᾳ τῇ οὔ[cη] ἐν τῷ Δέλτα.

3272. List of District Names

33 4B.83/C(1–2)a   9 × 34·5 cm.   *c.* A.D. 61/2

The list occupies the middle of a tall strip of papyrus. Upside down in relation to it was a list of personal names, with patronymics and ages, preceded by a heading which may be conjecturally restored as:

6–8-letter name κωμο]γραμματεὺς Ταλαὼ{ι}
κατ' ἄνδρα λαογ]ραφίας τοῦ η ἱεροῦ Νέρωνος
Καίcαροc C]εβαcτοῦ Γερμανικοῦ Αὐτοκράτοροc
                                    ] (vac.) ἔτουc   (vac.)

'N., village scribe of Talao: individual list of the poll-tax for the sacred 8th year of Nero Caesar Augustus Germanicus Imperator.'

On ἱεροῦ in this formula see O. Montevecchi in *Aegyptus* 51 (1971) 212–20. If Professor Montevecchi's theory is right the heading should be dated between 29 August and 12 October, A.D. 61, see op. cit. 213–14, but there is the possibility that the heading may have been copied later from a document out of which this list was extracted. Most of the meagre remains are of the ages and the ends of the patronymics.

At first sight it looks as if this list of names was the original use of the papyrus, which is blank on the back. However, the displacement of one of the ages to a spot higher than the end of the patronymic which precedes looks as if it was done to avoid the end of the first line of the list of districts and indicates rather that the list of districts stood there first. A possible explanation might be that the piece which included the district list and the blank spaces above, below, and to the right, was cut from a used roll, and that on this a scribe wrote the list of personal names, avoiding the seven-line district list as best he might. The back is blank.

The interest and the puzzle of the district list is the meaning of the heading δ̄ τόμοc μητροπόλεωc. Does it mean 'fourth roll for the nome capital' or 'fourth section of the nome capital'? Six names of districts follow. The total of district names attested is rather more than twenty-four, see H. Rink, *Strassen- u. Viertelnamen von Oxyrhynchus*, 52, perhaps more than thirty, see *HSCP* 79 (1975) 17 n. 50. It is difficult to be sure how many of these existed at any one time as administrative units, but it is possible that these six district names might represent about one-fourth or one-fifth of the city and form a convenient administrative division.

It seemed proper to make the text available in case that explanation is the correct one, but the usage of the word τόμος to mean 'roll' is common, whereas I have found no good parallel to suggest that it might mean 'section' in this sort of context.

Perhaps the text was a table of the contents of a roll and possibly it formed the first column of the roll and was followed by a register containing information arranged in six sections corresponding to the district names.

$$\overline{\delta}\ τόμος\ μητροπόλεως$$
$$Λυκίων\ Παρεμβολῆς$$
$$Δρόμου\ Θοήριδος$$
$$Δρόμου\ Γυμναςίου$$
$$5\qquad Μητρῴου$$
$$Ἡρακλέους\ τό(πων)$$
$$Πλατείας$$

6 το᾽

'Fourth roll for the nome capital. Lycians' Camp, Thoeris Street, Gymnasium Street, Metroum, District of Heracles, Square.'

3273. Communication to an Epistrategus

29 4B.63/C(6–7)a   17·5 × 24 cm.   First century

The recipient of this document is a new epistrategus, Q. Sanquinius . . .inius Maximus, presumably related to the senatorial Sanquinii listed in *PIR*¹ iii 172–3, Nos. 133–6. The last of these also had the *praenomen* Quintus and the *cognomen* Maximus; he was twice suffect consul and died in office as legate of Lower Germany just before A.D. 47. It might be that the new epistrategus is an adopted son of this Q. Sanquinius Maximus and that the damaged element of the name is his original *nomen*.

There is no internal evidence for the date except from the handwriting, a good-sized and carefully written documentary script. It is best paralleled in P. Lond. II 276 (p. 148; Facsimiles II Pl. 12, illustrated also in F. G. Kenyon, *Palaeography of the Greek Papyri*, Pl. IV opp. p. 42); that document dates from A.D. 15, but there is no guarantee that **3273** is very close to it in date. P. Lond. II 177 (p. 167; Facsimiles II Pl. 14) of A.D. 40–1 is also not very dissimilar. It would be reasonably prudent to put **3273** down as belonging to the first century and more probably earlier in that century than later.

It is evident from the text that Oxyrhynchus lay in the division of Egypt administered by the epistrategus, but the division is not named. Oxyrhynchus lay well within the area known as the Heptanomia and presumably became part of it as soon as it was created, having previously belonged to the Thebaid. The creation of the Heptanomia 'cannot be later than Vespasian and may go back to Augustus' (J. D. Thomas in *Akten d. XIII. Intern. Papyrologenkongresses*, p. 402 n. 18). However, no epistrategi of the Heptanomia are known before the reign of Vespasian, see M. Vandoni, *Gli Epistrategi*, p. 21. The combination of uncertainties about the date of this document and the date of the creation of the Heptanomia make it impossible to say for sure whether Sanquinius was epistrategus of the Thebaid or of the Heptanomia.

The subject of the text is a mistake made in nominating to the office of sitologus a man too poor to guarantee possible deficiencies by confusion with another man who had the same name, but not the same patronymic, and who was rich enough to serve. Obviously the aim of the writer was to have the right man appointed, but the text breaks off before it becomes clear whether the document should properly be described as a report or a complaint or a petition. The sender's description of his own position is sufficiently ambiguous to add to the difficulty of deciding what his point of view was, see 2–3 n.

The back of the document is blank.

$$Κοΐντωι \ Cανκυινίωι \ [3–4] \ ινίωι \ Μαξίμωι \ ἐπιcτρατή(γῳ)$$

παρὰ Εὐδαίμονος Μάρ[κ]ου Ἀντωνίου Cπένδοντος

φορολό[γ]ου. ἐν τοῖς εἰcδοθε[ῖc]ι εἰc cειτολογίαν

τοῦ Ὀξυρυγχίτου νομοῦ ἀνδράcι κατὰ πλάνην

5 ἐνεγράφη ἀντὶ Βελλέους τοῦ Διονυcίου

εὐπόρου καὶ εὐθετοῦντος ε[ἰc τ]ὴν χρεί-

αν ὁμώνυμος ἕτερος Βελ[λῆc] Πατερμού-

θιος ἄθετος καὶ π[ε]νιχρός. ἀμφοτέ-

ρων δὲ ὄντων ἀπ[ὸ κ]ώμης Τακόνα

10 τοῦ αὐτοῦ Ὀξυρυγχίτου νομοῦ, ἀλλα-

γέντος ὡς πρόκε[ιται κ]ατὰ πλάνην τοῦ

πατρωνύμου [8–10 letters]του [6–8 letters

...ειμηνυθ[

Βελλῆν Διο[νυcίου

15 ἐπιδί[δ]ωμ[ι

..βη[

...[

.]..[

 · · · · ·

1 επιcτρατ^η

'To Quintus Sanquinius ...inius Maximus, epistrategus, from Eudaemon, (slave?) of Marcus Antonius Spendon collector. Among the men nominated to serve as sitologi in the Oxyrhynchite nome was listed by mistake instead of Belles son of Dionysius, financially sound and fit for the service, another man of the same name, Belles son of Patermuthis, unfit for the service and poor. Since they are both from the village of Tacona in the same Oxyrhynchite nome and since the patronymic was mixed up by mistake, as stated above, ...'

1 [3–4]. *ινίωι*. The traces appear to come from a crossbar; the best possibility is]$_T$ and]$_\chi$ is the next best, though perhaps κ, ς, and ν are also possible. At base-line level on the edge before the gap there is a tiny and faint trace of ink; the wide spacing between the other words in this line suggests that it is accidental ink rather than part of a letter. There are at least twenty-eight known possible *nomina*: Arquinius, Asinius, Atinius, Avinius, Catinius, Clusinius, Corvinius, Cosinius, Cusinius, Fulcinius, Graecinius, Latinius, Licinius, Lisinius, Mescinius, Oclatinius, Ovinius, Prastinius, Rasinius, Reginius, Saevinius, Sicinius, Stertinius, Titinius, Tutinius, Vatinius, Verginius, Volcinius. This list is based on a cursory search of *PIR*² (A–L) and *PIR*¹ (M–Z) and is not likely to be complete.

2–3 The version given in the translation is not certain. A survey of the references to *φορολόγος*, and its cognates *φορολογέω* and *φορολογία*, given in WB and in S. Daris, *Spoglio Lessicale*, shows that they are rare words and the passages cited are unhelpful. Some from the late Byzantine period clearly refer to private rent-collecting. In the Ptolemaic and Roman periods the words refer to tax-collection but the contexts are mostly vague. In PSI VII 792 *φορολογία* is used (in lines 7, 8, and 13; correct *Spoglio*) in connection with the transport of grain received by the state as tax and the delivery of it to the department of the *procurator ad Mercurium*, see XXXI **2567** 9 n.

Most relevant to our case, however, is the lately published P. Vindob. Tandem 9, where the issue of seed corn for A.D. 11/12 by a sitologus is authorized by the strategus, the royal scribe, and one *Ϲιφίλου* (reading uncertain) *Χρηϲίμου Καίϲαρ*[ο]*ϲ φορωλώγου* (19–20). The editors point out (20 n.) that in the related P. Lond. II 256(d) and (e)—pp. 95–8—a man called *Φαῦϲτος Πρίϲκου Καίϲαρος* appears to perform the same function for A.D. 10/11 though his title is not specified. These persons are plausibly regarded as imperial slaves, but their nomenclature is odd, for though the translations call them respectively the sons of Chresimus and Priscus no slave or freedman ought to have an official filiation. However, the addition of *Καίϲαρος* makes it clear that they are in the imperial service, probably as slaves, cf. P. R. C. Weaver, *Familia Caesaris*, 48, so the solution may be to regard Chresimus and Priscus as the former owners from whose possession the slaves Siphilus (*sic*) and Faustus passed into the *familia Caesaris*. To this I can produce no good parallel, the nearest being the *agnomina* derived from the names of former owners and ending in *-ianus*, *-anus*, and *-inus*, see Weaver, op. cit., 212–26. If these men are indeed imperial slaves, M. Antonius Spendon may be an imperial freedman deriving his name from Mark Antony through, probably, one of the two daughters of Antony and Octavia, cf. M. Antonius Pallas, M. Antonius Felix. The juxtaposition of the names indicates that Eudaemon was Spendon's slave.

Other hypotheses, which appear less probable at the moment, might be that Spendon was a *publicanus* (concessionary of a farmed tax), see H. J. Mason, *Greek Terms for Roman Institutions*, 97, s.vv. *φορολογέω*, *φορολόγος*, or that he was a soldier assigned to tax-collecting duties.

12 *πατρωνύμου*. This word is new in the papyri. Very possibly *ὀνόματος* is to be supplied in the lacuna that follows it.

13 ...*ειμηνυθ*[. Articulate probably *μηνυθ*[, whether it alludes to information laid in the present document or not.

15 Above *ἐπιδί*[δ]*ωμ*[ι there are remains of about ten letters interlined. Very little has been read, viz.]..*ιτο*.....[, and it is not possible to say whether the word or words should have been inserted before or after *ἐπιδί*[δ]*ωμ*[ι.

3274. Petition

A 16/3(h)   24×20 cm.   *c.* A.D. 99–117

The chief interest of this and the following item is the name of a procurator of the *idios logos*, Aulus(?) Prifernius Augurinus, who has previously appeared in P. Ryl. II 291 in the unrecognizable form]Φερενίωι Ἀγ..[, which can now be re-read from a photograph kindly supplied by the John Rylands Library and plausibly restored as Πρ]ι-φερ{ε}νίωι Ἀγορ[ίνωι, in spite of the poor spelling. In H.-G. Pflaum, *Les carrières* iii 1107 his name is given from P. Ryl 291 as Herenius Ag . . . (cf. *PIR*² iii 124, iv 71, H 101) and by an oversight he is listed as a *iuridicus*. This reference does not appear at all in the latest list of heads of the *idios logos*, P. R. Swarney, *The Ptolemaic and Roman Idios Logos*, 127–8.

His exact date is hedged about with difficulties. Of **3274** it can be said that it is of the reign of Trajan and after some unspecified time in the third regnal year, A.D. 99/100 (18, 46). In **3275** the day is partly preserved, Payni 2(0–29) = 14–23 June, but the regnal year number is lost. One clue is offered by the name of the addressee, the strategus Apion who is otherwise known only from XXXVIII **2852** dated in 8 Trajan, A.D. 104/5, but this cannot be pressed too closely since Apion's neighbours in office are dated to 2 December, A.D. 99 (XLI **2958**) and A.D. 110/11 (XXXVI **2758** 1 n.). Augurinus' named neighbours in office are even further away on both sides, see P. R. Swarney, *Idios Logos*, 127. Trajan's victory title *Dacicus*, acquired at the end of A.D. 102 (*RE* Suppl. Bd. X col. 1069), shows that the earliest possible date for **3275** is 14–23 June, A.D. 103. The absence of *Optimus* on the other hand allows no limitation of the date, see P. Bureth, *Les titulatures*, 51–2.

The description of P. Ryl. II 291 says that the tenth year of Trajan or Hadrian is mentioned, which is based on line 9]δεκάτου ἔτους Τραι[ανοῦ . . . We can now be fairly confident that the emperor is Trajan, but since the papyrus is broken immediately on the left any year between the tenth and nineteenth might have stood here and we can even envisage the possibility of τοῦ εἰσιόντος] δεκάτου ἔτους Τραι[ανοῦ κτλ., which would allow us to bring the range of dates to include Trajan's ninth year, A.D. 105/6.

This range of possible dates compels us to consider the fragment of the name of a holder of this office apparently functioning in 8 Trajan which survives in BGU IV 1033. 20. The first edition has]μνου τοῦ πρὸς τῷ ἰδίῳ λόγῳ τῷ η (ἔτει). Wilcken corrected this to]λίνου in *Archiv* 3 (1906) 505. A photograph supplied by Dr. W. Müller of the Staatliche Museen zu Berlin shows that as well as]λινου, which is not compelling, we might read]αινου (cf. G. Plaumann, *Der Idioslogos*, 68),]βινου,]κινου, or]μινου. In my opinion, therefore, this is not Augurinus but a previous holder of the office.

The unusual names make it certain that there is some connection with the procurator of Achaea A. Pomponius C. f. Quirina Augurinus T. Prifernius Paetus, see H.-G. Pflaum, *Les carrières* i 167–8 (No. 72). This person had had a successful military career and was decorated by Trajan after a victory over the Getae, probably belonging to the first Dacian war concluded in A.D. 102 since there is no specific mention that it was part of the second expedition (so Vollgraff, *BCH* 28 (1904) 426). Pflaum repeats Groag's argument that the absence of *Dacicus* from Trajan's titles in the Argive dedication to the procurator of Achaea indicates that he held the post already in A.D. 102, that is after the victorious conclusion of the first Dacian war but before the bestowal of the title at the end of the same year. The same argument appears also in *RE* xxii 2 col. 1967. Unfortunately the omission of Dacicus is a modern error beginning, as far as I can see, with *ILS* 8863; at any rate Δακικοῦ is in the first edition, *BCH* 28 (1904) 425, likewise in *AÉ* 1905. 6, and in R. H. Lacey, *The Equestrian Officers of Trajan and Hadrian*, 9. This procuratorship, a centenarian post, is attested for some moment after Trajan acquired the title *Dacicus*. The charge of the *idios logos* was a ducenarian post which could well have been the next step in the same man's career, and I suggest that this is a likely hypothesis.

For the procurator of Achaea and other Prifernii of the same period see also *RE* xxii 2 coll. 1967–70, Suppl. Bd. xiv (1974) 484–5, and for another equestrian one see especially H.-G. Pflaum, *Les carrières* i 166–7 (No. 71).

This text is a petition to Augurinus from a lady about her dead brother's estate. Half of it was confiscated by Augurinus as a result of a case brought by an informer and she claims that she had paid out the equivalent to settle the deceased's debts. Another brother had apparently taken possession of the estate in any case. The damaged and lost portions at the foot would perhaps have given us more details.

The tops of two copies survive in a rubbed and broken state. They were glued together edge to edge after being written, as is shown by the fact that the initial letter of line 46 is partly under the left-hand sheet. The writing is probably all by the same hand, though there is a possibility that two scribes wrote one copy each and that the resemblance is due to the use of the same style of handwriting. I am unable to say why the duplicate copies were filed in this way or whether they are from official or private records. The back was used, after the join was made, for some sort of account, probably arranged by daily entries, though the damage is so very severe that it is difficult to say anything about it for certain.

i

Αὔλωι Πριφε]ρνίωι Αὐγουρίνωι
    c. 8   κα]ὶ πρὸς τῷ ἰδίῳ λό[γῳ
παρὰ c. 6]ίας τῆς Θέωνος
διὰ   c. 7]ς Διον[υς]ίου τοῦ
5   Ἁρποκρατ]ί[ων]ος τῷ[ν ἀπ' Ὀ]ξυρύγχ(ων)
πόλεως.] ἐ[κ] μηνύσεως Ἀ[μ-

5 ο]ξυρυγχ

μωνίου Ἀ]μμωνίου κατηγόρου
ἐκρίθ]ην ἐπὶ coῦ τοῦ κυρίου περ[ὶ
ὑπαρχ]όντων Διδύμου ἀδελφοῦ
10 μου] ἀναιρεθέντων ὑπὸ τοῦ ἀδελ-
φοῦ] ἡμῶν Διονυτᾶτος καὶ ἔδοξεν ἀν]αλαβεῖν τὴν ἡμίcιαν τῶν
ὑπαρχ]όντων τοῦ Διδύμου ʼὑπὲρ ἧc διετέθηʼ καὶ
ἐ]δήλωcά coι τῷ εὐεργέτῃ ʼτὴν αὐτὴν ἡμίcιανʼ ἀποδε-
15 δωκέναι με ὑπὲρ αὐτοῦ χρέα δα-
νιcταῖc καὶ ἀπεφήνω ἐπιδοῦναί
μ]έ coι ἀναφόρ[ιον] περὶ τούτων,
ὧν] ἐcτιν τ[ὸ] κα[θ' ἕν.] τῷ μὲν τρίτῳ
ἔτει] Τραιανοῦ Κ[αίcαροc το]ῦ κυρίου
20 ἀπέ]δωκα .[*c.* 12 letters].c κατὰ
　　　　　　c. 20 letters 　　　]ακοcίων
　　　　　　c. 23 letters 　　　].μαιω
　　　　　　c. 22 letters 　　　]ο.τρυ
　　　　　　c. 22 letters 　　　] Πτολλίωʼνʼ
25 　　　　　　*c.* 22 letters 　　　].αρτα
　　　　　　c. 30 letters 　　　]. Τραιανο.
　　　　　　c. 30 letters 　　　] Διονυcιο( )
　　　　　　c. 27 letters 　　δρα]χμάc

　　　　·　　·　　·　　·

12, 14 l. ἡμίcειαν　　　15–16 l. δανειcταῖc

ii

Α[ὔλωι Πρι]φερνίωι Αὐγουρείνωι
30 δ[*c.* 8 letters]. καὶ πρὸc τῷ ἰδίῳ
(vac.) [λόγῳ] 　　　(vac.)
π[αρὰ *c.* 4]τρίαc τῆc Θέωνοc διὰ
c. 8 letters] Διονυcί[ο]υ τοῦ Ἁρποκρατίωνοc τῶ]ν ἀπ' Ὀξυ[ρ]ύγχων πόλ[εωc.
35 ἐ[κ] μηνύcεωc Ἀ[μ]μωνίου Ἀμμων[ίου
κατηγόρου ἐκρίθην ἐπὶ coῦ το[ῦ κυρίου
περὶ ὑπαρχόντων Διδύμου το[ῦ ἀδελ-

φοῦ μου ἀναιρεθέντω[ν ὑπὸ τοῦ ἀδελφοῦ ἡμῶν Διονυτᾶτος [καὶ ἔδοξεν
40 ἀναλαβε[ῖν τὴν ἡμίσειαν τῶν ὑπαρχόντων τοῦ [Διδύμου καὶ ἐδήλω-
cά coι τῷ εὐε[ργέτῃ ἀποδεδωκέναι με
ὑπὲρ αὐτοῦ χρέ[α δανεισταῖς καὶ ἀπεφήνω ἐπιδο[ῦναί μέ coι ἀναφόριον
45 περὶ τούτω[ν ὧν ἐcτιν τὸ καθ' ἕν.
τῷ μὲν γ (ἔτει) [Τραιανοῦ Καίcαρος τοῦ κυρίου
ἀπέδωκ[α   *c.* 25 letters
ρογραφ.[*c.* 25 letters
καὶ το.[*c.* 25 letters

. . . . .

'To Aulus(?) Prifernius Augurinus the ... and (procurator) in charge of the *idios logos*, from Demetria(?) daughter of Theon by agency of ... son of Dionysius, grandson of Harpocration, inhabitant of the city of the Oxyrhynchi. As a result of information laid by Ammonius son of Ammonius, accuser, I was brought to trial before you, my lord, in a case concerning the property of Didymus my brother taken by our brother Dionytas and the decision was to confiscate the half of Didymus' property concerning which provision was made in his will and I informed you, my benefactor, that I had paid back the said half as debts to creditors on his behalf and you delivered judgement that I should submit a memorandum to you about these matters, of which the detailed story is as follows. In the third year of Trajan Caesar the lord I paid back...'

2 See 30 n.
3 See 32 n.
4 Possibly the text had διὰ τοῦ ἀνδρό]ς Δ. τοῦ Ἁ., 'by agency of her husband, D. son of H.', but for the purposes of the translation the other possibility has been preferred.
7 κατηγόρου. See *CÉ* 49 (1974) 145–6.
10 It is not quite clear what ἀναιρεθέντων means, but it seems that she is claiming that although she had settled the debts of her dead brother it was her other brother who actually took possession of the estate.
13–14 The interlineations in both lines come earlier than it seems possible to insert them, i.e. over -ων τοῦ Διδ- and over -λωcά coι τῷ ε-. In the duplicate no trace of them survives, but they may have come in a more suitable position at the ends of lines 41–2.
22].μαιω. The first letter looks like]ρ; possibly this is a name Ἑ]ρμαίῳ.
23 Possibly the name Τρύ[φων occurred here.
24 The syllabification indicates that Πτολλίων is nominative.
26 Read probably Τραιανοῦ, as part of a date.
27 Διονυcιο( ). Cf. perhaps 4 and 33.
29 Ἀ[ὔλωι. The trace is a clear diagonal descending to the right. The connection with the procurator of Achaea suggests that we should restore Ἀ[ὔλωι rather than Ἀ[ππίωι, Δ[εκίμωι, Δ[ουκίωι. Usually the *praenomen* goes with a specific *nomen*. Since this man preferred Prifernius, which was probably his original *nomen*, to Pomponius, which was probably that of an adoptive father, he would be expected to retain Titus as well. It is clear, however, that the remains will not suit any part of Τ(ε)ίτωι. In spite of this difficulty of nomenclature, it seems more likely that the head of the *idios logos* is the same man as the procurator of Achaea than that he is another relative.
30 δ[*c.* 8 letters].. This is very puzzling. In spite of the isolated case of Norbanus Ptolemaeus, δικαιοδότης καὶ πρὸς τῷ ἰδίῳ λόγῳ in A.D. 63 (P. Fouad 21. 5), it is not usual to find a second post being

held by a procurator, and there seems to be no way of restoring here a formula with διέποντι or διαδεχομένῳ indicating a temporary administration, whether of this office or another. It is clear that **3275** gives Augurinus no additional office and fairly clear that P. Ryl. II 291 does not do so either. The final traces do not suggest, though they do not absolutely exclude, δ[ικαιοδοτ]ῇ or -δοτ]ῆι, and the same applies, of course, to δ[ιοικητ]ῇ, -ῆι. They consist of parts of an upright preceded by traces which would combine best to form a diagonal such as that of]ν. Alternatively, all the traces might be part of the right-hand half of]ω and this seems to offer less grammatical difficulty. An escape from the implication that Augurinus held two posts might be to read δ[ουκηναρί]ῳ. The objection to this is that the custom of advertising official salaries in the titulatures is first attested for the reign of Commodus, even though there are traces of an informal classification of posts by this criterion from the reign of Augustus, see *RE* v coll. 1752–3, s.v. *ducenarius*.

It is perhaps worth adding that the remains do not suggest ἀρχιερεῖ, cf. *CÉ* 49 (1974) 146–7, *ZPE* 13 (1974) 32–3, XLV **3263** 9–10 n.

32]τρίας. If the traces on the edge of the break are indeed of tau, no alternative to Δημη]τρίας is offered by F. Dornseiff–B. Hansen, *Rückl. Wb. d. gr. Eigennamen*, 23.

41–2 See 13–14 n.

47–8 The end of line 20 suggests that κατὰ χει-]|⁴⁸ρόγραφο[ν stood here, with χειρόγραφον at the beginning of line 21.

3275. REPORT OF PRIESTS

33 4B.84/K(6–9)a   *c.* 7·5 × 12 ; 8·5 × 14 cm.   14–23 June, *c.* A.D. 103–117

The mention of Prifernius Augurinus, see **3274** introd., is the main point of interest in this text, which is a report from representatives of the priesthood of a village temple addressed to the governor of the district, who was apparently expected to pass on the information to the procurator in charge of the *idios logos*. The relations between the temples and the *idios logos* in this period are studied by P. R. Swarney, *The Ptolemaic and Roman Idios Logos*, 83–96.

The sheet, which is blank on the back, has been broken across the middle and the damage in the neighbourhood of this break is so severe that very little of the detail of the report can be recovered and it is not known how much may be missing between the two fragments. Only one of the several tiny scraps which are entirely detached bears ink and on that only a single iota can be read with confidence.

The number of priests was reported, and this was preceded by amounts in grain and money, some of which look as if they record expenditure.

No exact parallel has been identified, though we may compare in a general way parts of P. Tebt. II 298 and VIII **1143–4**. For the standard type of report from priests, the γραφαὶ ἱερέων καὶ χειρισμοῦ, which contained lists of priests by name and inventories of temple furniture, see E. H. Gilliam, 'The Archives of the Temple of Soknobraisis', in *YCS* 10 (1947) 181–281, esp. 191–8.

> Ἀπίωνι στρ(ατηγῷ)
> παρὰ Ὥρου Κεφάλωνος καὶ
> Πανεσνέως Ὥρου ἀμφοτέρων

1 στρ̄

ἀπὸ κώμης Ϲενοκώμεωϲ

5   ἱερέων Ἄμμωνος θεοῦ με-
γίϲτου ἱεροῦ τοῦ ὄντος ἐν
τῇ αὐτῇ κώμῃ προκεχειριϲ-
μένων ὑπὸ τῶν ϲυνιερέων.
πρὸς τὴν γραφεῖϲάν ϲοι ὑπὸ

10   Πρειφερνίου Ἀουγουρείνου
τοῦ κρατίϲτου πρὸς τῷ ἰδίῳ
λόγῳ ἐπιϲτο[λὴν π]ερὶ τοῦ κα-
τ' ἔτος αὐτῷ [λ]όγον ἀκρει-
βῆ πεμφθῆναι τῶν ὑπαρ-

15   χουϲῶν τ[ο]ῖϲ ἱεροῖϲ ο[....
ἔτι δὲ κ[αὶ τ]ῷ α...ου[..
νων πρ[οϲ]φων[οῦμεν] ὑ[πο-
κεῖϲθαι [ἡ]μεῖν κ[αὶ το]ῖϲ ϲυν-
ιερεῦϲι .[.....]ργ[..... ἐν 'Ο]ξυ-

20   ρύγχων [.....].ϲ.[..........
...]...[......]ιαϲ[..........
c. 12 letters]ϲκω[..........

.   .   .   .

.   .   .   .

.].…[
ἐξ ὧν …[

25   .ι..... (πυροῦ ἀρτ.) .ι..[.].[
(πυροῦ ἀρτ.) α (ἥμιϲ.?) ξ.[.]ητη (πυροῦ ἀρτ.) (ἥμιϲ.?) [.].[
... τῶν τεϲϲάρων (ἥμιϲ.?) ..[
ἱερεῦϲι Θοήριδος (δραχμ.) .....
τῶν τεϲϲάρων (δραχμ.) κβ. γείνον-

30   ται (πυροῦ ἀρτάβαι) ... χ(οίνικες) δ ......
αἳ ..( ) ἐκ (δραχμῶν) η (ἀρτάβαι) ..χ
γείνονται (πυροῦ ἀρτάβαι) ιβ. ἐϲμ[ὲν
δὲ τὸν ἀριθμὸν ἄνδρε[ϲ ..
περιτετμημένοι [τῶν λει-

13–14 l. ἀκριβῆ

35 τουργούντων ἐπι[κεκριμέ-
    νοι ἐπὶ (δραχμαῖς) λ. καὶ ὀ[μνύομεν
    Αὐτοκράτορα Καί[σαρα Νέρουαν
    Τραιανὸν Cεβαστὸ[ν Γερμανικὸν
    Δακικὸν μὴ ⟨ἐ⟩ψεῦc[θαι ἢ ἔνο-
40 χοι εἴημεν τῷ ὅρ[κῳ. ἔτους (?)
    Αὐτοκράτορος Καίc[αρος Νέρουα
    Τραιανοῦ Cεβαστο[ῦ Γερμανικοῦ
    Δακικοῦ, Παῦνι κ[(?). (m. 2) Ὧρος
    Καιφάλωνος καὶ [Π]α[νεc-
45 νέως Ὧρου ὠμωμέκαμε[ν
    τὸν ὅρκον. Πλουτίων ἀ-
    πελεύθερος Θέωνος ἔ-
    γραψα ὑπὲρ αὐτῶν μὴ
    εἰ]δώτων γράμματα.

44 l. Κεφάλωνος   44–5 l. [Π]α[νεc]νεύς, ὀμωμόκαμε[ν   49 l. εἰ]δότων

'To Apion, strategus, from Horus son of Cephalon and Panesneus son of Horus, both from the village of Senocomis, priests of the temple of Ammon, most great god, which is in the same village, appointed representatives by their fellow priests. In response to the letter written to you by Prifernius Augurinus, *vir egregius* in charge of the *idios logos*, concerning the dispatch to him annually of an accurate account of the properties(?) belonging to the temples and also of the ... we report that we have had granted to us and our fellow priests ... (in?) Oxyrhynchus ...'

'... total 12 artabas of wheat. We are men to the number of ..., circumcised, of the class of serving priests, examined (and approved to pay the εἰcκριτικόν) at 30 drachmas. And we swear by Imperator Caesar Nerva Traianus Augustus Germanicus Dacicus that we have told no lies or may we be liable to the (penalty of our) oath. Year ... of Imperator Caesar Nerva Traianus Augustus Germanicus Dacicus, Payni 2(0–29). (2nd hand) We, Horus son of Cephalon and Panesneus son of Horus have sworn the oath. I, Plution, freedman of Theon, wrote on their behalf because they do not know letters.'

1 For the strategus see XXXVIII 2852, dated to 8 Trajan, A.D. 104/5.

4–7 This temple of Ammon is new, see 3292 9 n. for others in Oxyrhynchite villages.

15 Perhaps restore ο[ὐcιῶν, or, since space is short, ο[ncιῶ = ο[ὐcιῶ(ν) may have been written.

16–17 It is palaeographically attractive to read ἀνηλου[μέ]νων and expenditures may be recorded in lines 26 and 28, but ἀνηλόω is a very rare form of ἀναλίcκω, cf. B. G. Mandilaras, *The Verb in the Greek Non-literary Papyri*, p. 66 § 61(2).

17–19 For the sense attributed to ὑποκεῖcθαι in the translation see *LSJ* s.v. ὑπόκειμαι II 7 b. If ἐ[λαιου]ργ[εῖον vel sim. is to be supplied in 19, it may be that it means that the priests hold a mortgage on an oil-factory or other real property which thus brings in an income, cf. ibid. 7 a. The same word is used in a similar document at P. Tebt. II 298. 52, but the passage is too damaged to be of any help.

26 ξ.[.]ητη. Comparing the dative in 28 and envisaging the possibility that this is an account of expenditure, see 16–17 n., we might guess ξυ[ρ]ητῇ, 'to the barber'. Since Egyptian priests wore the head shaved, this has some plausibility, but ξυρητής is known only from BGU II 630 verso 10, the common word being κουρεύς.

35–6 On the meaning of ἐπικεκριμένοι ἐπὶ (δρ.)λ see *YCS* 10 (1947) 203–4.

39 ⟨ἐ⟩ψεῦc[θαι. Cf. XXXVI 2761 13, XXXVIII 2855 18; F. T. Gignac, *Grammar*, 319–20. In spite of VII 1028 37 μὴ ψε(ύcαcθαι) I can find no certain example of any tense but the perfect.

3276–3284. APPLICATIONS FOR EPICRISIS

46 5B.49/K(6)a–f and (7)a–d   A.D. 148/9

These items are the better preserved examples of the remains of a *syncollesimon* or roll-file made up of applications for epicrisis glued together side by side. When all the remains are put together in a logical succession the lower edges, though broken, give the impression of a straight line, indicating that the bottom of the roll was torn away while it was still rolled up and has not been preserved with the top. It is noticeable that the items were of different heights and that the top edge of the roll was very uneven.

Each document has or had a number at the top and we seem to have remains of numbers 109 or 110 up to 121. These numbers all seem to be in the same hand, which may also have added the occasional annotations of district names.

3276 has a number at the top which might be either $\rho\iota$ (= 110) followed by an oblique stroke or $\rho\iota\alpha$ (= 111). There are remains of the flanking numbers, 109 and 111, or 110 and 112. The first of these is too damaged to repay transcription; the second is **3277**.

3278 has the number $\rho\iota\gamma = 113$; it therefore follows the previous group either immediately or after a gap which contained one item, no. 112. On the right of **3278** (113) are traces in a hand which matches remains adhering on the left of **3279**, which should therefore be 115 ($\rho\iota\epsilon$).

3280 has the heading $\rho\iota\varsigma$ (116), and though there is no join to **3279**, the last five items can be placed side by side on the evidence of overlap of text or fibres and their numeration is assured by the clear heading $\rho\kappa$ (120) at the top of **3283**. The damaged item falling between **3280** and **3281**, which must have been no. 117, has not been transcribed.

The format, as reconstructed, may be summed up in the following scheme:—

(109 or	110 or	(111 or										
110?)	111?	112?)	113	(114)	(115)	116	(117)	(118)	119	120	(121)	
om.	*3276*	*3277*	*3278*	om.	*3279*	*3280*	om.	*3281*	*3282*	*3283*	*3284*	

The section of the roll from which the fragments came must have been about 110 cm. long, by very rough measurement. The greatest height preserved is *c.* 12·5 cm. (*3279*).

The epicrisis has been studied recently in *Acts of the XIVth International Congress of Papyrology*, 227–32, by Professor O. Montevecchi, who is preparing a re-edition of the texts relating to it. The new items are all concerned with entry to the gymnasial class as distinct from the metropolitan.

The chief novelty is an expanded version of a clause already known from X **1266** concerning admission to the gymnasial class of persons who had no ancestor in the list of the 34th year of Augustus. This special entry is dated to years 3 and 4 of Nero, A.D. 56/7 and 57/8, and the examining officer's name and rank are given in such a way as to clear up a confusion between him and a prefect of Egypt also called Paulinus, see **3279** 20 n.

3276

ρι. [..] (vac.) Ἄ[ν]ω Παρ[εμβολῆς

παρὰ Πετ[.....]ϲ Ἀπο[λ]λωνίου τ[οῦ] Πετεύριοϲ

μητρὸϲ [.....]τηϲ ....ου τῶν ἀπὸ Ὀξυρύγχων

πόλεω[ϲ. κατὰ τ]ὰ κελευϲθέντα περὶ ἐπικρίϲεω[ϲ

5   τῶν π[ροϲβαινόντ]ων εἰϲ τοὺϲ ἐκ τοῦ γυμ[ναϲ]ίου

ἤ εἰϲι τ[οῦ γένου]ϲ τού[το]ν ἐτάγη ὁ υἱ[ιό]ϲ μου Ἀμμώνιοϲ

μητρὸ]ϲ Ἡρᾶτοϲ Ἀμόιτοϲ [π]ρ[ο]ϲ[βε]βηκὼϲ εἰϲ (τρειϲκαιδεκαετεῖϲ)

τῷ ἐ]νεϲτῶτι ιβ (ἔτει) Ἀντωνί[ν]ου [Κ]αίϲ[α]ρ[οϲ τοῦ κυρίου.

ὅθεν] παραγενόμενοϲ πρὸϲ τὴν τούτου ἐπίκρ[ι]ϲιν

10   δηλῶ κατὰ τὴν γενομένην τῷ ε (ἔτει) θεοῦ Οὐεϲπαϲιανοῦ

ὑπ]ὸ Ϲουτ[ωρίου] Ϲωϲιβίου ϲτρ(ατηγήϲαντοϲ) καὶ Νικάνδρου γενομέ-

νο]υ βα[ϲιλ(ικοῦ) γρ](αμματέωϲ) καὶ ὧν ἄλλ[ων] καθήκει ἐπίκριϲιν

τῶν ἐκ τ]οῦ γυμναϲίο[υ ἐπι]κεκρίϲθαι τὸν πατέρα

μου ἐπ᾽ ἀμ]φόδου Δρόμο[υ Γυ]μναϲίου καθ᾽ ἃϲ ἐπήνεγ-

15   κεν ἀποδ]ε[ί]ξ[ειϲ] ὡϲ ὁ πάπ[πο]ϲ αὐτοῦ Εὐβίων Πτολλί-

ωνόϲ ἐϲτιν] ἐν τῇ τοῦ λδ (ἔτουϲ) θεοῦ Καίϲαροϲ γρ(αφῇ)

ἐμὲ δὲ προϲβάντα] εἰϲ (τρειϲκαιδεκαετεῖϲ) τῷ α (ἔτει) θεοῦ Τραιανοῦ

c. 20   ].ταιϲ ἀποδείξεϲι

c. 25   ] τῆϲ μητρὸϲ

.   .   .   .   .

20   Back, downwards   ]υίου

                ] Ἄνω Παρεμ(βολῆϲ)

6 l. εἰ   7 ιγϛ   8 ιβϛ   10 εϛ   11 ϲτρϛ   12 βα[ϲιλ γρ]ϛ?   16 λδϛ, γρϛ   17 ιγϛ, αϛ   21 παρεμ

'No. 111(?). Upper Camp district.

'From Pet... son of Apollonius grandson of Peteyris mother ... daughter of (Pyrrhus?), inhabitant of the city of the Oxyrhynchi. In accordance with the orders concerning scrutiny of those entering the gymnasial class (to discover) if they are of this stock, my son Ammonius, mother Heras daughter of Amois, was registered as having entered the class of thirteen-year-olds in the present twelfth year of Antoninus Caesar the lord. Therefore I have presented myself for his scrutiny and declare that in the scrutiny of the gymnasial class which took place in the fifth year of the deified Vespasian under Sutorius Sosibius then strategus and Nicander then royal scribe and the other proper persons my father was scrutinized in the Gymnasium Street district in accordance with the evidences which he presented that his grandfather Eubion son of Ptollion is in the list of the thirty-fourth year of the deified Caesar, and (I declare) that I on entering the class of thirteen-year-olds in the first year of the deified Trajan...'

1 Ἄ[ν]ω Παρ[εμβολῆϲ. Cf. 21, **3278** 8. Perhaps Παρεμβολῆϲ was abbreviated as in 21, **3277** 1. The number may be ριᾱ = 111 or ρι´ = 110, see Introd. If it is 111, no item is unrepresented between 110 and 121.

2 Perhaps restore Πετ[εύριο]ϲ, the grandfather's name, since names often recur in alternate generations, but other names are also possible, e.g. Petsiris, Peteësis.

3 The mother's patronymic may be Πύρρου; τηϲ could be either the article τῆϲ or the end of her name.

8 12 Pius = A.D. 148/9.

10 5 Vespasian = A.D. 72/3.

16 34 Augustus = A.D. 4/5.

17 1 Trajan = 27 January–28 August, A.D. 98.

18–19 Restore something like ἐπικεκρίϲθαι ἐπὶ ταῖϲ α]ὐταῖϲ ἀποδείξεϲι [ἀμφόδου τοῦ αὐτοῦ (or ἀμφόδου Ἄνω Παρεμβολῆϲ) καὶ τὸν] τῆϲ μητρὸϲ [τοῦ υἱοῦ μου πρόπαππον κτλ., cf. **3283** 16.

20 Probably this is the applicant's patronymic, Ἀπολλω]νίου, which would be preceded by his name.

3277

(vac.) [Ἄ]νῳ Παρεμ(βολῆϲ) [

παρὰ Δι[c. 10   Πτ]ο[λ]εμαίου τοῦ Π[c. 20

Πετοϲίρι[οϲ ἀπ' Ὀξυρύγχων] πόλεωϲ. κατὰ τ[ὰ κελευϲθέντα περὶ ἐπικρίϲεωϲ

τ]ῶν πρ[οϲβαινόντων εἰϲ τοὺϲ ἐκ] τ(οῦ) [γ]υμναϲίου ἤ [εἰϲι τοῦ γένουϲ τούτου

5   ἐπ' ἀμφόδου Ἄνω Παρεμβολῆϲ ἐτάγ]η ὁ υἱόϲ μο[υ   c. 20

..[.]..[c. 15   προ]ϲβεβη[κὼϲ εἰϲ (τρειϲκαιδεκαετεῖϲ) τῷ ἐνεϲτῶτι

ιβ [(ἔτει)] Ἀντ[ωνίνου Καίϲαρ]οϲ τοῦ κυ[ρίου, ὅθεν παραγενόμενοϲ

π]ρὸϲ τὴν τ[ούτου ἐπίκριϲιν] δηλ(ῶ) κατ[ὰ τὴν γενομένην τῷ ε (ἔτει) θεοῦ

Οὐ]ε[ϲ]παϲι[ανοῦ ὑπὸ Σου]τορίου Cωϲιβίου ϲτρατηγήϲαντοϲ καὶ Νικάνδρου

10   γ]ενομέν[ου βαϲιλικοῦ] γραμματ[έωϲ   c. 20

.].·[.]...[c. 8   τῶ]ν ἐκ τοῦ γυ[μναϲίου   c. 15

c. 18   ].[.]. Πτολ[c. 20

·   ·   ·   ·   ·   ·

4 εκ]ᵗ; l. εἴ [8 δη^λ

'[No. 112?] Upper Camp district.

'From Di... son of Ptolemaeus grandson of P... mother... daughter of Petosiris, from the city of the Oxyrhynchi. In accordance with the orders concerning scrutiny of those entering the gymnasial class (to discover) if they are of this stock, my son... mother... daughter of... was registered in the Upper Camp district as having entered the class of thirteen-year-olds in the present twelfth year of Antoninus Caesar the lord. Therefore I have presented myself for his scrutiny and declare that in the scrutiny of the gymnasial class which took place in the fifth year of the deified Vespasian under Sutorius Sosibius then strategus and Nicander then royal scribe...'

1 Ἄ]νῳ. The traces are indeterminate, but since the flanking items **3276** (ριᾱ?) and **3278** (ριγ) are both from the Upper Camp district, Ἄνω seems preferable to the two other possibilities, Ἱππέων and Λυκίων. Before this a number, ριβ or ριᾱ, see introd., is lost.

2 Restore Δι[ονυϲοδώρου, Δι[ονυϲάμμωνοϲ vel sim.; after the grandfather's name, of which Π[is the beginning, supply μητρόϲ followed by the mother's name. Petosiris, in 3, is her father.

3 The restoration at the end is standard but too long to have been written here in full; probably it was abbreviated, e.g. επι^κ = ἐπικ(ρίσεως) would suit. Cf. 4, 5 and nn., 8.

4 Apparently εκ]ͭ = ἐκ] τ(οῦ) was written, cf. δηλ(ῶ) in 8. The beginning is also somewhat long; perhaps προσβαινον^τ was written.

5 Παρεμβολῆς: perhaps written παρε^μ, cf. 1 and 3, 4 nn.

5–6 To fill the gap we need the son's name, his mother's name preceded by μητρός, and her father's name. Since the space is so long, perhaps one of the three had a double name.

9 στρατηγήσαντος was presumably abbreviated to στρ弓 vel sim.

10–11 We expect here καὶ ὧν ἄλλων καθήκει ἐπίκρισιν τῶν ἐκ τοῦ γυμνασίου, but this gives only 26 letters before τῶν ἐκ τοῦ γυμνασίου, which seems too little for the space available. The meagre traces at the beginning of 11 do not fit comfortably into the formula, though no letter there can be identified with certainty.

3278

ριγ
παρὰ Τερεντ[ί]ου Δι[ο]γένους τοῦ
Μικκάλου μητρὸς Θαήσιος Ποσ[ει-
δωνίου ἀπὸ Ὀξυρύγχων πόλεως.

5   κατὰ τὰ ⟨κε⟩λευσθέντα περὶ ἐπικ(ρίσεως) τῶ[ν
προσβ(αινόντων) εἰς τοὺς ἐκ τοῦ γυμνασίου ἤ ε[ἰ-
σι τοῦ [γ]ένους τούτου ⟨ἐτάγη⟩ ἐπ' ἀμφόδου
Ἄνω Παρ[ε]μβολῆς ὁ υἱός μου Ἀμόις
μητρὸς Θαήσιος Πτολεμαίου προσβ(εβηκὼς)

10   εἰς (τρεισκαιδεκαετεῖς) τῷ ἐνεστῶτι ιβ (ἔτει) Ἀντωνίνου
Καίσαρος τοῦ κυρίου. ὅθεν παραγε-
νόμενος πρὸς τὴν τού[του] ἐπίκ(ρισιν)
δ[η]λῶ κατὰ τὴν γενομ⟨έν⟩η[ν τ]ῷ ε (ἔτει)
θεοῦ Οὐες(πασιανοῦ) ἐπίκ(ρισιν) ἐπικεκρίσθαι τὸν

15   πατέρα{ν} μ(ου) Διογένην προσβ( ) Μικκάλου υφ..[...]...[.].[.....]...

    •   •   •   •   •

5 επι^κ   6 προσ^β; ἤ, l. εἴ   9 προσ^β̄   10 ιγ弓, ιβL   12 επι̣^κ   13 ε弓   14 ουες)επι^κ
15 πατεραν^μ, προσ^β

'No. 113.'
'From Terentius son of Diogenes grandson of Miccalus mother Thaesis daughter of Posidonius from the city of the Oxyrhynchi. In accordance with the orders concerning scrutiny of those entering the gymnasial class (to discover) if they are of this stock, my son Amois mother Thaesis daughter of Ptolemaeus was registered in the Upper Camp district as having entered the class of thirteen-year-olds in the present twelfth year of Antoninus Caesar the lord. Therefore I have presented myself for his scrutiny and declare that in the scrutiny which took place in the fifth year of the deified Vespasian my father Diogenes, the elder(?), son of Miccalus, was scrutinized . . .'

13–14 It is noticeable that the names of the local officials conducting the scrutiny of 5 Vespasian are not mentioned here as they are in the other documents of this file.

15 In spite of the misleading circumstance that προϲβ( ) is used above (6, 9) for parts of προϲ-βαίνειν, we should probably expand here to προϲβ(ύτερον) = πρεϲβύτερον, 'the elder', indicating that Diogenes was to be distinguished from a younger namesake. This is a common vulgar spelling of the word, see Mayser–Schmoll I i p. 45 lines 38–42 (§ 6, 5).

3279

ρι.[

παρὰ Παυϲιρίωνο[ϲ   c. 10   τοῦ Ἀ-
περῶτος μητρὸς Διδ[ύ]μ[ης ἀπ' Ὀξυρύγχων πόλεως. κατὰ τὰ κελευ[ϲθέντα
5 περὶ ἐπικρίϲεως τῶν προϲβα[ινόντων
εἰϲ τοὺϲ ἐκ τοῦ γυμναϲίου ἤ εἰϲ[ι τοῦ γένους
τ]ούτου ἐτάγη ἐπ' ἀμφόδου Ἱππέ[ων Παρεμ-
β[ο]λῆϲ ὁ υἱόϲ μου Ϲαραπίων μη[τρὸϲ   c. 5
ριοϲ Πανεχώ[το]υ προϲβεβηκ[ὼϲ εἰϲ (τρειϲκαιδεκαετεῖϲ)
10 τῷ ἐνεϲτῶτι ιβ (ἔτει) Ἀντων[ίνου Καίϲαροϲ
τοῦ κυρίου. ὅθεν παραγενόμ[ενοϲ εἰϲ τὴν
τούτου ἐπίκριϲιν δηλῶ κατὰ [τὴν γενομένην τῷ ε (ἔτει) θεοῦ Οὐεϲπαϲιαν[οῦ ὑπὸ Ϲουτω-
ρίου Ϲωϲιβ[ί]ου ϲτρατηγήϲαντοϲ [καὶ Νικάνδρου
15 γενομένου βαϲιλικοῦ γραμμ[ατέωϲ καὶ
ὧν ἄλλων καθήκει ἐπ[ί]κριϲιν [ἐπικεκρίϲθαι
τὸν πάππον μου Ἀπερῶτα Ἀπε[c. 12
ωνοϲ ἐν ὑπερετέϲι ἐπὶ τοῦ α[ὐτοῦ ἀμφόδου
ἐν εἴδει τῶν τῷ γ (ἔτει) καὶ δ (ἔτει) Ν[έρωνος ὑπὸ
20 Κουρτίου Παυλείνου χειλιάρ[χου ἐπικε-
κριμένων καὶ τὸν [π]α[τ]έρα [μου προϲ-
βάντα γεγενῆϲθαι ἐν ταῖϲ ....[c. 2 τοῦ γυμναϲίου γραφαῖϲ ἀμφόδου τοῦ [αὐτοῦ c. 2
....[....].[.].[........]..[.....].[c. 7

·   ·   ·   ·   ·

6 l. εἴ   10 ιβL   13 εL   19 γL, δL

'No. 115.

'From Paysirion son of... grandson of Aperos mother Didyme from the city of the Oxyrhynchi. In accordance with the orders concerning scrutiny of those entering the gymnasial class (to discover) if they are of this stock, my son Sarapion mother …ris daughter of Panechotes was registered in the Cavalry Camp district as having entered the class of thirteen-year-olds in the present twelfth year of Antoninus Caesar the lord. Therefore I have presented myself for his scrutiny and declare that in the scrutiny which took place in the fifth year of the deified Vespasian under Sutorius Sosibius then strategus and Nicander then royal scribe and the other proper persons my grandfather Aperos (son of Aperos grandson of …ion?) was scrutinized among those over age in the same district in the category of those scrutinized in the third and fourth year of Nero by Curtius Paulinus military tribune and (I declare) that my father entered and took his place in the (subsequent?) lists of the gymnasium in the same district. . . .'

1 ρι.[. This item must be no. 115, ριε, because adhering to its left edge are remains of a document in the same hand as that on the remains which adhere to the right of **3278**, which is no. 113, ριγ. The traces just before the break are mostly below the line; probably the explanation is that only part of the traces belong to ε, while below there is either stray ink or part of an annotation of the district name. We should perhaps print two lines, i.e.

$$1 \qquad ρι ε[$$
$$1a \qquad .[$$

but since for 1a ʿΙ[ππέων Παρεμβολῆς, cf. 7–8, looks unsatisfactory, I am inclined to think that the remains are stray ink.

17 It looks as if the patronymic of this Aperos was the same, i.e. Ἀπε[ρῶτος, followed by τοῦ and then by the grandfather's name, which must have been a short one with a vowel before the omega, e.g. Ἀπί]ωνος, Ὡρί]ωνος.

18 The applicant's grandfather was scrutinized 'among those over age', which makes it clear that these words refer to the person scrutinized and not to the person applying to have him scrutinized, as was supposed in XII **1452** 44–56, 51 nn. The wording there is [ἀκολ(ούθως)] αἶς—οἶς ed. pr., but a photo shows the expected αἶς—ὁ πατ(ὴρ) αὐτοῦ ἐν ὑπ(ερ)(ετέσιν)—υ)L pap.—ἐπήνεγ[κ(εν)] ἀποδείξε(σιν).

Usually ὑπερετής means 'beyond the age of liability to poll-tax', that is, in the sixties, see *Archiv* 3 (1904–6) 232–3. In these cases, however, it seems better to suppose that it means 'beyond the normal age for scrutiny', that is, 'over thirteen'. Note that each of these cases relates to an important and anomalous stage in the development of the gymnasial scrutiny, the new one to A.D. 56–8, that in **1452** to the enrolment of A.D. 72/3, see next note.

20 Κουρτίου Παυλείνου. The *nomen* is clear to read and the passage removes a difficulty from the list of prefects. This is the person mentioned in a similar connection in X **1266** 25, where the *nomen* was read by Grenfell and Hunt as Καυρτίου and by C. H. Roberts as Καυνείου (*JRS* 44 (1954) 116–19, cf. *BASP* 4(1967) 84). The papyrus, now Bodleian MS. gr. class. d. 119 (P), has been inspected and does in fact have Κουρτίου.

The passage of **1266**, less precise than this one, seemed to be dated to 5 Vespasian = A.D. 72/3; consequently Paulinus was wrongly taken to be identical with the Παυλῖνος διαδεξάμενος τὴν ἡγεμονίαν in Josephus *BJ* vii 10, 4. Now **3279** not only reveals his true *nomen* as Curtius but shows that he was a military tribune active in 3 and 4 Nero, i.e. A.D. 56/7 and 57/8. The tribune Paulinus who interviewed Josephus in A.D. 67 (*BJ* iii 8, 1) could perhaps have been our Curtius Paulinus, but, far more important, the way is now open to accepting the identification of the prefect Paulinus with the Valerius Paulinus described in *PIR*[1] iii p. 373 (V 105), cf. H.-G. Pflaum, *Les carrières*, i p. 94, No. 40. P. Strasb. 541 refers in a damaged context to a prefect with the *nomen* Valerius in the reign of Vespasian. The regnal year number is lost and so is the prefect's *cognomen*. Very possibly we should restore the *cognomen* as Paulinus.

It should be noted that we have now no fixed date in the prefecture of Paulinus. Josephus tells us that he succeeded on the death of Ti. Julius Lupus, last known in office some time in 5 Vespasian = A.D. 72/3, cf. XXXVI **2757** i 2.

The words διαδεξάμενος τὴν ἡγεμονίαν, used by Josephus to describe Paulinus, would in a document mean quite precisely 'then acting prefect'. In Josephus they may mean something less precise, 'the successor to the prefecture', but since Lupus died in office there is some suggestion that they should be taken in the narrower sense. The titulature in P. Strasb. 541 indicates that the Valerius there was a prefect in his own right, but it would be possible that Valerius Paulinus should have had his appointment as acting prefect confirmed by promotion to full prefect.

Information from this document has been used in *JRS* 65 (1975) 143 (no. 28 a), 183 (§ vi), and a similar document from the Michigan collection has allowed similar conclusions, see P. J. Sijpesteijn, *Flavius Josephus and the Prefect of Egypt in 73 A.D.*, forthcoming in *Historia*.

The new dates of 3 and 4 Nero make it worth while retracing the important stages in the history of the gymnasial epicrisis. All the applications that are complete enough to check make a statement about the scrutiny of 5 Vespasian = A.D. 72/3. Clearly this was a date of some special significance; perhaps an effort was made to compile a complete record in that year. In all but three instances the claim is made that the person scrutinized in A.D. 72/3 passed the scrutiny by proving that an ancestor's name was to be found in the list of 34 Augustus = A.D. 4/5, which date also, therefore, marks an important stage in the institution of gymnasial epicrisis, the earliest known to us and very possibly the initial one.

In the three exceptional cases the persons passed the scrutiny of A.D. 72/3 because of the admission of the applicant or an ancestor to the gymnasial class by Curtius Paulinus, who was active, as we now learn, in A.D. 56/7 and 57/8.

It appears, therefore, that most members of the gymnasial class after A.D. 72/3 derived their right from an ancestor approved in A.D. 4/5, some derived it from one approved in A.D. 56/7 or 57/8, and all had their right finally established by a review held in A.D. 72/3. See now also *BASP* 13 (1976) 182–5.

20–1 ἐπικε]κριμένων. This is restored in accordance with the reading of X **1266** 25, though in the note there the first editors suspected that εἰσκεκριμένων should be read. However, there is no real analogy with P. Flor. I 57. 73, which they cite, and ἐπικρίνειν seems to be the word which is appropriate to this context.

22 At the end μετ.[is possible. This would imply something like ἐν ταῖς μετὰ [ταῦτα (or τοῦτο) τοῦ γυ]μνασίου γραφαῖς, cf. **3283** 18, but the space available should accommodate only about seven letters as the most, to judge from neighbouring lines. It is, of course, common to find writing particularly cramped at the ends of lines, so that a long supplement remains possible, though unattractive.

3280

ριϛ

παρὰ Πνεφερῶτος Ἡρᾶτος τοῦ Πνεφ[ερῶτος
μητ(ρὸς) Θατρῆτος ἀπ' Ὀξυρ(ύγχων) πόλ(εως). κατὰ τὰ κ[ελευ-
σθέντ(α) περὶ ἐπικρίσεως τῶν προσβα[ινόντων
εἰς τοὺς] ἐκ [τ]οῦ γυ[μν]ασίου ἥ εἰσι τ[οῦ]

5 (at left margin of line 4)

· · ·

3 μη^τ, οξυρ‾πὁλ   3–4 κ[ελευ]σθεν^τ   5 l. εἰ

'No. 116.

'From Pnepheros son of Heras grandson of Pnepheros mother Thatres from the city of the Oxyrhynchi. In accordance with the orders about scrutiny of those entering the gymnasial class (to discover) if they are of . . .'

(The remains of no. 117, identified by a fragment of 118 (**3281**) adhering to its right side, are too fragmentary to repay transcription.)

3281

ρι[η   ]

παρὰ Διονυcίου Διον[υcίου τοῦ] καὶ Ἀμόι Διονυ-

cίου μητρὸc Ἀρcινόη[c Cαρα]πίωνοc ἀπ' Ὀ-

ξυρύγχων πόλεω[c. κατ]ὰ τὰ κελ[ε]υcθέν-

τα περὶ ἐπικρίcεωc [τῶν] προcβαινόντ(ων) εἰc

το]ὺc ἐ[κ το]ῦ γυμ(ναcίου) ε[ἴ ε]ἰ[cι το]ῦ [γ]ένου[c τ]ούτ[ο]ν

. . . . .

5 προcβαινον^τ   6 γυ^μ

'No. 118.

'From Dionysius son of Dionysius alias Amois grandson of Dionysius mother Arsinoe daughter of Sarapion from the city of the Oxyrhynchi. In accordance with the orders concerning scrutiny of those entering the gymnasial class (to discover) if they are of this stock . . .'

2 Ἀμόι. On short Egyptian genitives such as this see XLIII **3102** 5 n.

3282

[ριθ   ]

παρὰ Cαραπ[ί]ωνοc Ἁρ[ποκρατίω]νοc τοῦ

Cαραπίωνοc μητρ[ὸc Δη]μητρίαc

τ[ῆ]c καὶ Ἀcκλαταρίου Ἡρακλείδου ἀπ' Ὀξ(υρύγχων) πόλ(εωc).

κατὰ τὰ κελευcθέντα περὶ ἐπικρίcεωc

τ[ῶ]ν προcβαινόντων εἰc (τρειcκαιδεκαετεῖc) εἰ ἐξ ἀμ-

φοτέρων γονέων εἰcὶ τάγματοc ἀπὸ

γυμναcίου ἐτάγη`ν´ ἐπ' ἀμφόδου Δεκά-

τηc προ[c]βεβηκὼc εἰc (τρειcκαιδεκαετεῖc) ἔτ[ει

ιβϛ θεοῦ Ἀδριανοῦ. ὅθεν παραγ[ενόμε-

νοc πρὸc [τ]ὴν ἐμαυτοῦ ἐπίκ[ριcιν

δηλῶ τὸν πάππον μου Cαραπίω[να

Ἁρποκρατίωνοc ἐπικεκρίcθαι [τῇ γε-

νομένῃ τῷ ε (ἔτει) θεοῦ Οὐεcπαcια[νοῦ

ὑπὸ Cουτωρίου Cωcιβίου cτρατηγή(cαντοc)

καὶ Νικάνδρου γενομένου βαcι[λ]ικοῦ

. . . . . .

4 οξ'πο^λ   6, 9 ιγϛ̅   10 ιβϛ   14 εϛ   15 cτρατηγ^η

'[No. 119].

'From Sarapion son of Harpocration grandson of Sarapion mother Demetria alias Asclatarion daughter of Heracleides from the city of the Oxyrhynchi. In accordance with the orders concerning scrutiny of those entering the class of thirteen-year-olds (to discover) if they are born of parents both of the category of the gymnasial class, I was registered in the Tenth district as having entered the class of thirteen-year-olds in the twelfth year of the deified Hadrian. Therefore I have presented myself for my own scrutiny and declare that my grandfather Sarapion son of Harpocration was scrutinized in the [scrutiny] which took place in the fifth year of the deified Vespasian under Sutorius Sosibius then strategus and Nicander then royal scribe. . . .'

6–8 εἰ . . . ἀπὸ γυμνασίου. This is a more specific equivalent of εἴ εἰσι τοῦ γένους τούτου. Apparently it has not occurred before in connection with gymnasial epicrisis, but cf. VIII **1109**, X **1306**, PSI X 1109, 10, all relating to the metropolitan epicrisis.

9–10 The applicant was thirteen years old in 12 Hadrian = A.D. 127/8 and therefore aged thirty-four at the date of the document, presumably 12 Pius = A.D. 148/9, like the other items in the roll. For late epicrisis in unusual circumstances see *CÉ* 31 (1956) 109–17.

3283

ρκ

παρ[ὰ] Θέωνος Θέων[ο]ς τοῦ Θέωνος μητρὸς
Διογ]ενοῦτος Διονυσίου ἀπ' Ὀξυρύγχων π[ό]λ[ε]ως.
κατ]ὰ ‵τὰ′ κελευσθέντα περὶ ἐπικρίσεως τῶν προσβαινόν-
5　　των εἰς τοὺς ἐκ τοῦ γυμνασίου εἴ εἰσι τοῦ γένους τούτου ἐτάγη ἐπ' ἀμφόδου Ἱππέων Παρεμβολ(ῆς) ὁ υἱός μου
Π]αυσῖρις μητρὸς Θαήσιος Διδύμου γεγονὼς (τρεισκαιδεκαετὴς) τῷ
διελθ(όντι) ια (ἔτει) Ἀντωνίνου Καίσαρος τοῦ κυρίου. ὅθεν παρα-
γενόμενος πρὸς τὴν τούτου ἐπίκρισιν δηλῶ κατὰ τ[ὴ]ν
10　　γενομένην τῷ ε (ἔτει) θεοῦ Οὐες(πασιανοῦ) ὑπὸ Κουτωρίου Σωσιβί[ου
στρατηγή(σαντος) καὶ Νικάνδρου γενο(μένου) βασιλ(ικοῦ) γρ(αμματέως) καὶ ὧν
ἄλλων καθήκ(ει) ⟨ἐπίκρισιν⟩
ἐπικεκρίσθαι τὸν πάππον μου Θέωνα Ἀμμω(νίου) ἐπ' ἀμφόδ(ου)
Πα]μμένους Παραδ(είσου) ἀκολούθ(ως) αἷς ἐπήνεγκεν ἀποδείξεσι
ὡ[ς] ὁ πάππος αὐτοῦ Θέων Ἀμμω(νίου) ἐστὶν ἐν τῇ τοῦ λδ (ἔτους)
15　　θεοῦ Καίσαρος γραφῇ καὶ τὸν πατέρα μου Θέωνα προ[σ-
βάντα ἐπικεκρίσθαι τῷ ια (ἔτει) Δομιτιανοῦ ἐπὶ ταῖς προκ(ειμέναις)
ἀποδείξεσι ἀμφόδ(ου) τοῦ αὐτοῦ, ἐμὲ δὲ προσβάντα γεγονέναι
ἐν ταῖς τοῦ γυμνασίου γραφαῖς ἐπ' ἀμφόδ(ου) τοῦ α(ὐτοῦ) Παμμένο[υς
Παραδ(είσου) καὶ τὸν τῆς μητρὸς τοῦ υἱοῦ μου πρόπαππον
20　　　　　　　*c*. 35　　　　　　　　].[*c*. 3

．　　．　　．　　．　　．

4 τω of τῶν corr. from πρ　　　6 παρεμβο̅λ　　　7 ιγ̅ϲ̅　　　8 διελθιαϛ　　　10 εϛ,
ουεϲ)　　11 στρατηγη̅, γενο̅βασι̅γρϛ, καθη̅κ　　12 αμμω̅, αμφο̅δ　　13 παραδακολουθ　　14 αμμω̅,
λδϛ　　16 ιαϛ, προ̅κ　　17 αμφο̅δ　　18 αμφο̅δτουα̅　　19 παραδ

'No. 120.

'From Theon son of Theon grandson of Theon mother Diogenous daughter of Dionysius from the city of the Oxyrhynchi. In accordance with the orders concerning scrutiny of those entering the gymnasial class (to discover) if they are of this stock, my son Paysiris mother Thaesis daughter of Didymus was registered in the Cavalry Camp district as having reached the age of thirteen in the past eleventh year of Antoninus Caesar the lord. Therefore I have presented myself for his scrutiny and declare that in the ⟨scrutiny⟩ which took place in the fifth year of the deified Vespasian under Sutorius Sosibius then strategus and Nicander then royal scribe and the other proper persons my grandfather Theon son of Ammonius was scrutinized in the Pammenes' Garden district in accordance with the evidences which he presented that his grandfather Theon son of Ammonius is in the list of the thirty-fourth year of the deified Caesar, and (I declare) that my father Theon entered and was scrutinized in the eleventh year of Domitian on the aforesaid evidences in the same district, and that I entered and took my place in the gymnasium lists in the same Pammenes' Garden district, and that the great-grandfather of the mother of my son. . . .'

11 ⟨ἐπίκρισιν⟩. This is the minimum required to supply the sense, cf. e.g. **3278** 14, and is usually all that is present. One document has ἐπίκρισιν τῶν ἐκ τοῦ γυμνασίου at this point, **3276** 12–13; **3277** 10–11 had something similar but apparently longer.

16 11 Domitian = A.D. 91/2.

3284

[ρκα

π[αρ]ὰ Καλλίου .[.]..[*c.* 15   ]......[*c.* 30

νιος ἀπὸ η.[.]....[*c.* 15   ].......[*c.* 12   ].[*c.* 10   τῷ τοῦ

νομοῦ βασιλ(ικῷ) γρ(αμματεῖ) Cερήνῳ τῷ [κ]αὶ Cαραπίωνι ὑπὸ .[......].νο...[.].[.].[*c.* 8   πε-

5   ρὶ τοῦ δεῖν ἀποδεῖξαι ἐνθά[δ]ε ὡς ἔcτιν ὁ ἀδελφός μου Ἁρθοῶνις .[*c.* 10

γένους τάγματος τῶν ἐκ τοῦ γυμναcίου καὶ ὑπὸ τοῦ Cερήνου τοῦ καὶ Cαραπίω(νος)

ἔ]χων ἐπιστάλματα ἐξετάcαι περὶ τ[ο]ύτου δηλῶ αὐτὸν προcβεβηκέναι

εἰc (τρειcκαιδεκαετεῖc) τῷ   *c.* 10   (ἔτει) Ἀντωνίν]ου Κ[α]ίcαρος τοῦ κυρίου καὶ εἶναι αὐτὸν

     c. 50   ]..

     .   .   .   .   .

4 βαcὶ γρϚ   6 ἐκ corr. from ἀπό; cαραπι ͫ

'No. 121?

'From Callias . . . from . . . (to?) the royal scribe of the nome Serenus alias Sarapion by . . . concerning the necessity of proving here that my brother Harthoönis is in the category of the gymnasial class by descent(?), and having received official instructions from Serenus alias Sarapion to make inquiry concerning him I declare that he entered the class of thirteen-year-olds in the current twelfth (*or* past *n*th) year of Antoninus Caesar the lord and that he is . . .'

3–4 After ἀπό it might be possible to read Ἡλ[ίο]υ πόλ[εως. The name of Heracleopolis cannot be read, nor can any other possibility that has been thought of. It is not even certain that a place-name is required here, though it looks likely.

In the absence of a parallel it is not possible to say exactly what is happening here, though it is clear that the case was not quite routine. The fact that Callias applies on behalf of his brother probably means that the father was dead and his death may have occasioned the neglect of some proper procedure.

The pattern may have been something like κατὰ τὰ γραφέντα (or ἐκ βιβλιδίων ἐπιδοθέντων) . . . τῷ . . . βαcιλικῷ γραμματεῖ . . . ὑπὸ τοῦ δεῖνος . . . δηλῶ, 'in accordance with what was written to (or 'as a result of a petition submitted to') the royal scribe by so-and-so . . . I declare'. The royal scribe was very probably one of the board to which these applications were addressed, cf. XII **1452** of A.D. 127/8, addressed to the strategus, royal scribe, and 'other proper persons'.

On the royal scribe Serenus alias Sarapion see XLI **2961** 11–12 n.

5 The trace at the end of the line suggests the loop of a large alpha coming well below the line. If the rest was on the same scale ἀ[πὸ τοῦ is probably enough to complete the line, though about ten letters have been crammed into the same space in line 6.

8 For the restoration cf. e.g. **3276** 7–8. The ending of the imperial titulature indicates that the current reign is mentioned and before τῷ ἐνεcτῶτι ιβ (ἔτει)—or διελθόντι nth (ἔτει)—there is not room for more than εἰc ιγϛ.

3285. LEGAL CODE

23 3B.3/H(4–5)c	8·5 × 14 cm. (fr. 1) 7 × 14 cm. (fr. 2)	Second half of the second century A.D.

For the moment the chief interest of the text from which these fragments come is the surprise of its mere existence. It was a Greek version, written down in the second half of the second century A.D., of a legal code which has survived in part in a famous demotic papyrus of the third century B.C., lately published as G. Mattha, *The Demotic Legal Code of Hermopolis West* (IFAO, Bibliothèque d'Étude xlv, Le Caire, 1975).

Until the experts in juridical papyrology have discussed the subject and agreed, only very tentative suggestions can be made about the implications of the existence of this copy. A basis for the discussion might be the hypothesis put forward here that **3285** and the demotic document represent what is referred to in Greek papyri of the Ptolemaic period as the νόμοc τῆc χώραc and in Roman papyri as the νόμοc (or νόμοι) τῶν Αἰγυπτίων. The suggestion that the two are the same or equivalent was made by Professor H. J. Wolff, *ZRG* 70 (1953) 43–4. There is a convenient discussion of this and other views by Professor J. Modrzejewski in *Proceedings of the XIIth International Congress of Papyrology*, 331–4, where it is pointed out that Roman judges were not bound by this codification but delivered judgements sometimes accepting it and sometimes in disagreement with it.

It is clear enough from the references to the νόμοc τῶν Αἰγυπτίων that it did in the Roman period form a basis on which people founded their actions and that Roman judges were accustomed to take advice from experts (νομικοί) on questions relating to it, see XLII **3015** and perhaps XXXVI **2757**. P. Tebt. II 488 refers to it in connection with building in a way which very well could, though there is no absolute certainty that it does, relate to the regulations about illegal construction in fragment 1 of this papyrus, which are the equivalent of col. vi 3–11 of the demotic document.

The hypothesis, therefore, seems to explain why the provisions set down in demotic in the third century B.C. should be worth preserving in a Greek version in the second century A.D. If it is correct, this Greek version is probably the descendant of a translation made in the early Ptolemaic period.

The circumstances of the compilation of the code can only be guessed at. It is recorded that Darius I ordered his satrap to have Egyptian scholars make a compilation of Egyptian laws in Aramaic and demotic, the first obviously in the *lingua franca* of the Persian empire for the use of the officials of the occupying forces (W. Spiegelberg, *Die sogenannte demotische Chronik*, 30–1). Later the occupying Greeks would soon feel the need of a similar version of their own and may even have taken the code of Darius as a basis. I owe both the reference and the tentative suggestion to Professor G. R. Hughes, to whom I am also very grateful for much information from the demotic code given in advance of Mattha's posthumous book, which he revised for publication and furnished with additional notes and a glossary. Passages of translation from the demotic marked (GRH) are cited from a new version kindly supplied by Professor Hughes.

I must also acknowledge here a great debt to Dr. W. J. Tait, who removed some misunderstandings arising from my ignorance of demotic from a draft of this edition and made many helpful suggestions.

The remains written along the fibres on the backs of the fragments are very much damaged and are in difficult documentary hands. Consequently the nature of the texts has not been determined, but it is clear that on the back of fr. 2 there are two hands both different from the one on the back of fr. 1. The code may have been written on the back of a roll file of related documents (τόμος cυγκολλήcιμος), or a roll may have been made up out of used pieces of papyrus specially to take the code.

A useful date is given in fr. 2 back 10, which reads:]. (ἔτους) ιγ̄ Αὐτοκ(ράτορος) Καίcαρος Τίτ(ου) Αἰλ(ίου) Ἀδριανοῦ Ἀ[ντωνίνου; the abbreviations are in the forms L, αυτοκ, τιτ, αιλ.

Regnal year 13 Pius is equivalent to A.D. 149/50. This is therefore the earliest possible year for the writing of the code, since it is clear that the code was written on the back of a roll made up of these documents. The ill-written documents look as if they were ephemeral and likely to be regarded as waste paper not very long after this date, so it will probably be safe to assign this copy of the code to the period A.D. 150–200, which also suits the handwriting.

The regulations are written in a careful documentary hand across the fibres. A top margin of *c.* 2 cm. is preserved on fr. 1, which contains lines 1–23, and, although the top of fr. 2 is more damaged, there was clearly a space there which was probably again part of a top margin. From the demotic text a very rough calculation can be made which shows that fr. 2 is not likely to come from the column succeeding that of fr. 1, but was probably separated from it by anything from two to seven columns. The calculation is as follows:

1–23 = M(attha) vi 3–11; 25–46 = M. viii 14–22, i.e. 18 demotic lines = 45 Greek.

Between M. vi 11 and M. viii 14 there are about sixty-six demotic lines. If 18 demotic = 45 Greek,

$$\text{then 66 demotic} = \frac{45 \times 66}{18} = \frac{2970}{18}$$
$$= 165 \text{ Greek.}$$

If 24, the first line of fr. 2, is the top of the column succeeding fr. 1, the height of fr. 1's column is $23 + 165 = 188$ lines, which is absurdly high and virtually impossible.

If one column of text of x lines is missing, $2x = 188$, $x = 94$ lines.

If two columns are missing, $3x = 188$, $x = c.$ 63 lines;

    if three columns are missing, $4x = 188$, $x = 47$ lines;

    if four columns are missing, $5x = 188$, $x = c.$ 38 lines;

    if five columns are missing, $6x = 188$, $x = c.$ 31 lines;

    if six columns are missing, $7x = 188$, $x = c.$ 27 lines;

    if seven columns are missing, $8x = 188$, $x = c.$ 23 lines.

Since we can see that the columns were at least 23 lines high in both fragments, seven columns missing is the absolute maximum possible number. There is no way of ascertaining which of these formats is the correct one. A column of about ninety lines is not outside the bounds of possibility, cf. C. H. Roberts, *Greek Literary Hands*, No. 15 c, with 87–89 lines to the column, but it is not very likely, because it would in this hand require a very tall roll of *c.* 55 cm. Among the other possibilities there is nothing to choose. Anything from two to seven columns missing would produce a reasonable format.

The calculation necessarily assumes that the Greek followed the demotic text fairly closely. This is an assumption which such Greek text as survives appears to justify, but it does remain possible that there were discrepancies even greater than those which can be observed in fragment 1.

It is also tentatively assumed that the Greek comes from a complete text or at least from a continuous text of a substantial portion of the code. Even if what we possess is an excerpt or excerpts, the implication is strong that the code existed in a complete Greek text.

fr. 1

    τὸν κ]αὶ τόν, πατρὸς τοῦ καὶ τοῦ, κατῳκοδομη[κέναι ψιλόν τι οἰ-

    κόπ]εδον, τοῦτο δὲ φῇ αὑτοῦ εἶναι καὶ τοῦ πατρ[ὸς αὑτοῦ, ὃς

    ἐών]ηται αὐτὸ κατὰ συνγραφήν, ὁ δὲ καταβοη[θεὶς φῇ ὡς τοῦτο

    αὑ]τοῦ εἶναι καὶ τοῦ πατρὸς αὑτοῦ καὶ ἠγορακέ[ναι κατὰ συγγρα-

5   φή]ν, ἐπερωτῶσι οἱ δικασταὶ τὸν καταβοη[θέντα εἰ ἀξιοῖ

    αὐτὸς ἐπι]δεῖξαι ὡς εἶναι τὸ οἰκόπεδον αὑ[τοῦ καὶ τοῦ πα-

    τρός, ὃς] ἐώνηται αὐτὸ κατὰ συγγραφήν, [ἢ τὸν καταβο-

    ήσαντα] καθάπερ προγέγραπται. ὡς ἂν τ[ῷ καταβοηθέντι

    δοκῇ ἐπιχ]ωρεῖται αὐτῷ καὶ ἐπιδείξαντο[ς   *c.* 12–14 letters

10   ....].....[.]..γγρα.[..].ι αὐτῷ ὁ καταβοηθείς [*c.* 11–15 letters

    ἐὰν δ]ὲ ὁ καταβοηθεὶς ὁμολογήσας ἐπιδείξει[ν μὴ ἐπιδείξῃ, συγ-

3, 7 l. συγγραφήν

χωρεῖ]ται ἡ οἰκία τῷ καταβοήσαντι καὶ γράφετ[αι αὐτῷ ὁ καταβο-
ηθε]ὶς cυνγραφὴν ἀποcταcίου. [

ἐὰν δ]ὲ ὁ ἡccηθεὶc βούληται καθελεῖν τὴν οἰκ[ίαν ἣν αὐτὸc ᾠ-
15 κοδό]μηcε ἐν τῷ οἰκοπέδῳ καὶ ἀπενέγκαc[θαι τὰ οἰκοδομηθέντα,] ἐπιχωρεῖται αὐτῷ λύειν αὑτὸν ἀπε[νεγκάμενον τὰ
οἰκ]οδομηθέντα. (vac.) [

ἐὰν] δὲ ὁ καταβοηθεὶc ἀξιώcῃ τὸ[ν] καταβ[οήcαντα ἐπιδεῖ-
ξα]ι ὡc ἔcτιν αὐτοῦ τὸ οἰκόπεδ[ο]ν, προc[τάccουcι αὐτῷ οἱ
20 δι]καcταὶ ἐπιδει[κνύ]ναι, κἂν [ἐ]πιδε[ί]ξ[ῃ, cυγχωρεῖται αὐ-
τ]ῷ ἡ οἰκία. (vac.) [

ἐὰν δὲ ὁ κ]αταβοηθ[εὶc
......].α cυνχ[

. . . . .

fr. 2

..] τοιχο.. {ἐὰν δὲ μὴ τύχῃ ἡ οἰκία} (vac.) [
25 ἐὰν] δὲ μὴ τύχῃ 'ἡ' οἰκία οὖcα ἐν τῇ αὐτῇ πόλει ἐν ᾗ ο[ἱ δικαc-
ταὶ] διατρείβουcι, ἐπιδεικνύναι δεῖ τοὺc κρεινομέν[ουc πε-
ρὶ] τοῦ τοίχου καθάπερ ἐπὶ τῶν οἰκιῶν γέγραπτα[ι.

ἐὰ]ν δέ τιc καταβοήcῃ κατά τινοc περὶ ῥύμηc, φάμ[ενοc αὐ-
τὴν] εἶναι τῆc ἑαυτοῦ οἰκίαc, ὁ δὲ καταβοηθεὶc φῇ ὡc τ[αύτην εἶ-
30 ναι] τὴν ῥύμην τῆc ἑαυτοῦ οἰκίαc, τοὺc τοιούτουc διακ[ρίνεcθαι
δεῖ] κατὰ τὰ ἄνω γεγραμμένα. (vac.) [

ἐὰ]ν δέ τιc καταβοήcῃ κατά τινοc, φάμενοc τὴν χολέ[δραν
τῆc] οἰκίαc τοῦ ἀντιδίκου καταρραίνειν τὴν ἑαυτοῦ ο[ἰκίαν
τῷ] ἀπορρέοντι ὕδατι, περὶ τῶν τοιούτων ἐπιcκ[οποῦcι
35 οἱ] δικαcταὶ ἐνχέοντεc ὕδωρ εἰc τὴν χολέτρ[αν. ἐὰν δέ
τι] ῥαίνῃ τὴν οἰκίαν τοῦ καταβοήcαντοc, ἀπ[οτέμνου-
cι] ἀπὸ τῆc χολέτραc ἕωc ἂν μηκέτι ῥαίνῃ. [

ἐὰ]ν δέ τιc καταβοήcῃ κατά τινοc, φάμενοc αὐ[τὸν τὴν
θύ]ραν τῆc ἑαυτοῦ οἰκίαc ἀνεῳχέναι εἰc τ[ὸ αὐτοῦ οἰκό-
πε]δον, ἐὰν μὴ εὑρεθῇ ἐν τῷ τόπῳ τούτῳ ἐν ᾧ ἀ[νέῳ-
40 χε] τὴν θύραν ἴδιον οἰκόπ[ε]δον ὑπάρχον τῷ{ν} ἀντ[ιδί-

13 l. cυνγραφήν   15 ἐν: ε corr. from ν   20 l. καί, ἐὰν ἐπιδείξῃ, κτλ.   26 l. δια-
τρίβουcι, κρινομέν[ουc   35 l. ἐγχέοντεc, χολέδρ[αν   37 l. χολέδραc

D

κ]ῳ, ἀναγκάζεται ἀνοικοδομεῖν τὴν θύραν ἣν ἀ[νέῳχε.

ἐ]ὰν δέ τις καταβοήσῃ κατά τινος, φάμενος αὐτὸν [ὑπο-

ρύ]ξαι ὑπὸ τὴν αὐτοῦ οἰκίαν καὶ ποιῆσαι αὐτὴν [πεσεῖ-

45   ν,] προστάσσεται τῷ καταβοηθέντ[ι ὀ]μόσαι τῷ κατ[αβοήσα-

ν]τι εἰ μὴν ὅτι οὐ πονηρεύεσθα[ι π]ρὸς τὸ πεσε[ῖν

    •   •   •   •   •

('If a man raises an outcry against another, alleging) that So-and-so, whose father is So-and-so, has built upon a vacant plot and says that this belongs to him and to his father, who bought it according to contract, and the man complained against says that this belongs to him and to his father and that he bought it according to contract, the judges ask the man complained against if he wishes to prove himself that the plot belongs to him and to his father, who bought it according to contract, or the plaintiff (to prove) as written above. It is granted to the man complained against (to proceed) as he likes and . . .'

'If the man complained against agrees to give proof and does not do it, the house is granted to the plaintiff and the person complained against writes a contract of withdrawal for him.'

'If the defeated party wishes to dismantle the house which he himself built on the plot and carry away the construction, it is permitted to him to purge himself(?) by carrying away the construction.'

'If the man complained against requires the plaintiff to give proof that the plot belongs to him, the judges order him to give proof and, if he gives it, the house is granted to him.'

'If the man complained against . . .'

'. . . wall. If the house does not happen . . .'

'If the house does not happen to be in the same city as the judges, the persons seeking judgement must present their evidence about the wall in accordance with what has been written in the section on houses.'

'If a man raises an outcry against another concerning an access, alleging that it belongs to his own house, and the man complained against says that this is the access to his house, such persons must have their dispute settled in accordance with what has been written above.'

'If a man raises an outcry against another, alleging that the gutter of his antagonist's house splashes his own house with the water that flows from it, in such cases the judges make a test by pouring water into the gutter. If it splashes the house of the plaintiff at all, they cut off sections from the gutter until it no longer splashes.'

'If a man raises an outcry against another, alleging that he has opened the door from his own house on to his (the plaintiff's) ground, if there be not found in this place in which he has opened the door private ground belonging to the antagonist, he is compelled to wall up the door which he has opened.'

'If a man raises an outcry against another, alleging that he dug beneath his house and caused it to fall, it is enjoined upon the man complained against to swear an oath to the plaintiff that he is truly not acting maliciously to cause the collapse . . .'

1–21 These lines are equivalent to Mattha vi 3–11. The order of sections is not the same, i.e. Mattha vi 1–7 = 1–9, M. vi 7–8 = 11–13, M. vi 8–10 = 18–21, M. vi 10–11 = 14–17. There are difficulties in matching 9–10 to the demotic, and there are other discrepancies in detail. The chief difference, however, is that the Greek makes use of indirect speech, a construction which does not exist in demotic, wherever it is appropriate.

2 αὐτοῦ. Cf. 4, 6 etc., but ἑαυτοῦ in 29, 33, and 39. The form αὐτοῦ had disappeared from the papyri by the first century B.C., according to Mayser, *Grammatik*[1], i § 69. 5 (p. 305); the weakening of the aspirate made it indistinguishable from αὑτοῦ, ibid. n. 1, cf. § 45 (p. 199), ii 2, § 66 b (pp. 71–3). Very likely the forms αὑτοῦ and αὑτόν (16, if correct) go back to a version of the early Ptolemaic period.

2–3 ὃς ἐών]ηται αὐτὸ κατὰ συνγραφήν. Cf. 4–5 and especially 6–7. In the same and a similar context the demotic has 'he wrote for me concerning it' (M. vi 4: GRH) and 'he was written for regarding it' (M. vi 6: GRH), which seem to refer to a deed by which the fathers confer title on their sons rather than to the deeds of purchase by which they acquired it.

The restoration at the end of 2 is rather short, nine letters instead of the usual eleven to fifteen letters, but 6–7 seems to be a good parallel and probably the text here was not longer. The traces do not suit ἠγορακ]έναι, so it is not possible to use 4–5 as the model for the restoration here.

4 καὶ ἠγορακέ[ναι κατὰ cυγγραφή]ν. The demotic apparently has no space for an equivalent at this point. Cf. 7 n.

5 The δικαcταί can have no relevance to the real procedure under Roman rule. Obviously the Roman procurators used the regulations as a guide line only.

For the restoration of ἀξιοῖ, cf. ἀξιώcῃ (18) in a passage answering to this one. The demotic has 'if it happens that you have worthiness' (M. vi 9), previously interpreted as 'if you are able', see Mattha, op. cit., p. 104 n. line 9, but it looks rather as if the Egyptian expression meant 'think fit' and had a derivation similar to that of ἀξιοῦν from ἄξιος. However, it should be noted that ἀξιώcῃ in 18 does not correspond to the same demotic phrase—the demotic in that place (vi 8) has simply, 'If the man against whom action is brought says to the judges, "Let him who brings action against me prove" etc.' So the basis of the interpretation of the demotic suggested here is not strong. Note also, however, that the Greek text will hardly adapt itself to the sense 'if he is able', e.g. εἰ δύναται αὐτός or εἰ ἔξεcτι αὐτῷ, because this requires the use of a different verb for the second half of the sentence and space seems too limited to allow one.

7 ὃc] ἐώνηται αὐτὸ κατὰ cυνγραφήν. At this point the demotic (M. vi 5) has again apparently no space for an equivalent, cf. 4 n.

7–8 [ἢ τὸν καταβοήcαντα] καθάπερ προγέγραπται. It is clear that the last two words are intended to save writing out again ἐπιδεῖξαι ὡc . . . cυνγραφήν as in 6–7, which in the indirect speech of the Greek would have been word for word the same. The ellipse is very abrupt. It would be more comfortable if we could restore ἐπιδεῖξαι before καθάπερ προγέγραπται, as I have felt obliged to add '(to prove)' in the translation, but the space does not allow it, and no better form of words has been discovered.

Dr. Tait informs me that harsh ellipses, sometimes by a method rather like the English use of 'ditto', are not uncommon in demotic. He cites *OMRO* 44 (1963) 14 n. b., *Enchoria* 2 (1972) 33–6, and *P. dem. Zen.* 22 ii 12 *et al.* (Tafel 10). Some such demotic usage may be reflected in the Greek text here.

9 ἐπιχ]ωρεῖται. Cf. 16.

9–10 There appears to be no demotic equivalent to this passage, though there is a short lacuna (M. vi 7). No really satisfactory reconstruction of the Greek text has been achieved. The only hypothesis which I can put forward must assume that καταβοηθείς in 10 is a mistake for καταβοήcας. This is a very dangerous assumption, but it can be pointed out in extenuation that the demotic in M. vi 7 has 'to the one against whom complaint is made' (GRH) when the sense requires 'to the one who complains', as is also confirmed by the Greek, τῷ καταβοήcαντι (12).

The hypothesis depends on an analysis of the clauses in both demotic and Greek. Both documents prescribe that the judges are to ask the defendant whether he chooses to have the case depend on the proof of title which he himself advances or on the proof of title presented by the plaintiff. After this the eventualities considered in the clauses of the demotic may be summarized and tabulated as follows:

1. The defendant chooses to give proof of title and fails (M. vi 7–8).
2. The plaintiff is required to give proof of title and succeeds (M. vi 8–11).
3. The plaintiff is required to give proof of title and fails (M. vi 11).

It is very plain that one important eventuality is not considered, namely, what happens if the defendant chooses to give proof of title and succeeds.

The Greek may be summarized as follows:

I. Uncertain (9–10).
II. The defendant chooses to give proof of title and fails (11–17).
III. The plaintiff is required to give proof of title and succeeds (18–21).
IV. Uncertain (22–3).

The order of eventualities is not the same, and if I is in fact a separate eventuality, even though it is not framed in a conditional sentence in the same way as the others, the Greek contains one more eventuality. It would be satisfactory if the uncertain clauses I and IV could represent the demotic eventuality 3 and the missing eventuality of the defendant choosing to give proof of title and succeeding.

The only way I have found of restoring the text in this way involves the correction of the text mentioned above, viz:

I (Missing from the demotic?).

ὡς ἂν τ[ῷ καταβοηθέντι
δοκῇ ἐπιχ]ωρεῖται αὐτῷ καὶ ἐπιδείξαντο[c ὡς ἔcτιν αὐ-
10 τοῦ τὸ] οἰκόπ[ε]δον γράφ[ετ]αι αὐτῷ ὁ καταβοηθεὶc (sic l. καταβοήcαc) [περὶ ἀποcταcίου.

'it is granted [to the man complained against (to proceed)] as [he likes] and on his giving proof [that the] plot [is his] the plaintiff writes for him [in relinquishment].'

For περὶ ἀποcταcίου cf. 13, but it is perhaps slightly too long. An alternative might be simply ἀποcταcίου, cf. P. Grenf. I 11 ii 19 καὶ ἀποcταcίου ἐγράψατο τῶι Πανᾶι.

Moreover, if IV is to equal 3, it is very difficult to account for κ]αταβοηθ[εὶc in 22. So little remains that some escape might probably be found, but I have been forced to make the same emendation again, viz:

22 ἐὰν δὲ ὁ κ]αταβοηθ[εὶc (sic l. καταβοήcαc) ἀξιωθεὶc ἐπιδεικνύναι μὴ ἐπιδεί-
ξη, ἡ οἰκ]ία cυνχ[ωρεῖται τῷ καταβοηθέντι.

'If the plaintiff on being required to give proof does not give proof, the house is conceded to the man complained against.'

If the analysis is basically correct, the Greek text seems to have a more logical order. First it considers what happens if the defendant chooses to prove title himself and divides the clauses according to his success or failure. Then it considers what happens if the defendant requires the plaintiff to prove title and divides the clauses according to the success or failure of the plaintiff.

Nevertheless, we can perhaps retain the advantage gained from the analysis and yet escape from the disadvantage of being forced to emend the text in 22. It was pointed out to me by Dr. Tait that the provision that the builder may, if he chooses, remove his construction instead of ceding it to the landowner (14–17), occupies a different place in the demotic. Its position in the Greek is logical, for it follows and accompanies the eventuality that the builder agrees to give proof of title and fails. In the demotic its position is also logical, but it follows and accompanies the eventuality that the landowner chooses to give proof of title and succeeds (M. vi 10). Now this suggests that the demotic should have had this provision twice and that the Greek may indeed have it twice, the second version beginning in 22, viz.:

ἐὰν δὲ ὁ κ]αταβοηθ[εὶc βούληται ἀπενέγκαcθαι τὰ ᾠκοδο-
μημέ]να, cυνχ[ωρεῖται κτλ. on the lines of 16–17.

In this version, besides some abridgement of the first version, we would have κ]αταβοηθ[εὶc for ἡccηθεὶc (14), ᾠκοδομημέ]να instead of οἰκ]οδομηθέντα (15?, 17), and cυνχ[ωρεῖται instead of ἐπιχωρεῖται (16). Still, this result seems more satisfactory than emending κ]αταβοηθ[εὶc to καταβοήcαc. To retain the analysis of the clauses of the Greek given above, all we have to do is to attach lines 22–3 to clause III and assume that clause IV, the equivalent of the demotic eventuality 3, came after the point where the Greek text breaks off.

There is still, obviously, considerable room for doubt about the relationship between the Greek and the demotic and about the reasons for the differences.

It should perhaps be mentioned that the Greek of 5–10 could be restored to be consistent with itself but contrary in sense to the demotic, i.e. read and restore in 5 καταβοή[cαντα not καταβοη[θέντα, in 7–8 καταβοηθέντα not -ήcαντα, in 8 καταβοήcαντι not -ηθέντι. The sense would then be, '. . . the judges ask the *plaintiff* if he wishes himself to give proof that the ground belongs to him and his father, who bought it by contract, or (if he wishes) the *defendant* (to give proof) as before. Whatever the *plaintiff* decides is conceded to him and if he gives proof that the ground belongs to him, the *defendant* writes for him in relinquishment.'

However, this is clearly only an accident of the state of preservation of the Greek. Besides the evidence of the demotic, the Greek itself in 18–19, ἐὰν] δὲ ὁ καταβοηθεὶc ἀξιώcῃ τὸ[ν] καταβ[οήcαντα ἐπιδεῖξα]ι, κτλ., shows that the choice of procedure is given to the defendant.

13 The right arm of the final hypsilon is prolonged as a thin horizontal, acting as a filler sign, running across all the unwritten papyrus at the end of the line.

14-17 On the position of this clause see p. 36 para. 5.

In Mattha, op. cit., 105 n. line 10, Professor Hughes concluded that the demotic equivalent of τὰ οἰκοδομηθέντα referred primarily to the woodwork, but καθελεῖν τὴν οἰκ[ίαν indicates that complete removal of all the building materials belonging to the offender was envisaged. The intention, presumably, was that the site should be returned to its original condition as far as possible and that the owner should suffer no disadvantage from the trespass.

16 λύειν αὐτόν. On αὐτόν cf. 2 n. In spite of considerable damage to αὐτόν each letter seems to have left characteristic traces. In particular it would not be possible to read αὐτήν (= τὴν οἰκίαν), which would give a much easier sense, 'it is permitted to him to demolish it and carry away (read ἀπε[νεγκα-μένῳ) the building materials'. If λύειν αὐτόν is correct, it seems to mean that he atones for the offence of building on someone else's ground by clearing the site. Perhaps we should emend to αὐτήν.

20 κᾶν [ἐ]πιδε[ί]ξ[η. In spite of some damage it seems certain that κᾶν was written, where we would write καί, ἐάν. Cf. Mayser–Schmoll, *Grammatik* I i § 30. 2 (p. 137). Of the references given there the relevant ones are P. Cair. Zen. II 59236. 4-5, III 59440. 10, P. Tebt. III (i) 780. 20, UPZ I 2. 27; 70. 11; 110. 133, 176, II 218 i 24; 224 iii 3. For the Roman period cf. e.g. P. Achmim 8. 15-17 of A.D. 197.

21 The demotic (M. vi 9-10) has a longer version, 'If he gives proof, they shall award [the house to him (and) they shall require that his ad]versary [write for him] in relinquishment' (GRH). The written relinquishment is mentioned in the Greek at 10, probably, and 13. The first is apparently not in the demotic, the second is.

22-3 See 9-10 n. for attempts to recognize the sense of this passage. The theta of κ]αταβοηθ[εὶς is certain.

24 ..]τοιχο.. It is not possible to recognize this for certain as part of the same provisions as the demotic.

Evidently the scribe wrote the next six words before deciding that they ought to begin a separate section on a new line, see 25. No attempt to cancel the false start can be seen, but the damage to the top edge may have removed some indication of omission or cancellation.

25-46 These lines are equivalent to M. viii 14-22 and the deviations are minor compared with those in fragment 1.

27 καθάπερ ἐπὶ τῶν οἰκιῶν γέγραπτα[ι. This is more specific than the demotic: 'If it happens that it is not in the town in which the judges are that the house is, giving proof regarding the wall is what shall be done in accord with the rule for giving proof which shall be applied' (GRH). For the procedure to be followed in giving proof the Greek appears to refer to an earlier section relating to houses.

29-30 The demotic has no equivalent for ὁ δὲ καταβοηθεὶς . . . τῆς ἑαυτοῦ οἰκίας.

32 χολέ[δραν. The word is new in the papyri. The restoration follows the orthography of *LSJ* even though the papyrus has χολέτρα twice below (35, 37) and may well have had the same here. For the phonetic confusion of δ and τ see Mayser–Schmoll I i § 33. 3a (pp. 146-7).

The basic meaning appears to be 'groove' or 'channel', e.g. Eratosth. *ap.* Eutoc. *in Archim.* p. 94 H. πινακίσκοι ἐπωστοὶ ἐν χολέδραις, 'movable plates in grooves'. The same open shape is implied by Apollod. *Poliorcet.* 182, 7 κάμαξ . . . ἐκκεκολαμμένος κοιλάσματι ἡμικυκλίου χολέδρας τὸ σχῆμα, 'a rod . . . with a hollow gouged out in the shape of a semi-circular channel'. Another passage seems to apply the word to a decorative finial on the outflow pipe from the basin of a fountain, Horap. 1, 21 τὰς χολέδρας καὶ τοὺς εἰσαγωγεῖς τῶν ἱερῶν κρηνῶν λεοντομόρφους κατεσκεύασαν οἱ ἀρχαῖοι τῶν ἱερατικῶν ἔργων ἐπιστάται, 'the masters of the temple works in ancient times fashioned the outflows and inflows of the sacred fountains in the shape of lions.' See below for gargoyles in the same shape.

For this context, however, the most promising reference is Hesych. s.v. χολέρα (which it seems essential to emend to χολέ⟨δ⟩ρα)· cωλὴν δι' οὗ τὸ ὕδωρ ἀπὸ τῶν κεράμων φέρεται ἐξακοντιζόμενον, 'a channel along which water is carried from the (roof-)tiles and discharged'. The final Greek word graphically describes the function of the gutter—to throw the rainwater well away from the wall of the house. The trouble arises if it throws the water on to a neighbour's wall.

Unfortunately, comparatively little is known of Egyptian domestic architecture, and the upper parts of old buildings are the least likely to survive. However, a certain amount is known of roof drainage systems from the temples. Cf. A. Badawy, *A History of Egyptian Architecture*, 242 (of Karnak): 'There was a system of water drains on the roof with three gargoyles on each side of the temple'; 358 (of Medinet Habu): 'Adequate provision for the drainage of rainwater'—from the roof—'featured large waterspouts in the shape of the forepart of a lion projecting at the top of the external faces.' Cf. also J.-L. de Cénival, *Living Architecture: Egyptian*, 139–40, G. Jéquier, *Les éléments de l'architecture* (*Manuel d'archéologie égyptienne*), 55–6.

The demotic expression has a 'wood'-determinative, see Mattha, op. cit. 112–13, suggesting that Egyptian gutters were customarily made of wood.

37 After the last word there is the beginning of a horizontal which was probably a filler sign, cf. 13 n.

40 ἐν ᾧ. The traces are very meagre. It may be that we ought to prefer to read εἰ[ς ὅ]ν, which is what is suggested by 39–40, εἰς τ[ό . . . οἰκόπε]δον.

3286. PETITION TO THE TOWN COUNCIL

48 5B.28/A(1)a   9·5 × 8·5 cm.   A.D. 222/3

An early attestation of the process of nomination (ὀνομασία) in the town council is given here, the next earliest dating from A.D. 247, see A. K. Bowman, *Town Councils*, 98–9. The writer, who had previously served as gymnasiarch, was nominated again to that office on the same day on which he submitted this petition protesting that it was beyond his ability and appealing to the prefect.

The prytanis has been attested in office for A.D. 222/3, see 2 n., and the prefect Aedinius Julianus had a short term lasting from summer or autumn A.D. 222 to summer A.D. 223, see 12 n., so the year of this document is guaranteed to be A.D. 222/3.

A diagonal line begins in the left margin opposite line 7 and runs into the middle of the top margin. Also in the top margin is a trace of a very much shorter diagonal above and to the left of the first and parallel to it. The longer line might have been the beginning of a cancellation by chiasm, cf. P. Mich. XI 613 and Pl. III, but if so the process was never finished and it is a process usually adopted to nullify contracts.

On the back are the top 11 lines of a very much damaged document addressed to Flavius Harpocration, strategus of the Oxyrhynchite nome, already attested by XII **1433** (September/October, A.D. 238) and XLIII **3133** (25 January, A.D. 239). The sender is a former gymnasiarch and mentions of the town council, appeal, and petition to an unnamed epistrategus suggest that it concerns another case of contested nomination. The hand is different from that on the front.

'Οξυρυγχειτῶν τῇ κρατίστῃ βουλῇ
διὰ Μ[ά]ρκου Αὐρηλίου Ἀμμωνίου
γυμνασιάρχου ἐνάρχου πρυτάνεως
παρὰ Μά[ρ]κου Α[ὐρ]ηλίου Νεπωτιανοῦ
5   υ[ἱοῦ Αὐρη]λίου Διονυσάμμωνο[ς
γυμνασιαρχήσαν`τος´ τῆς αὐτῆς π[ό]λεως.
πρὸς τ[ὴ]ν γενομένην τῇ ἐνεστώ-

ϲη ἡμ[έ]ρᾳ ἐν τῇ α[ὐτ]όθι κρατίϲτῃ βο[υλῇ
ὀν[ο]μαϲίαν μου ὡϲ εἰϲ γυμναϲι[αρχίαν
10 καὶ οὐκ ἀ[ν]αλογῶν πρὸϲ τὴν τηλ[ι]κα[ύ-
την ἀρχὴν ἐπικαλούμενοϲ τὸ[ν λ]α[μ-
πρότατον ἡγεμόνα Αἰδείνιον Ἰ[ο]υλι[ανόν

. . . .

12 ἰ[ο]υλι[

'To the excellent council of the Oxyrhynchites by agency of Marcus Aurelius Ammonius, gymnasiarch, prytanis in office, from Marcus Aurelius Nepotianus son of Aurelius Dionysammon, former gymnasiarch of the same city. With reference to my nomination to the gymnasiarchy made the present day in the excellent council of the same place, since I am not equal to so great a magistracy, calling to my aid the most glorious prefect Aedinius Julianus . . .'

2 The *praenomen* of the prytanis is new but not surprising. His titles are as in I **77** of 19 May, A.D. 223, cf. P. J. Sijpesteijn, *Liste des gymnasiarques*, 28 no. 273, A. K. Bowman, *Town Councils*, 131.

4–5 Nepotianus does not appear in P. J. Sijpesteijn, op. cit.; neither Nepotianus nor Dionysammon appears in the index of A. K. Bowman, op. cit.

12 For this prefect see J. Modrzejewski, *Les préfets d'Égypte au début du règne d'Alexandre Sévère* (in *Antidoron M. David = Pap. Lugd. Bat.* XVII), 62–3, *ZPE* 17 (1975) 308–9.

The last two syllables of his name belonged probably to the next line.

3287. APPLICATION FOR PAYMENT

29 4B.45/G(1–2)b   8 × 17 cm.   27 March–25 April, A.D. 238?

This document is addressed to Geminius Valerianus, ὁ κράτιϲτοϲ ἐπίτροποϲ, known also from VIII **1114** 5, and described in CPR V 4. 12–13 as head of the *idios logos*, cf. also XLIII **3103** introd. He is the last holder of the post whose name is known to us and I have suggested in XLV **3263** introd. and in CPR V 4. 12 13 n. that his department may have been abolished during the financial reforms of Philip the Arabian.

The applicant is described as φρο(ντιϲτὴϲ) Φοβώου, which probably means that he was the steward of property administered by the *idios logos* in the neighbourhood of that village and he applies for an additional allowance of 700 drachmas to be spent on agricultural work on land described as ἐδάφη ἰδιόϲ(πορα). Probably this means that the estate was worked by tenant farmers under the supervision of the steward, as was normal in Egypt, see *Studies in Roman Property*, ed. M. I. Finley, 45. See P. R. Swarney, *Idios Logos*, 111–19, for the functions of the *idios logos* as administrator of government property.

The back of the sheet is blank.

Γεμεινίῳ Οὐαλεριανῷ τῷ κρ(ατίςτῳ) ἐπιτρό(πῳ)

διὰ Αὐρηλίων Ἡρακλείδου καὶ

Χαιρή(μονος) ἀμφο(τέρων) βουλ(ευτῶν) τῆς λαμ(προτάτης) πόλ(εως) τῶν

Ἀλεξ(ανδρέων) τῶν ἀξιολ(ογωτάτων)   (vac.)

5   παρὰ Αὐρηλίου Πτολλᾶ φρο(ντιστοῦ)

Φοβώου. αἰτοῦμαι ἐπιςταλ(ῆναι)

καὶ νῦν εἰς κοπὴν . . . ιγην

καὶ [ς]υλλογὴν χόρτου τῶν ἰδιος(πόρων)

ἐδαφῶν ἀπὸ κλήρου . . . . εως

10   ἄλλας δραχμὰς ἑπτακοςίας, γ(ίνονται) (δραχμαὶ) ψ,

ὦν λόγον δώςω.   (vac.)

(ἔτους) δ″ Φαρμοῦθι.   (vac.)

(vac.) (m. 2) Αὐρή(λιος) Θέων ςεςημ(είωμαι).

---

1 κρϛ επιτρο)   3 χαιρῆαμφ°βου̣λ, λαμϛπο̅   4 αλεξ′, αξιο̅   5 φρο̅   6 ϛπιςτα   8 ιδιος)
10 γϛψ   12 Lδ″   13 αυρη′, ςεςη̅ͫ

'To Geminius Valerianus, the most excellent *procurator*, through Aurelius Heracleides and Aurelius Chaeremon, both councillors of the most glorious city of the Alexandrians, most worthy gentlemen, from Aurelius Ptollas, steward of Phoboou. I beg to have paid to me immediately towards cutting . . . and gathering fodder on privately sown lands from the allotment of . . . another seven hundred drachmas, total 700 dr., of which I shall render account. Year 4, Pharmuthi. (2nd hand) I, Aurelius Theon, signed.'

2–4 It is not clear whether these intermediaries were acting as bankers and would have advanced the money themselves or whether they were agents of the *idios logos* who would have authorized a payment from a state bank.

7 . . . ιγην. The only reading I can think of is ὀλ{λ}ίγην, which is thoroughly unsatisfactory. Preferable would be another noun parallel with κοπήν and [ς]υλλογήν, preceded by καί. The traces represented by the first two dots end in a descender, which suggests that καί, rapidly written, is a possibility. For γ, ς is a less attractive possible reading.

8 On χόρτος see M. Schnebel, *Landwirtschaft*, 211–18, esp. 216–17 on the harvest.

9 . . . . εως. At first sight this looks as if it ought to be identifiable with the κλῆρος Τοκέως in XII **1534** 3, but a photograph of that document seems to show rather ϛτοκέως; see *Aegyptus* 55 (1975) 200, 202; cf. perhaps the man of Thracian origin called ϛποκῆς who had connections with the Oxyrhynchite village of Mermertha in the mid third century B.C. (P. Sorb. 17, cf. F. Uebel, *Die Kleruchen*, p. 324 No. 1368). Here, however, though the letter before -εως is an undamaged κ or β, the first letter begins with an upright topped by a crossbar which extends back to the left (tau is best, pi possible) and there are probably two damaged letters between it and κ or β.

12 Year 4 is probably of the reign of Maximinus and Maximus, A.D. 237/8, the year following the date of VIII **1114**, where Valerianus also appears. The 4th year next preceding, 4 Severus Alexander = A.D. 224/5, is clearly too far away; the next following, 4 Gordian, A.D. 240/1, is possible but not so likely as A.D. 237/8.

13 It is not clear what Aurelius Theon was. He might have been assistant to the steward. Perhaps more likely he was an official or clerk who countersigned the application.

3288. Petition

38 3B.82/G(1)b   9 × 10·5 cm.   A.D. 252/3

This is a fragment from near the foot of a petition concerning a dispute about the boundaries of agricultural land, cf. e.g. P. Petaus 24, and, for the law, R. Taubenschlag, *Opera Minora* ii 395–6, *Law*² 254–5. The petitioner had previously taken his case to the dioecetes, who had issued an order instructing the recipient of this petition to survey the land and determine the boundaries.

The name of the dioecetes, Septimius Apollonius, and the date allow a misunderstanding to be cleared away. He has appeared also in P. Théad. 14. 18–19 and is there described as κοσμήσας τὴν διοίκησιν, which means that at the date of that reference he was out of office. P. Théad. 14 is assigned to the fourth century A.D. by the first editor, to the third century by V. Martin in *Archiv* 6 (1913) 170 n. 3 (followed by G. Bastianini, *Gli strateghi dell'Arsinoites*, 58), and to the end of the third or the beginning of the fourth by J. Lallemand, *L'Administration*, 82 n. 9. To judge from a photograph a date inside the third century would be quite acceptable, though it is not impossible that proceedings before a procurator could still be worth citing half a century later. Whatever the date of P. Théad. 14 may be, the new document makes it clear that the Septimius Serenius Apollonius, ἀπὸ ἐπιτρόπων, who acknowledged the return of a loan in A.D. 333, see XIV **1716**, cannot be identified with the dioecetes, as tentatively suggested by Lallemand, op. cit. 90 n. 4, 262. On the other hand it may very well be that the κράτιστος Ἀπολλώνιος in SB VI 9387. 11 is the same man, since he receives a petition relating to an οὐσία.

The back of the papyrus is blank.

.   .   .   .   .

Ἀδύμου κληρ[..].[.].[.....
μόνας δὲ γεωργῶ (ἀρούρας) γ.
νῦν δὲ τοῦ κρατίστου διοικητοῦ
Σεπτιμίου Ἀπολλωνίου
5   κελεύσαντός σοι καταπατῆσαι
καὶ παραδῶναι ἑκάστῳ τὴν
ἰδίαν κτῆσιν αὐτὸ τοῦτό σε
ἀξιῶ τὴν παράδοσίν μοι ποι-
ήσῃ τῆς (ἀρούρης) α, ὅπως δυνη-
10   θῶ τὰ ὑπὲρ τούτων δημόσια
εἰσενεγκεῖν τῷ ἱερωτάτῳ ταμείῳ.
(ἔτους) γ′ Αὐτοκρατόρων Καισάρων

2 ʊγ   6 l. παραδοῦναι   7 ἴδιαν   9 ʊα   11 ἱερωτατω   12 Lγ′

Γαίου Οὐιβίου Τρεβωνιανοῦ
Γάλλου καὶ Γαίου Οὐιβίο[υ

.   .   .   .   .

'. . . (from the) allotment of Adymus four (?) aruras (?), but I farm three aruras only. Now, since the dioecetes Septimius Apollonius, *vir egregius*, has ordered you to make a survey and deliver to each person his own private property, it is this very thing that I request of you—that you make delivery to me of the one arura, so that I may be able to contribute the public taxes on them to the most sacred treasury. Year 3 of Imperatores Caesares Gaius Vibius Trebonianus Gallus and Gaius Vibius . . .'

1 The allotment name is new, see *Aegyptus* 55 (1975) 159–244. The first trace visible after κληρ[could well belong to the bottom of the arura symbol and the second to a delta representing the numeral 'four'. The wide spacing would also suit this interpretation. The text envisaged for the purposes of the translation is ἐκ τοῦ] Ἀδύμου κλήρ[ου] (ἀρουρ-) δ, μόνας δὲ γεωργῶ (ἀρούρας) γ.

6–7 παραδῶναι (l. παραδοῦναι) ἑκάστῳ τὴν ἰδίαν κτῆσιν. This is an allusion to the legal formula '*suum cuique tribuere*', see P. Petaus 24. 10 n.

8–9 ποιήςῃ. Cf. BGU I 159 (=W. *Chr.* 408). 10–11 ἀξιῶ ἀκοῦσαι μου πρὸς αὐτοὺς καὶ τὸ δοκοῦν σοι κελεύςῃς γενέσθαι; SPP XXII 87. 13–14 ἀ[ξιῶ] τὸ δόξαν σοι κελεύςῃς γενέσθαι.

12–14 Since attested dates cover virtually the whole of this Egyptian year, running from Thoth 4 (1 September, A.D. 252; PSI VII 795. 15) to Mesore 29 (22 August, A.D. 253; VIII **1119** 30), cf. P. Bureth, *Les titulatures*, 116–17, the date of this document cannot be narrowed further than the regnal year number allows, i.e. the extreme limits are 29 August, A.D. 252, and 28 August, A.D. 253.

3289. PETITION TO A STRATEGUS

37 4B.106/J(1–3)b   11·5 × 14·5 cm.   A.D. 258/9

This is a straightforward report of thefts from the house of the petitioners' father. There is perhaps a guarded implication that their brother, mentioned in 10 as the father's third heir, is the person suspected of having made away with the papers and other lost articles.

The date clause, though not complete, gives us more information about the length of the term of office of the strategus concerned, see 1 n.

The back is blank.

Αὐρηλίῳ Ϲαρ[απ]ίωνι στρ(ατηγῷ) Ὀξυρυγχίτου
παρὰ Αὐρηλίων Θεωνείνου τοῦ καὶ Ϲαραπίωνος
ἀρχιερατεύσαντος [καὶ] Θέωνος ἀμφοτέρων
ἐξηγητῶν βουλευ[τ]ῶν τῆς Ὀξυρυγχιτῶν πόλεως.
5   καὶ ἔτι περιόντος τοῦ πατρὸς τοῦ ἡμετέρου Ϲαραπίωνος Ϲαραπίωνος ἐξηγητεύσαντος τῆς αὐτῆς
πόλεως καὶ καθ' ἑαυτὸν οἰκοῦντος ἕκαστος καὶ
ἡμῶν ἐπὶ τῆς ἰδίας ἀνεχώρει οἰκίας, τελευ-
τήσαντος δὲ τούτου ἐπὶ κληρονόμοις ἡμεῖν τε

1 στρ〴

10 καὶ ἑτέρῳ ἡμῶν ἀδελφῷ Ἀμμωνίῳ καθ' ἃς ἔ-
λιπεν διαθήκας τὰς καὶ `μετὰ᾽ τελευτὴν αὐτ[ο]ῦ ἀνοιγεί-
cαc γενόμενοι ἐν τοῖc τούτου πράγμα[ci]ν ἔγνω-
μεν ἀφαιρέcειc βιβλίων καὶ ἄλλω[ν ....]ων
οὐκ ὀλίγων γεγενῆcθαι. περὶ ὧν ἀ[cφα-
15 λιζόμενοι ἐπιδίδομεν τὰ βιβλείδια πρὸc τὸ
εἶναι αὐτὰ ἐν καταχωριcμῷ ἵν' εἰ πολυπρα-
γμονήcαντεc καταλαβώμεθά τι μένῃ ἡμεῖν
ὁ λόγοc πρὸc τοὺc φανηcομένουc τὴν ἀφαίρε-
cιν πεποιῆcθαι. (ἔτουc) ϛ᾽ Αὐτοκρατόρων Καιcάρων
20 Πουπλίου Λικιννίου Οὐαλεριανοῦ καὶ Πουπλίου
Λικιννίου Οὐαλεριανοῦ Γαλλιηνοῦ Γερμανικῶν
Μεγίcτων Εὐcεβῶν Εὐτυχῶν κα[ὶ Πο]υπλίου

· · · ·

19 Lϛ᾽

'To Aurelius Sarapion strategus of the Oxyrhynchite nome, from Aurelius Theoninus alias Sarapion, ex-chief-priest, and Aurelius Theon, both exegetae, councillors of the city of the Oxyrhynchites.
While our father, Sarapion son of Sarapion, ex-exegetes of the same city, was still alive and living by
himself, each of us also departed to his own house, and after he died, with us and another brother of
ours, Ammonius, as heirs according to the will which he left and which was opened after his death,
when we visited his property we discovered that there had been thefts of papers and not a few other
[articles?]. To secure ourselves in respect of these we submit this petition so that it may be upon record,
in order that, if after inquiries we find out anything, our case may continue to lie against those who
shall be discovered to have perpetrated the theft. Year 6 of Imperatores Caesares Publius Licinius
Valerianus and Publius Licinius Valerianus Gallienus Germanici Maximi Pii Felices and Publius . . . '

1 The strategus is otherwise known from P. Mich. IX 614. 1 and 3290 5, both undated. It could
easily be incautiously assumed from P. Mich. 614. 7, which gives a date sometime in 3 Valerian and
Gallienus (= A.D. 255/6) for a communication addressed simply 'to the strategus of the Oxyrhynchite
nome', that Aurelius Sarapion was in office in that year. However, we know from XXXIV 2714 that
on the first day of 4 Valerian and Gallienus (29 August, A.D. 256) the strategus was Aurelius Sabinus.
The present document, therefore, gives the best evidence for the date of Aurelius Sarapion, sometime in
A.D. 258/9, though it seems not unlikely that the communication mentioned above, which was eventually
delivered to Aurelius Sarapion, reached him sometime in A.D. 256/7. His successor is first known in
office on 24 November, A.D. 260, according to a justified restoration of XII 1411, cf. 3292 1–2 n.

2 Although the names are common, it is quite likely that Theoninus alias Sarapion is the same as
the prytanis known from the undated XII 1515 (lines 1–2). If so, 3289 dates from before his service as
prytanis and provides a *terminus post quem* of A.D. 258/9 for 1515, which is assigned to the late third
century.

Incidentally, instead of Cκυβᾶτοc, in 1515 14, a photo shows Cκύβαλοc; delete the entry for the
former in NB.

8 ἀνεχώρει. The use of the imperfect is unusual. Cf. perhaps B. G. Mandilaras, *The Verb in the
Greek Non-literary Papyri*, §§ 288–92, on the aoristic imperfect.

13 βιβλίων. These are most likely to have been papers of some kind. There is admittedly a possibility, though nothing can now be made of it, that they were books, cf. e.g. Julian, *Ep.* 38, on the library
of George, late bishop of Alexandria. Julian writes to Porphyrius the *rationalis* instructing him to

persuade or compel those under any suspicion of having stolen from the library (τοὺς ὁπωςοῦν ὑπονοίας ἔχοντας ἀφῃρῆςθαι τῶν βιβλίων) to make full restitution.

Restore perhaps [cκευ]ῶν. Cf. BGU VIII 1774. 6–8 περὶ ἐκφορήςεως cκευῶν τε καὶ βιβλίων ʽπατρικῶνʼ. 16–17 For εἰ with the subjunctive see R. C. Horn, *The Use of the Subjunctive and Optative*, 64–6.

22 The Caesar whose name once followed was in all probability Saloninus, who was promoted after his brother's death in summer A.D. 258, cf. XLIII **3134** 12 n. There seems to be no example as yet of Valerian Caesar appearing in a date clause of the sixth year, though it is conceivable that one might be found, if news of his death failed to reach some part of Egypt before 29 August, A.D. 258.

3290. APPLICATION FOR PAYMENT

43 5B.70/C(14–17)a   9·5 × 12 cm.   c. A.D. 258–60

Another mention of the strategus Aurelius Sarapion occurs in this document, cf. **3289** 1 n. The earliest limit of its date is established by the mention of Mussius Aemilianus as prefect of Egypt. He was promoted from acting prefect between 24 September, A.D. 258 and September/October, A.D. 259, see XLIII **3112** introd. By 24 November, A.D. 260 Sarapion himself had been replaced by the next strategus, see **3292** 1–2 n.

The application comes from a known person, Aurelius Spartiates alias Chaeremon, see 1 n., who requests payment for wine supplied by him to provision troops serving, apparently, under the direct command of the prefect. See **3292** introd. for the probable cause of this military activity. Other references to provisioning troops in this period are XLIII **3111**, a freight contract for wine, and P. Wisc. I 3, a petition from an unwilling liturgist who had just performed duties connected with supplies for troops. On the military *annona* of the time see D. van Berchem, 'L'annone militaire . . . au IIIᵉ siècle', in *Mémoires de la Société Nationale des Antiquaires* 10 (1937) 117–202.

On the back is the left half of a six-line letter written downwards along the fibres, which is transcribed as item **3291**.

Αὐρήλιος Cπαρτιάτης ὁ καὶ Χαιρή-
μων γυμνασιαρχήcας βουλευτὴc τῆc
Ὀξυρυγχιτῶν πόλεωc δι' ἐμοῦ Αὐρηλί[ο]υ
Ἀγάθου γραμματέωc.   (vac.)

5   Αὐρηλίῳ Cαραπίωνι cτρατηγῷ Ὀξ[υ-
ρυγχίτου τῷ φιλτάτῳ χα[ίρ]ειν.
αἰτοῦμαι ἐπ[ιcτ]αλῆναι τε.[.]α.[....
τωc εἰc τιμ[ὴ]ν οὗ παρέcχον οἴνο[υ
κεραμίων τριακοcίων ἐκ προcτάξεω[c
10   τοῦ διαcημοτάτου ἡμῶν ἡγεμόν[οc
Μουccίου Α[ἰ]μιλλιανοῦ εἰc χρείαc [ἀννώ-

νης τῶν [ἅμ]α αὐτῷ γενναιοτάτων

cτρατιωτῶν ἀ]κολούθωc τοῖc γραφεῖ-

．　　　．　　　．　　　．　　　．

'Aurelius Spartiates alias Chaeremon, ex-gymnasiarch, councillor of the city of the Oxyrhynchites, through me, Aurelius Agathus, secretary, to Aurelius Sarapion, strategus of the Oxyrhynchite nome, his dearest colleague, greeting. I request that payment be made . . . for the price of 300 jars of wine which I supplied by order of our most perfect prefect Mussius Aemilianus for the needs of the *annona* of the most valiant soldiers in his company, in accordance with what was written . . .'

1 This man was already known as an ex-gymnasiarch and councillor of Oxyrhynchus, cf. P. J. Sijpesteijn, *Liste des gymnasiarques*, 30 No. 292, A. K. Bowman, *Town Councils*, 147, and also as strategus of the Hermopolite nome, cf. e.g. XXXI **2560** 1 n. If XVII **2108** of 25 February A.D. 259 rightly belongs to him, as suggested in **2560** 1 n., he may have been in Hermopolis as strategus at the date of this papyrus, which would neatly explain the presence in 3–4 of the secretary who acts as intermediary. One might have expected him to have been given his title in that case, but it is noteworthy that his name appears first in the prescript, which implies that he was not inferior to the strategus of the Oxyrhynchite nome though his titles as given are inferior.

7–8 After τε omicron or omega seems best. Any other letter would probably have left traces on the papyrus below the small curve which is visible. τέω[c] is hard to avoid, but not easy to understand. The use of the word became more frequent in late Greek, but the meaning is always vague, see D. Tabachovitz, *Études sur le grec de la basse époque*, 70–73. Here 'now' would suit. After]α is a letter with an upright and a crossbar or diagonal, e.g. λ, ν, π, τ. At the end four letters lost is a generous estimate, though it is possible that more could have been crowded in. Something like ἀρ[υπερθέ]]τωc would suit.

3291. Letter

43 5B.70/C(14–17)a　　　　　9·5 × 12 cm.　　　　　*c*. A.D. 258–60 or later

This letter is written downwards along the fibres on the back of **3290**. The left half is well preserved at top and bottom and it seems certain that there was no prescript, though a farewell formula may easily have been lost from the lower right. Since wine is mentioned, as in **3290**, and Spartas (6) might be related to or even identical with the Spartiates in **3290**, it seems worth while to transcribe it, even though a good deal must be lost from the ends of the lines.

If the present document does concern the same people and the same transaction as **3290**, that can hardly be the copy that was actually submitted to the strategus. However, it is probably unprofitable to speculate how it came to be re-used by the writer of the letter, who was a woman.

εὐθέωc ἀναβᾶca εὗρον Cαραπίωνα τὸν ˌ[

παρέλαβα παρ' αὐτοῦ τὴν ἀποχ(ὴν) καὶ ἔπεμψά coι [

κέν μοι τὴν ἐ(πιcτολὴν?) τὴν (πρὸc) τὸν κυν.[.]...ου[

πόλεωc. εὐθέωc οὖν διαπεμφθῆναί coι [

5　ὁ οἶνοc του.....[....].δετη.[

τὴν ἀδελφὴν αὐτοῦ καὶ Cπαρτᾶν καὶ ...[

2 αποχ̅　　　3 ε‧, ρ‧

'As soon as I got up here I found Sarapion the . . . I received the receipt from him and I sent (it?) to you . . . he (delivered?) to me the letter(?) for the . . . city. Immediately, therefore, . . . to be sent to you . . . the wine . . . (greet so-and-so and?) his sister and Spartas and . . .'

1 At the end ϛ[is a possibility, which might suggest ϲ[τρατηγόν, as **3290** is addressed to a strategus called Sarapion, but ạ[looks more likely and there are more possibilities.

3 Among the least unattractive possibilities are κυνη[γ]όν, after which there is a long descender, and Κυνọ[π]ọλ(ίτην), the long descender being taken as an abbreviation mark.

3292. COMMUNICATION TO A STRATEGUS

48 5B.30/G(1–2)f   6·5 × 10 cm.   *c.* A.D. 259–64

This document, probably either a report or a petition, breaks off at an interesting point just when it seems to be about to speak of the events of a sudden dawn attack, presumably on the village of Nesmeimis, from which the sender came.

By mentioning the name of an approximately datable official and specifically describing the tribe of the Goniotae as Libyans it draws together into a single period several items of evidence about barbarian raids on Egypt, cf. J. Lallemand, *L'Adminis-tration*, 31. We may plausibly conclude that the Libyan invasion which reached Philadelphia in the Fayum in A.D. 258 (P. Princ. II 29), the undated disturbances by the Goniotae and Mastitae in the region of Heracleopolis (BGU III 935), and the undated appearance of these two tribes in the Oxyrhynchus area (XXXIII **2681**), are all episodes of the same series and to be connected with the invasion mentioned in this document of *c.* A.D. 259–64.

As the evidence accumulates it grows more and more likely that the troop movements under Mussius Aemilianus, acting-prefect and then full prefect of Egypt, and under the two *correctores* of this period, were associated with disturbances like these, cf. **3290**, XLIII **3111**, **3112** introductions.

The back is blank.

Αὐρηλίῳ Πτολεμαίῳ τῷ
καὶ] Νεμεϲιανῷ ϲτρ(ατηγῷ) Ὀξ(υρυγχίτου)
παρ]ὰ Αὐρηλίου Παμούνι-
οϲ] Θώνιοϲ μητρὸϲ Θατρῆ-
5 τοϲ] ἀ[π]ὸ κώ[μ]ηϲ Νεϲμίμε-
ωϲ ἱε]ρέωϲ καὶ προφή-
τ]ου Ἄμμωνοϲ καὶ τῶν
ϲ]υννάων θεῶν με[γ]ίϲτω(ν)

2 ϲτρϛοξ'.   8 με[γ]ιϲτῶ

ἱ[ε]ροῦ τοῦ ὄντος [ἐν τῇ] αὐτῇ

10 Νεϲμίμι. ἐπεὶ ἐν τῇ γε-
νομένῃ καταδρομῇ τῶν
ἐπε[λθ]όντων Λιβύων Γω-
νιωτῶν ἐπὶ τῆϲ ιθ τοῦ
ὄντ]οϲ μηνὸϲ Παῦνι

15 ἐξα]ίφνηϲ ὑπὸ τὸν ὀρθ⟨ρ⟩ο(ν)
...]ομενοι...[.].[....

. . . . . .

10 l. Νεϲμίμει   15 ορθο̄

'To Aurelius Ptolemaeus alias Nemesianus, strategus of the Oxyrhynchite nome, from Aurelius Pamunis son of Thonis, mother Thatres, from the village of Nesmeimis, priest and prophet of Ammon and the associated very great gods of the temple which is in the same Nesmeimis. Whereas, during the the late invasion of marauding Goniotae from Libya, on the nineteenth of the current month of Payni suddenly at dawn . . .'

1–2 This strategus is known from XII **1411**, **1502**, and **1555**. According to a well justified restoration **1411** dates from 24 November, A.D. 260; **1555** certainly belongs to the brief reign of Macrianus and Quietus, which ran from autumn A.D. 260 to near the end of A.D. 261. His next known predecessor is Aurelius Sarapion, on whom see **3289** 1 n., last known some time in A.D. 258/9. His next known successor is the strategus who appears for the first time in the next item, dated to 26 May of an unknown year falling in the period A.D. 262–5, see **3293** 1–2 n., 23–6 n. The service of our strategus must, therefore, lie between 29 August, A.D. 258 and 26 May, A.D. 265. The day of the present document is limited by lines 13–14 to the period 20–30 Payni = 14–24 June and consequently the possible years are A.D. 259 to A.D. 264. No doubt the earlier part of this period is more likely, since P. Princ. II 29 dates from 8 or 18 September, A.D. 258.

9 This temple is not recorded in G. Ronchi, *Lexicon Theonymon*, Vol. i. Two other Oxyrhynchite villages are credited there with temples of Ammon, namely Peenno (p. 112) and Teis (p. 114), and there was also one at Senocomis, see **3275** 4–7.

12–13 The Goniotae (and Mastitae) lived in Mareotis, which in the time of Ptolemy the geographer (ii A.D.) was in Libya and much later was in Egypt, according to J. Lallemand, *L'Administration*, 47.

15 ὑπὸ τὸν ὀρθ⟨ρ⟩ο(ν). For the correction cf. *LSJ* s.v. ὑπό C III, 2, citing this same phrase from N.T. Acts 5:21 and Geoponica 2. 4. 3. The misspelling is perhaps due to a phonetic difficulty, cf. Mayser–Schmoll I i 159–60 (§ 36). It occurs also in P. Warren 17. 9.

3293. NOTICE TO SERVE AS A COSMETES

32 4B.3/K(1–2)b   11 × 28·5 cm.   26 May A.D. 262, 263, 264, or 265

Similar documents to this are XLIV **3182** (gymnasiarch, A.D. 257), VI **891** (exegetes, A.D. 294), **3297** (cosmetes, A.D. 294), and P. Ant. I 31 (cosmetes, A.D. 347). It is interesting that here the cosmetes is given notice to serve by the strategus, whose involvement in the business of the town council and the boards of magistrates was not expected, see **3182** introd., where the possibility that the sender of **3182** might have been the strategus was regarded as unlikely. The similarity of the new text now makes it very likely. Since the dates in **3182** are within a week of that of XXXIV **2714**, it may well have been sent by the strategus Aurelius Sabinus acting through his deputy Aurelius Petronius.

It is not yet clear whether a magistrate could expect as a matter of routine to receive notice both from the local prytanis and/or council and from the strategus as the representative of the Roman government, or whether the strategus only intervened in exceptional circumstances. In this connection we should note that in **3182** the gymnasiarch is liable only for a quarter share of the duty for one day, and that in **3293** there is a passage, unfortunately damaged, which seems to refer to the absence of one of the interested parties, see 15–17 n.

The remains of the date clause and of the name of the strategus show that a previously unknown strategus was the sender of this notice, cf. 1–2 n. We also learn the name of a new prytanis. The back is blank.

$$Αὐρήλιος \ Πα.....[...]..[$$
$$κ....ας \ στρ(ατηγὸς) \ Ὀξυρυγχ[ίτου$$
$$Αὐρηλίῳ \ Διοςκόρῳ \ Χω-$$
$$cίωνος \ κοςμητῇ \ τῷ$$
5 $$φιλτάτωι \ χαίρειν.$$
$$δι' \ ὧν \ μοι \ ἐπέςτε[ι]λεν$$
$$ἡ \ κρατίςτη \ τῶν \ αὐτόθι$$
$$βουλὴ \ διὰ \ Αὐρηλίου \ Θέω-$$
$$νος \ Cαραπίωνος \ ἐνάρχου$$
10 $$πρυτάνεως \ ἐδήλω[cε]ν$$
$$δεῖν \ cε \ ἀναδήςα[c]θ[αι] \ τὸν$$
$$τῆς \ κοςμ[ητείας \ ςτ]έφα-$$
$$νον \ ἀπὸ \ νε[ομηνίας \ ἕως \ .$$
$$τοῦ \ ὄντος \ μ[ηνὸς \ Παῦνι$$
15 $$τω \ τὸν \ κ...[.........$$
$$ἀγόμενόν \ cο. \ ἀποδη[...$$
$$τυγχάνειν. \ ἵν' \ οὖν \ εἰ[δῇς,$$
$$φίλτατε, \ καὶ \ τῶν \ [τῇ \ ἀρχῇ$$
$$διαφερόντων \ π[ρόνοιαν$$
20 $$ποιήςῃ \ ἐπέςτε[ιλά \ cοι. \ (m. \ 2) \ ἐρρῶ-$$
$$](vac.) \ cθαί \ cε \ εὔχομ[αι, \ φίλ(τατε). \ (m. \ 3) \ Αὐρ(ήλιος)$$
$$](vac.) \ Cαραπάμ[μων \ ὑ(πηρέτης) \ ἐπήνεγκα.$$

2 στρ$\mathcal{S}$

(m. 1) (ἔτους) .. Ἀ]ὐτοκράτ[ο]ρος Κα[ίσαρος Πουπλίου
Λικιν]γίου Γαλλιην[οῦ Γερμανικοῦ
25   Μεγίςτ]ου Εὐςεβοῦς Εὐ[τυχοῦς
Ϲεβαςτοῦ,] (vac.) Παῦνι α[

'Aurelius P . . . alias . . ., strategus of the Oxyrhynchite nome, to Aurelius Dioscorus son of Chosion, cosmetes, his dearest colleague, greeting. The most excellent town council of the local people in a communication addressed to me by agency of Aurelius Theon son of Sarapion, prytanis in office, has declared that you are required to put on the crown of the office of cosmetes from the first to the *n*th of the current month of Payni . . . For your information, then, dearest colleague, and so that you may make provision for matters relating to the magistracy, I have sent you this communication. (2nd hand) I pray for your health, dearest colleague. (3rd hand) I, Aurelius Sarapammon, assistant, served the notice. (1st hand) Year (9–12?) of Imperator Caesar Publius Licinius Gallienus Germanicus Maximus Pius Felix Augustus, Payni 1.'

1–2 The strategus is evidently new. Since the remains do not suit the formulas indicating an acting strategus—διαδεχόμενος | διέπων τὰ κατὰ τὴν ϲτρατηγίαν or the like—the spacing probably indicates that he had an alias. Of the numerous patterns theoretically possible the best are Πα.....[. ὁ κ]αὶ | ² Κ....ας and Πα.....[...].. [ὁ] | ² καὶ ..ας. His term of office must fall between those of Aurelius Ptolemaeus alias Nemesianus, for whom 24 November A.D. 260 is the one virtually certain date, see 3292 1–2 n., and Aurelius Heraclius alias Asterius, first known on 11 October, A.D. 265 (P. Giss. 34). For the date of this papyrus see further 23–6 n.

3–4 The cosmetes has not been identified elsewhere.

8–10 The prytanis is new. Since the office is an annual one, see A. K. Bowman, *Town Councils*, 61–5, there is a hope that the exact year of this document may one day be fixed by a new papyrus. Cf. 23–6 n. for the possible years.

13–14 ἀπὸ νε[ομηνίας ἕως .] | ¹⁴ τοῦ ὄντος μ[ηνὸς Παῦνι. The date of the start of the cosmetes' term of service is given here as the first of the current month, which is Payni according to line 26, where the ambiguous trace of the number of the day must consequently belong to α. It is a little surprising, perhaps, that the document is dated on the very same day, 26 May, as the start of the term of service. One would have expected that longer notice would have been given, see XLIV 3182, where service begins on 27 August, the notification is dated 23 August, and the delivery of it took place on 25 August; also P. Ant. I 31, where the notice is dated 25 July and the service begins on the next day. Cf. 3297 1 n.

There is, of course, no way of guessing what figure between 2 and 30 inclusive stood at the end of line 13.

15–17 One can only guess at the meaning here. By way of conjecture I suggest τῷ τὸν κατὰ [τὸ ἥμιϲυ ϲυν-] | ¹⁶ αχόμενόν ϲοι ἀπόδη[μον] | ¹⁷ τυγχάνειν, 'because the person who is associated with you to do a half share of the duty is out of town'. The dative of the articular infinitive is comparatively rare according to B. G. Mandilaras, *The Verb in the Greek Non-literary Papyri*, 337–8; to his examples can now be added one which seems particularly relevant here, XL 2902 8–10 μέχρι δεῦρο μὴ ὑπακούϲας τῷ ἐπὶ τῇ[ϲ] ἀλλοδαπῆς ἀναγκαίας χρείας χ[ά]ριν παρεϲτρατεῦϲθαι, 'up to now not having answered to my name because of having been away from home on unavoidable duty following the army'. For ἀπόδη[μον] τυγχάνειν cf. XL 2899 13–15 ἀπ[όδη]μος τυγχάνων καὶ παρε[ίθην] κατ' ἄγνοιαν, 'because I was away from home I was also mistakenly passed over'; *LSJ* s.v. τυγχάνω A II 2. For the rest I have no single convincing parallel. For the sharing of public duties see 3182 introd., 7–8 n., XL 2915 17, 2940 5.

18 For the restoration of τῇ ἀρχῇ cf. W. *Chr.* 402 i 18–19, τὰ τῇ ἀρχῇ (= κοϲμητείᾳ) [δ]ιαφέροντα [π]άντα ἀ[π]οπληρώϲεις.

21–2 The name in 22 is not mentioned elsewhere in the text. Though the position is different, it probably belongs to a delivery docket corresponding to XLIV 3182 17–18 Αὐρήλιος Ἀμόις ὑπ(ηρέτης) ἐπήνεγκα [(ἔτους) δ]· Μεϲορὴ ἐπαγομένων β. Here no date was necessary because the notice was only written on the day of the commencement of service, see 13–14 n., and delivery must have taken place on the same day.

The beginnings of the lines appear to be blank and this does not seem to be due to abrasion of the

E

ink. However, the layout would be more usual if the sender's farewell formula and the assistant's docket occupied separate lines, and this may possibly have been the case here.

23–6 The date clause is that of the sole rule of Gallienus, which contained years 9–15, A.D. 261/2 to A.D. 267/8. It lacks the victory title Περςικὸς Μέγιςτος, which is attested in the papyri from the early part of year 14, A.D. 266/7, and never thereafter omitted in the cases cited in P. Bureth, *Les titulatures impériales*, p. 120. (In the damaged CPR p. 110 B, 18 it is virtually certain to have appeared and cannot be assumed not to have been written.) The present document, therefore, should be earlier than year 14. Year 13, A.D. 265/6 is extremely unlikely, because the office of prytanis is annual, see A. K. Bowman, *Town Councils*, 61–5, and another prytanis is already attested (XXXI **2569**). The same is apparently true of year 9, A.D. 261/2, which in its earlier part was designated 2 Macrianus and Quietus, but when I saw PSI IX 1070 on two occasions in 1970 in the Laurentian Library in Florence I concluded that the figure for the year was extremely doubtful and that the traces would be as much consistent with *a* as with β. Since Aurelius Dioscurides alias Sabinus is attested in XVII **2109** as the prytanis of 1 Macrianus and Quietus, PSI 1070 may well belong to that year. At the very least the doubtful figure should not be used to prove that Sabinus was in office as prytanis in two successive years, though this was accepted by Dr. Bowman, op. cit., p. 63.

For this document, therefore, years 9–12 of Gallienus are available and the possible dates are 26 May, A.D. 262, 263, 264, and 265.

26 The figure for the day is much damaged. It is consistent with *a* and this is the only date which will suit the details given in 13–14, see note.

Below and to the left of Παῦνι in this line there are some traces of ink, which might possibly be remains of a further short line, but they are so slight that it seems more likely that they are accidental.

3294. Nomination to Public Service

48 5B.30/G(3–5)a	5·5 × 20·5 cm.	Between 29 August, A.D. 271 and 4 March, A.D. 272

The date assigned to the strategus Aurelius Turbo in XL **2923** 1, 8 nn. is here confirmed, and since that dating itself depended on the dates assigned to the prefect Statilius Ammianus, those too receive general corroboration. We also learn the name of a new phylarch (3–4).

Two features of the format of the document are puzzling. First, the top margin is unusually deep, *c.* 8·5 cm. Second, the plural formula—εἰς τὰς ὑπογεγραμμένας χρίας δίδωμι τοὺς ἐνγεγραμμένους (8–10)—suggests that it should be followed by the titles of at least two offices and the names of at least two persons, but the blank space which follows the body of the document and precedes the date clause is deep enough and wide enough for only one short line.

Probably the top margin was intended to contain annotations for official use. In the Petaus archive documents which needed to be forwarded from the village scribe's office were copied out on a fresh sheet with a space left blank at the top for a covering letter, see P. Petaus p. 110, a reference which I owe to Professor E. G. Turner.

The Press reader has pointed out that, as well as leaving too little space after 13, the clerk slipped into the singular, writing ἔςτι δέ for εἰςὶ δέ. The sheet was probably regarded as spoiled for this use and put aside for the back to be used for a less formal purpose.

The writing is blurred and looks as if it was rubbed while the whole of the written part of the surface was damp, but there seems to have been no deliberate attempt to wash off the ink.

The back is occupied by **3300.**

Αὐρηλίῳ Τούρβωνι
  cτρ(ατηγῷ) τῆc λαμ(πρᾶc) Ὀξ(υρυγχιτῶν) πόλεωc
παρ' Αὐρηλίου Cτεφάνου
Ὡρίωνοc φυλάρχου
5 τῆc λαμπρᾶc Ὀξυρυγχει-
  τῶν πόλεωc τοῦ
  ἐνεcτῶτοc β (ἔτουc) καὶ ε (ἔτουc).
  εἰc τὰc ὑπογεγραμμέναc
  χρίαc δίδωμι τοὺc
10 ἐνγεγραμμένουc
  ὅπωc ἀντιλ . . . .
  ἔκαcτοc . . . .[.].του
  χρίαc. (vac.) ἔcτι δέ.
       (vac.)
  (ἔτουc) β' Αὐτοκράτοροc Καίcαροc
15 Λουκίου Δομιττίου Αὐρηλιαν[οῦ
  Εὐcεβοῦc Εὐτυχοῦc Cεβαcτοῦ
  καὶ (ἔτουc) ε' Ἰουλίου Αὐρηλίου
  Cεπτιμίου Οὐαβαλάθου
  Ἀθη]νοδώρου τοῦ λ[αμ-

          .   .   .   .   .

2 cτρ∫, λαμ∫οξ'   7 β∫'', ε∫''   9, 13 l. χρείαc   14 ⌐β'   15 δομιτ'τιου   17 ⌐ε'

'To Aurelius Turbo, strategus of the glorious city of the Oxyrhynchites, from Aurelius Stephanus son of Horion, phylarch of the glorious city of the Oxyrhynchites for the present second year and fifth year.'

'To the undermentioned services I nominate the persons named herein, so that each may (take up? his own?) service. Viz: (blank).'

'Year 2 of Imperator Caesar Lucius Domitius Aurelianus Pius Felix Augustus, and year 5 of Julius Aurelius Septimius Vabalathus Athenodorus, the most glorious . . .'

2 λαμ(πρᾶc). See *ZPE* 12 (1973) 277–92 for the dating of changes in the titulature of the city of Oxyrhynchus, and especially 281–5 for this one. The earliest secure date for the later title λαμπρὰ καὶ λαμπροτάτη remains 4 March, A.D. 272, ibid. 285, X **1264** 2, 6, and this date may be regarded as the *terminus ante quem* for **3294.** Note that XL **2923,** also addressed to Aurelius Turbo, has the later title and is to be dated, presumably, later than this document.

It is most unusual and is perhaps simply a scribal error that Turbo is described as strategus of the city. He should properly be called strategus of the Oxyrhynchite nome.

3–4 The phylarch is new. On the office see P. Mertens, *Les services de l'état civil*, 16–30, cf. XL Introd. pp. 7–8. The Shepherds' Quarter, or, as I have suggested, the tribe consisting of this and other quarters and designated by its name for short, was providing liturgists for this year, A.D. 271/2, see XL **2904** 8–10 n.

11–12 We expect something like ὅπως ἀντιλάβηται ἕκαστος τῆς ἑαυτοῦ χρίας. In 11 there is room for only about four letters after ἀντιλ—and they appear to have been altered by a pen with a broader point. In 12 ἑαυτοῦ by itself is too short; τῆς καθ' ἑαυτοῦ χρίας, cf. Mayser, *Grammatik*, II ii 429–30, would suit the space and will probably do as a conjecture, but I am unable to verify it.

14–19 For the chronology see XL Introd. pp. 15–26. According to the view adopted there 2 Aur. 5 Vab. began on 30 August, A.D. 271. In the course of the same Egyptian year it began to be designated as 3 Aurelian, the first example dating from 24 June, A.D. 272, see ibid. p. 23. For **3294**, therefore, the *terminus post quem* is 29 August, A.D. 271, and the *terminus ante quem* is 4 March, A.D. 272, as explained above in 2 n.

19 λ[αμ-] | 20 [προτάτου or λ[αμϛ = λ[αμ(προτάτου). For the titles see P. Bureth, *Les titulatures*, 122.

3295. REGISTRATION OF A CHILD

18 2B.65/G(1)b   10·5 × 20 cm.   24–28 August A.D. 285

The standard analysis of documents of this type is to be found in P. Mertens, *Les services de l'état civil*, 48–65. Examples published later are XXXVIII **2855**, **2858**, XLIII **3136**, **3137**, XLIV **3183**, and P. Köln II 87.

This new one is interesting for its date in the first year of Diocletian and for the exceptional address, best paralleled in P. Köln 87 of A.D. 271—τοῖς διοικοῦσι τὰ κατὰ τὴν φυλ(αρχίαν) τῆς . . . πόλεως, 'to the administrators of the affairs of the phylarchy of the city'. One of the members of this board is Aurelius Horion son of Theon, who is known from later years as a systates, i.e. in XLIII **3137** of A.D. 294/5 and in P. Fuad I Univ. 13 of A.D. 297/8. The phylarchs of the tribes were replaced by systatae near the beginning of Diocletian's reign, the earliest systates being attested in A.D. 287 (PSI III 164), see Mertens, op. cit., p. 31 and n. 174. It is an obvious possibility that at the time **3295** was written the change was imminent or even in progress. Another possibility is that the particular phylarch to whom the application would normally have been sent was for some reason unable to act. In XL **2936** 28–9 a subscription which would normally have been written by a phylarch was made by a person whose title should probably be restored as διοικ(ῶν) τὰ κατὰ τὴν [φυλαρχίαν and there are indications that this was because the phylarch was ill, see ibid. 9 n., 28–31 n. P. Köln 87 belongs to the same short period in A.D. 271.

The back is blank.

τ[ο]ῖς διοικοῦσι τὰ κατὰ τὴν φυλ(αρχίαν) τῆς λαμ(πρᾶς) καὶ
λαμ(προτάτης) Ὀξ(υρυγχιτῶν) πόλεως τοῦ ἐνεστῶτος α (ἔτους) διὰ
Αὐρηλίων Ὡρίωνος Θέωνος καὶ Νίλου τοῦ

1 φυλ, λαμ)   2 λαμ)οξ', αϛ''

καὶ Ἀθηναίου καὶ Μέλανος Μέλανος καὶ τῶν

5   cὺν αὐτοῖc π(αρὰ) Μάρ[κο]υ Αὐρηλίου Εὐδαίμο-

νος Ἡρακλείδου τοῦ Διοσκόρου μη(τρὸς) Ταύριος

ἀπὸ τῆς αὐτῆς πόλεως. β[ο]ύλομαι πρώτω[c

ἀ[ναγρα]φῆναι ἐφ' οὗ κἀγὼ ἀ[ν]αγράφομαι

αὐτὸc] ἀμφόδου ['Ιππέ]ων Παρεμβολῆc

10   τὸ]ν γεγονότα μ[ο]ι ἐκ τῆc cυνούcηc μοι

γυναικὸc Αὐρηλίαc Νίκηc ἤτοι Ταϊάδος

ἀπὸ τῆς αὐτῆς πόλεως υ[ἱ]ὸν Αὐρήλιον

Εὐδαίμονα (δωδεκάδραχμον) ἀπὸ γυμ(ναcίου) ὄντα πρὸς

τὸ ἐνεcτὸc α (ἔτος) (ἐτῶν) ια. διὸ ἐπιδίδωμι

15   τ[ὸ] ὑπόμ(νημα) ἀξιῶν ταγῆναι αὐτὸν διὰ τῆc

καταχωριζομένηc ὑφ' ὑμῶν γραφῆc

ἀφηλίκ[ω]ν ἐν τῇ τῶν ὁμηλίκων τάξει

ὡc καθήκει καὶ ὀμν[ύ]ω τὸν ἔθιμ[ον] Ῥωμαί-

οιc ὅρκον μὴ ἐψεῦcθαι.   (vac.)

20   (ἔτους) α″ Αὐτοκρά[τ]ορος Κ[α]ίcαρος Γαΐου Οὐαλ[ερίο]υ

Δι]οκλητιανοῦ Εὐcεβοῦc Εὐτυχοῦc Cεβαcτοῦ

ἐπ]αγομένω(ν) ..   (vac.)

(m. 2)   Αὐρήλιος Εὐδα[ίμ]ων ἐπιδέδω-

κα καὶ ὤμοσα τὸν ὅρκον ὡc

25   πρόκειται. Αὐρήλιος Ἀcκλ[ᾶc

ἔγραψα ὑπὲρ αὐτοῦ μὴ εἰδ[ό-

το]c γράμματα.   (vac.)

(m. 3?) 'Ιππέων Παρεμβολ(ῆc) ...[.]........

     ..].....[.] (v.) ....[.....]....

5 π′   6 μη⟩   11 ταϊαδος   13 ιβ., γυμϚ   14 αϚLιᾳ   15 υπομϚ   20 Lα″, γαϊου
22 επ]αγομενω   28 παρεμβδ

'To the administrators of the affairs of the phylarchy of the glorious and most glorious city of the Oxyrhynchites for the present 1st year, by agency of Aurelius Horion son of Theon and Aurelius Nilus alias Athenaeus and Aurelius Melas son of Melas and their associates, from Marcus Aurelius Eudaemon, son of Heracleides, grandson of Dioscorus, mother Tayris, from the same city. I wish to have registered for the first time in the district in which I am myself registered, the Cavalry Camp district, the son born to me from my wife who lives with me, Aurelia Nice or Taias, from the same city, Aurelius Eudaemon, who is liable to the twelve-drachma poll-tax and of the gymnasial class and is in the present 1st year 11(?) years old. Therefore I submit the application, requesting that he be enrolled in the list of minors registered by you in the category of his coevals as is proper and I swear the oath customary among Romans that I have made no false declaration. Year 1 of Imperator Caesar Gaius Valerius Diocletianus Pius Felix Augustus, *n*th intercalary day.'

(2nd hand) 'I, Aurelius Eudaemon, have submitted (the application) and I swore the oath, as aforesaid. I, Aurelius Asclas(?), wrote on his behalf because he does not know letters.'

(3rd hand?) 'Cavalry Camp district . . .'

3 Ὠρίωνος Θέωνος. See introd.

14 ια. The reading is doubtful; ι seems very likely and the fact that the son is to be enrolled in the list of minors (16–17) suggests that he was under fourteen years of age. It seems impossible to read the other theoretical possibilities, ιβ and ιγ.

28 The last three traces look like ∟ι . ; if so, this is the son's age, i.e. (ἐτῶν) ια(?), see 14 and n. It should be preceded at this point by his name, but this is difficult to verify. A possibility is Εὐδ[α]ίμονα, cf. XLIII **3136** 18–19, though the nominative case is expected, see XXXVIII **2855** 28, XLIV **3183** 22–3, P. Cornell 18. 26–9.

3296. Petition?

28 4B.61/G(24–25)a   9 × 23 cm.   10 June, A.D. 291

The earliest known date for the prefect of Egypt Titius Honoratus was hitherto 21(?) January, A.D. 292, see *ZPE* 17 (1975) 320. This document sets the date back some seven months to 10 June, A.D. 291. It also gives us the name of another equestrian official of high rank, Aurelius Antiphates, *vir perfectissimus*, and tells us that he was in office on and before the same fixed date. The loss of about forty-five letters from the ends of the lines deprives us of the knowledge of what that office was and makes it very difficult to gather what the document was about.

However, as far as at present understood or guessed, it seems to be a petition submitted by the heirs of Aurelia Stratonice and by a lady called Aurelia Lucilla alias Theonis. The story may have run somewhat as follows. On 10 June, A.D. 291 a letter dated Mecheir (January/February) of the same year was delivered. It is not clear by whom it was sent; very likely it was delivered to the petitioners. In the strangely long interval between the sending and the delivery of the letter proceedings had taken place in the court of Antiphates, during which he delivered some pronouncement which prompted the petitioners to appeal to the prefect of Egypt, Titius Honoratus.

At this stage we reach the main point of the petition, which is even less clear than the rest. It seems most likely that the letter in question was an official or semi-official letter requiring some action which the petitioners wanted to postpone to await the outcome of the appeal to the prefect. Possibly they required a subscription from Antiphates authorizing such a delay, but a clause mentioning the amount of the caution money payable in respect of the appeal may be the kernel of the matter. For the many difficulties and uncertainties see the notes.

On the back, upside down and across the fibres, there are the ends of 10 lines giving Oxyrhynchite place-names and areas of land in aruras, below which the papyrus is blank.

Αὐρηλίῳ Ἀντιφάτῃ τῷ διαϲημοτ[άτῳ
      (vac.)   [
παρὰ κληρονόμων Αὐρηλίαϲ Ϲτρατονείκηϲ [
νοέωϲ γυμναϲιάρχου βουλευτοῦ τῆϲ λαμπρᾶϲ καὶ λα[μπροτάτηϲ Ὀξυρυγχιτῶν πόλεωϲ
Λουκίλληϲ τῆϲ καὶ Θεωνείδοϲ θυγατρὸϲ Θέωνο[ϲ
5 χιτῶν πόλεωϲ. ἐπειδὴ τῇ ἐνεϲτώϲῃ ἡμ[έρᾳ
ἐπιτρόπου ἐπήνεγκεν ἐπιϲτολὴν ἐξ ὀνόμα[τοϲ
εἰϲ Μεχεὶρ μῆνα τοῦ ἐνεϲτῶτοϲ ζ϶ καὶ ϛ϶.[
ϲτουμένων ὑφ' ἡμῶν, τῆϲ δὲ ἐπιϲτ[ο]λῆ[ϲ] ..[
δέπω τοῦ πράγματοϲ παρὰ ϲοὶ γνωϲθέν[τοϲ
10 διὰ τοῦ υἱοῦ Ἡρώδου καί τινα διελάληϲαϲ δι..[
ἡμᾶϲ ἀκολούθωϲ τοῖϲ νόμοιϲ ἐκκαλουμεν[
Ὀνωρᾶτον, ᾧ παραθηϲόμεθα τὰ προϲόντ[α
ἀξι]οῦντεϲ, ὡϲ ἐκελεύϲθη, τὴν ϲυνήθη υ.[
ϲτρ]ατηγὸν ἐπιϲτολιμεα γράμματα πρὸϲ τὸ α[
15 ...] τοῦ τῆϲ ἐκκλήτου προϲτίμ[ο]υ ὄντοϲ ϲυν.[
τε]τρακιϲχιλίαιϲ ἑξακοϲίαιϲ εἴκοϲι πέντε του[
καὶ καθ' ἕνα ὡμολογήϲαμεν. (ἔτουϲ) ζ′ Αὐτοκράτ[οροϲ Καίϲαροϲ Γαΐου Αὐρηλίου
      Οὐαλερίου Διοκλητιανοῦ
καὶ (ἔτουϲ) ϛ′ Αὐτοκράτοροϲ Καίϲαροϲ Μάρκου Αὐ[ρηλίου Οὐαλερίου
      Μαξιμιανοῦ Γερμανικῶν Μεγίϲτων
Εὐϲεβῶν Εὐτυχῶν Ϲεβαϲτῶν, Παῦνι ιϛ⁻. [
20 (m. 2) δι' ἐ]μοῦ Αὐρηλίου Ϲαρᾶ του.[
ἐπ]ιδεδώκαμεν καὶ ε.[
(m. 3) Αὐρη]λία Λουκίλλα ἡ κ[αὶ Θεωνίϲ
ἐπερ]ωτηθεῖϲα ὡμολ[όγηϲα.
(m. 4) .....].....ων τὴν ἐκλ[
25   .....].......προϲέλθατε [
    ....]..[.].ατα. (vac.) [

2 l. Ϲτρατονίκηϲ   4 l. Θεωνίδοϲ   6 επηνεγ'κεν   8 ὑφ   10 ϋϊου   11 εκ'καλουμεν[
14 l. ἐπιϲτολιμαῖα   15 εκ'κλητου   17 Ⳑ ζ′   18 Ⳑ ϛ′

(No continuous translation is possible. The notes contain translations of passages where some sense seems to emerge.)

2–3 Restore Ἀντι]νοέωϲ. This may refer to Stratonice's father, but possibly the name of the subscriber of 20–1 appeared in 2, e.g. δι' ἐμοῦ Ϲαρᾶ κτλ. Ἀντι]νοέωϲ; cf. also 6 n.

5–8 In spite of the damage a clear grammatical relationship can be perceived: ἐπειδὴ τῇ ἐνεστώςῃ ἡμ[έρᾳ ... (subject)] ... ἐπήνεγκεν ἐπιςτολήν ... [... κεχρονιςμένην] εἰς Μεχεὶρ μῆνα ... [περὶ χρεω?]-ςτουμένων ὑφ' ἡμῶν, 'Whereas today So-and-so delivered a letter dated in the month of Mecheir about (sums owed?) by us ...'

6 ἐπιτρόπου. This might denote an official *procurator* of some kind or a guardian. It might be that Saras, the subscriber of 20–1, was the guardian of the heirs, cf. also 2–3 n.

ἐπήνεγκεν. This word is sometimes used of the delivery of official communications by ὑπηρεταί, e.g. I **59** 22, VI **899** 50, XLIV **3182** 17, BGU IV 1070. 13, 14. If the letter was equivalent to a summons delivered by an assistant of the strategus, that might explain why the strategus is apparently mentioned in 14.

6–7 Restore probably κεχρονιςμένην] εἰς Μεχεὶρ μῆνα. Why the letter took so long to be delivered (January/February till 10 June) is one of the puzzling questions to arise here. It suggests, however, that it was not a mere private letter, but probably a document passing through the machinery of the bureaucracy.

8 Restore perhaps χρεω]ςτουμένων, cf. 5–8 n. and introd. See P. Kretschmer and E. Locker, *Rückläufiges Wb. d. gr. Sprache* for possible verbs in -ςτέω. None of the others is more attractive.

8–12 The following outline can be conjectured: τῆς δὲ ἐπιςτ[ο]λῆ[ς ... ἔτι πάλαι γεγραμμένης μη]δέπω τοῦ πράγματος παρὰ coὶ γνωςθέν[τος ... ὅτε ὁ δεῖνα (= ἡ Λουκίλλα?) προςῆλθέ coι] διὰ τοῦ υἱοῦ Ἡρώδου καί τινα διελάληςας δι..[... κελεύων ...] ἡμᾶς ... ἐκκαλουμέν[ους ... ἀπαντᾶν πρός ...], Ὀνωρᾶτον, ᾧ παραθηςόμεθα τὰ προςόντ[α ἡμῖν δίκαια, 'and since the letter was drafted a long time ago, before the matter was heard in your court, when (Lucilla?) came before you represented by (her?) son Herodes and you delivered some pronouncements, ordering us to appeal and go before Honoratus, to whom we shall submit the rights that are ours'.

10 διελάληςας. In spite of the note to XVI **1829** 4 explaining that διαλαλία and διαλαλεῖν technically refer to an 'investigation' before a magistrate, all the passages cited in the dictionaries seem to suggest that they are used rather of solemn pronouncements, sometimes with an additional notion of commanding.

δι..[. Not δι' ὧν; possibly διᾳ.[or δι' ᾳ.[.

12 Ὀνωρᾶτον. See introd. The future verb immediately following makes it quite clear that he was still in office at the date of this document.

12–13 The main clause probably begins here with something like ἐπιδίδομεν τὰ βιβλίδια | 13 ἀξι]οῦντες, 'we submit the petition requesting ...'. The continuation is much more dubious. Perhaps it was something like τὴν cυνήθη ὑπ[οςημείωςιν ἐκδοθῆναι ἡμῖν, 'that the customary subscription be issued to us', cf. P. Lips. 33 ii 17. Note that there does seem to be an official subscription at the foot of this document (24–6).

14 ςτρ]ατηγόν. Cf. 6 n., but ἐπι|ςτρ]άτηγον is also at least a theoretical possibility, see J. Lallemand, *L'Administration*, 44.

ἐπιςτολιμέα (l. -αῖα) γράμματα. The phrase occurs twice in Philo (*De Josepho*, 168; *In Flaccum*, 109), and seems to mean no more than 'letter'; ἐπιςτολιμαῖος is new in the papyri. It is not quite clear that the letter is, or is to be, directed to the strategus (πρὸς τὸν ςτρατηγόν?), but that seems most likely.

πρὸς τὸ ᾳ[perhaps introduced an articular infinitive, the construction being equivalent to a final or consecutive clause, cf. B. G. Mandilaras, *The Verb*, § 861(1).

15–16 This passage was evidently about the surety required in cases of appeal, cf. N. Lewis in *Le Monde grec* (*Hommages à C. Préaux*), 762–3. In one of two cases in papyri the surety of 1,062½ drachmas was made up of a basic 1,000 dr. plus additional charges (προςδιαγραφόμενα) of 1/16 or 6¼% amounting to 62½ dr. (P. Achmim 8. 37–9); in the other the surety of 2,125 dr. is twice the amount in P. Achmim 8 and can clearly be regarded as made up in the same proportions of a basic 2,000 dr. plus 125 dr. (see CPR V 5. 3 n.). The sum here, 4,625 dr., cannot easily be divided in those proportions. No clear deduction can be made, but it is tempting to think that somehow the progress of inflation is reflected in these figures. The simplest hypothesis would be to divide the sum into a round 4,000 plus 625 extra charges, which would mean that the rate had risen from 1/16 (or 6¼%) to 5/32 (or 15⅝%).

There is also doubt about how many persons this surety covers. The figures here may be for each individual or for several together. In CPR V 5 the guarantors are paired and it is not clear if each is held responsible for 2,000 dr. plus charges or if they share the obligation.

Still less is it clear why the sum is stated here. The appearance of stipulation clauses at the foot may suggest that there is some element of contractual agreement about this document, even though it seems to be cast in the form of a petition, cf. 23 n.

17 καὶ καθ' ἕνα ὡμολογήσαμεν. This looks like part of a stipulation clause in some such form as ἐπερωτηθέντες ὑφ' ἓν καὶ καθ' ἕνα ὡμολογήσαμεν, 'the formal question having been put to us together and severally we gave our consent.' For ὑφ' ἓν καὶ καθ' ἕνα cf. I **94** 12 ἤτοι ὑφ' ἓν ἢ καθ' ἕνα, but I cannot claim to have seen any similar addition to a stipulation clause. Cf. 22–3 n.

17–19 For the imperial titles see e.g. XXXVIII **2855** 18–24. Here 46 letters are lost in 17 and 43 in 18, equivalent to just over half the width of the document.

20–1 Cf. 2–3 n., 6 n.

20 του.[. Some possibilities are (1) a patronymic, e.g. Τούρ[βωνος, (2) an alias, i.e. τοῦ κ[αὶ ..., (3) a description, e.g. τοῦ ἐ[πιτρόπου or τοῦ π[ροκειμένου. The trace is too tiny to allow any choice.

21 Very probably restore ἐπ[ερωτηθέντες ὡμολογήσαμεν vel sim., cf. 17, 23.

22–3 Restore probably ἐπιδέδωκα καὶ |²³ ἐπερ]ωτηθεῖσα ὡμολ[όγησα, cf. 21 and n. The stipulation clause is very rarely used in documents drafted in petition form, see D. Simon, *Studien z. Praxis d. Stipulationsklausel*, 51–2 (on p. 52, n. 48, correct Herm. 77 to refer to SPP V 74). Simon's four examples are applications for payment. This may suggest that here the passage in 15–16 relating to caution money was the essential part of the document, see 15–16 n.

24–6 This does not look like the subscription of a petitioner or amanuensis, and, in spite of printed appearances, the remains in 26 do not suit ἔγραψα ὑπὲρ αὐτοῦ μὴ εἰδότος (vel sim.) γ]ρά[μ]ματα. It looks much more like an official subscription containing instructions to apply elsewhere—προσέλθατε [(25), cf. 12–13 n. In 24 ἐκλ[may represent ἔκ⟨κ⟩λ[ητον, but need not.

3297. NOTICE TO SERVE AS A COSMETES

17 2B.63/G (d)   7 × 12·5 cm.   Shortly before 11 January, A.D. 294?

Similar documents to this are XLIV **3182** (gymnasiarch, A.D. 257), **3293** (cosmetes, *c.* A.D. 262–5), VI **891** (exegetes, A.D. 294), and P. Ant. I 31 (cosmetes, A.D. 347). Unfortunately the exact wording of **3297** cannot yet be restored, because none of these is an exact parallel. In fact, though each of the five documents is basically a notification that the recipient will shortly be required to serve as a magistrate, they come from at least four different sources.

In **3297** the source is the prytanis. In **891** it is the council with the prytanis acting as intermediary. This is probably only a formal difference and indeed the prytanis is the same in both. In **3293** the sender is the strategus. In P. Ant. 31 the sender is the logistes and in **3182** his identity is not known, though the wording makes it clear that he was not the prytanis and **3293** rather suggests that he was the strategus.

On the cosmetes see E. L. de Kock, *Die Kosmeet in Egipte*, (diss. Leiden, 1948).

The back is blank.

Αὐρήλιος] Κορνηλιανὸς διασημότατος
ἔναρχος π]ρύτανις τῆς λαμπρᾶς καὶ λαμ-
προτάτη]ς Ὀξυρυγχιτῶν πόλεως
.......] Τρύφωνι Διονυσίου
5   ....].. τῷ φιλτάτῳ χαίρειν.

......]ρχειν τὸν τῆc κοcμητείαc
cτέφ]ανον ἀπὸ ιϛ‑ Τῦβι ἕωc λ‑
τοῦ αὐ]τοῦ μηνὸc ἐν αἷc ἡμέραιc
.....] πανήγυριc, ἡμέραc ιε⁻,

10   ..... πρ]όνοιαν πάντων τῶν
τῇ ἀρχῇ] διαφερόντων
ἐπιcτέλλ]εταί coι, φίλτατε,

c. 8. (m. 2) ἐρ]ρῶcθαί cε εὔχ(ομαι), φίλτατε.

13 ευχ´

'Aurelius Cornelianus, *vir perfectissimus*, prytanis in office of the glorious and most glorious city of the Oxyrhynchites to [Aurelius?] Tryphon son of Dionysius . . ., his dearest colleague, greeting. [Since it is necessary for you to hold?] the office of cosmetes from 16th Tybi to the 30th of the same month, in which days . . . festival, for (a total of) 15 days, and to attend to everything which concerns [the magistracy, notice is sent] to you, dearest colleague, [for your information?]. (2nd hand) I pray for your health, dearest colleague.'

1 The prytanis is the same as in **891**, where we must now read in line 7 διαcῇ̄, i.e. διαcη(μοτάτου), in spite of the understandable doubts of the first editors. On the diffusion of the perfectissimate in this period and more especially later under Constantine see *RE* xix 668 ff., cf. XLIII **3124** 1–2 n. Some time before A.D. 317 councillors who had performed all the public duties of their native city could acquire the perfectissimate by application to an emperor, see C. Theod. XII i 5. Possibly this is the explanation of the unexpected rank of this prytanis, though one can only guess.

The date of **891** is A.D. 294, though the reading of the consular date clause needs revision in some details. The *ed. pr.* has in lines 1–3

['Εφ' ὑ]πάτων Οὐαλερίων Κων-
[c]ταντ[ίο]υ καὶ Μαξιμια[νοῦ
τῶν ἐπιφανεcτάτων Καιcάρων

I was able to inspect the papyrus, which is now in the Bodleian Library, Oxford, shelfmark MS. Gr. class. f. 89 (P), and propose the following version of lines 1–2:

[ἐπὶ ὑ]πάτων τῶν κυρίων ἡμῶ[ν
[Κων]cταντί[ο]υ καὶ Μαξιμιανοῦ

Compare SB VI 9044. 13. It is worth adding that the end of line 3 appears to be complete and that there is no space anywhere to restore at the end of the formula τὸ γ´ or τὸ ε´, which would turn the date clause into that of A.D. 300 (cf. XLIII **3141**) or A.D. 305 (cf. XLIII **3143**). For A.D. 299/300 a different prytanis is already attested, see XLIV **3187**; A.D. 304/5 is still vacant.

The prytanis was appointed for an annual term, see A. K. Bowman, *Town Councils* 61–5. Cornelianus, therefore, was the prytanis for A.D. 293/4, and there is a reasonable chance that **3297** also dates from this year, though it is quite possible that Cornelianus served more than once in this office. Since the period of the cosmetes' activity is given as 16–30 Tybi = 11–25 January, this document probably dates from shortly before 11 January of whatever year is in question, see **3293** 13–14 n., although **3293** is itself dated on the same day as the beginning of the cosmetes' term of office.

4 Supply probably Αὐρηλίῳ, but some other *nomen* is possible.

5 ....]... Probably we should assume that the line was indented and read simply κοcμη]τῇ, cf. **3293** 4–5. The reading is complicated by damage and by a descender from the rho of Τρύφωνι in the line above.

6]ρχειν. If it were not for the fact that the rounded trace before χ and the long descender visible in the next line strongly suggest ρ, there would be a temptation to satisfy sense and space by restoring [δέον cε] ἔχειν τόν . . . [cτέφ]ανον . . . | ¹⁰ [καὶ τὴν πρ]όνοιαν . . . The sense could also be represented by

restoring [δόξαν coι ὑπά]ρχειν τόν . . . [cτέφ]ανον . . . | ¹⁰ [καὶ τὴν πρ]όνοιαν . . ., but that is too long for line 6, unless it was in ecthesis, which seems improbable. Alternatively [δέον ce ἄ]ρχειν τόν . . . [cτέφ]ανον is perhaps a tolerable expression, cf. X **1252** verso 16 for cτέφανοc in the sense of 'office', but then it is not convincing simply to tack on [καὶ τὴν πρ]όνοιαν and space for another verb to govern πρόνοιαν is hard to find. In the circumstances the translation given above can only be a makeshift approximating to the right sense. Cf. **3293** 11–13 for the natural expression ἀναδήcαcθαι τὸν τῆc κοcμητείαc cτέφανον.

By way of conjecture Mr. Parsons suggests περὶ τοῦ cὲ ἄ]ρχειν (in ecthesis) . . . [ἵνα ποῇ πρ]όνοιαν . . . [ἐπιcτέλλ]εταί coι, 'Concerning your term of office . . . so that you may attend (to everything) . . . notice is sent to you.'

7 16–30 Tybi = 11–25 January, cf. 1 n.

9 Perhaps restore [ἐcτιν], but this word could easily be dispensed with; a name or description of the festival is equally likely.

In all probability the festival is the one mentioned in XVII **2127** 4 and in I **42** 3. The first passage records a payment apparently made in Pachon in respect of a festival held in Tybi, which involved a sacrifice conducted in the theatre. In I **42** (= W. *Chr.* 154) an official gave notice of a display by ephebes which was to take place next day on 24 Tybi = 19 January, A.D. 323 and somehow provide a διπλῆ τέρψιc.

It is not clear from the interrupted text of 8–9 whether the festival occupied the whole of the period of office or, as seems more likely, only part of it. Nor is it clear from **42** whether the ephebic display was part of the festival or a separate and later event. The phrase ἡ προάγουca πανήγυριc gave some difficulty to the first editors and was translated as 'the distinguished character of the festival' in spite of a note showing uneasiness and their recognition that προάγουca ought to mean 'previous', see already WB s.v. προάγω (5). However, even with this accepted the situation is still not clear. It seems that there are three possibilities. The most attractive to me is that 'the previous festival', which was over by 23 Tybi = 18 January, involved the ephebes, and their display of 24 Tybi = 19 January, not connected with the festival, would give the spectators 'a double pleasure'. Secondly, 'the previous festival' might mean the same event in the previous year, but the promise of a διπλῆ τέρψιc tells against that. Lastly, and more remotely, ἡ προάγουca πανήγυριc might possibly mean 'the festival up to now', 'the earlier part of the festival', in which case the display of 19 January would have been part of a celebration covering these two days and an unspecified period before them.

It is uncertain how much weight we should give to the fact that the ephebes were the particular concern of the cosmetes.

For other references to festivities in Tybi cf. *CÉ* 43 (1968) 344, line 5 with notes on 348–9, *CÉ* 49 (1974) 376 and n. 2.

11 Cf. **3293** 18 n.

12 Cf. VI **891** 17.

13 There is space to restore ἵν' εἰδῇc, following the lines of **891** 16–17 ἵνα τοῦτο εἰδέναι ἔχοιc, ἐπιcτέλλεταί coι, but the beginning of the line might have been blank.

There is a presumption that the subscriptions of both **891** and **3297** are by Aurelius Cornelianus and indeed it seems likely that they are by the same hand, which uses, however, a broader pen in **891** 18–19.

3298. HOROSCOPES AND MAGIC SPELL

38 3B.81/J(1–3)a   19 × 7 cm.   Later third century

The lingering notoriety of the emperor Elagabalus is illustrated by the rare and opprobrious term, κόρυφοc, 'catamite', applied to him in the date clause of one of these horoscopes, see 2 n. This description of him has been referred to by Dr. T. D.

Barnes in his article 'Ultimus Antoninorum' (*Bonner HA Colloquium* 10 (1972) 53–74) p. 53. In **3299** the disapproval is less colourfully expressed by calling him ἀνόϲιοϲ Ἀντωνῖνοϲ μικρόϲ. Official disapproval of Elagabalus resulted in a *damnatio memoriae*, which has manifested itself in the erasure of his name from some inscriptions (e.g. *ILS* I 466, 468, 470–2; SB VIII 9997. 65). The references in P. Bureth, *Les titulatures*, 106–7, do not lead to any instance of the erasure of his name in the papyri, but there exists one example in a forthcoming papyrus, inv. 69/19(a). Various interrelated periphrases are employed to allude to his reign in the papyri of subsequent reigns. Two papyri of 13 Severus Alexander (A.D. 233/4) describe A.D. 220/1 by this method: τῷ μετὰ τὴν τοῦ θεοῦ Ἀντωνίνου μεγάλου αὐτοκρατορ[εία]ν δ ἔτει (P. Flor. I 56. 12–13); τῷ μετὰ τὸ κε (ἔτοϲ) θεοῦ Ϲεουήρου Ἀντωνίνου δ (ἔτει) (P. Lips. 6. 16). The same method is used to refer to A.D. 221/2 in P. Mich. inv. 1935. 10 (τ]ῷ ε (ἔτει) τῆϲ μετὰ θεὸν Ϲεο[υῆ]ρον Ἀντωνῖνον βαϲιλίαϲ), and this papyrus dates from summer A.D. 272, in the reign of Aurelian. (The papyrus will be published in a Ph.D. thesis for the University of Michigan by Mr. Vincent P. McCarren, who very kindly communicated the text to me in advance of publication.) Similar is the use of τῆϲ προαγούϲηϲ βαϲιλείαϲ in P. Hamb. I 18 i 3–4, ii 3, 8, 13, see the introduction there, p. 79.

 In this connection it should be observed that the θεὸϲ Ἀντωνῖνοϲ in XXVII **2746** 11 is Caracalla, see n. ad loc., and not Elagabalus as implied by P. Bureth, *Les titulatures*, 107.

 The date of the latest of the horoscopes gives a *terminus post quem* for the papyrus of A.D. 249/250, see line 22 and n. The hand looks as if it belongs still to the third century.

 The foot of the sheet is lost. On the front, where the writing runs along the fibres, the left edge looks as if it has suffered very little damage and there are tops of two columns with a few complete lines as well as the beginnings of lines from a third column. On the other side there are complete lines only in the second column, to the right of which is a blank space *c.* 8·5 cm. wide. A few ends from a preceding column also survive.

 Probably all the writing is by the same person, though the first two columns on the front and the first three lines of the third are in a good cursive, flowing but careful, while the rest is far more rapid and careless.

 The second horoscope was cast for the son of the man named in the first. It is also noticeable that the first horoscope gives positions in degrees and minutes inside the zodiacal signs, while the second gives only the names of the signs. The others are too damaged to compare. The final, much damaged, item was a spell to conjure up a dream.

 The impression given is that this sheet is not the work of a serious astrologer, so to speak, but rather of a person interested in the fates of particular people. He probably collected the horoscopes rather than cast them himself.

 Professor Neugebauer was kind enough to make accurate modern computations for the horoscopes, which have been added in round brackets at the appropriate points in the translation.

i

γένεϲιϲ Ἀπολιναρίου
β (ἔτουϲ) Ἀντωνείνου τοῦ κορύφ(ου)
Παχὼν κβ‾ νυκτὸ(ϲ) εἰϲ
κγ‾ ὥρᾳ ζ   εχθ( )
⁵ ὡροϲκό(ποϲ) Ἰχθύϲι μοιρ(ῶν) ϛ
]υρμου   Ζεὺϲ Ἰχθύϲι μοιρ(ῶν) β λε(πτῶν) ιη
Ϲελήνη Τοξότῃ μοιρ(ῶν) γ
Κρ]όν[οϲ Ϲ]κορπίῳ [......]..

· · · · ·

ii

Ϲεουήρου υἱοῦ ὁμοί(ωϲ)
¹⁰ ϛ (ἔτουϲ) Γορδιανοῦ Φαῶφι ζ
νυκτὸϲ εἰϲ η‾ ὥρ(ᾳ)
ε‾ ἀρχῆϲ
Ἥλιοϲ καὶ Ἑρμῆϲ Ζυγῷ
ὡροϲκό(ποϲ) Διδύμοιϲ
¹⁵ [Κρ]όνοϲ ἀρχὰϲ Παρθένου
[Ἄ]ρηϲ Ϛκ[ορ]πίῳ
c. 12   ].ω

· · · · ·

iii

γένεϲ(ιϲ) Δη[
γ (ἔτουϲ) Φιλίπ[πων
²⁰ εἰϲ κα‾ ν[
γένεϲιϲ Ἀμμ[
α (ἔτουϲ) Δεκίου ..[
α‾ ἡμέ[ραϲ
ὡροϲκ[όποϲ
²⁵ Ἀφροδ[ίτη
Ζεὺ[ϲ
Κρό[νοϲ
..[

· · · · ·

2 βϛ, κορυφ′   3 νυκτ°   4 εχθ   5 ωροϲκο), μοιρ′   6 μοιρ′, λε)   7 μοιρ′   9 ομο^t
10 ϛϛ   11 ω monogram   14 ωροϲκο)   18 γενεϲ′   19 γϛ   22 αϛ

i

Back   ].

30   ὦ]ρᾳ ζ‾

     ] (vac.)

     ] (vac.)

     ] Ἀφροδίτης

     ] (vac.)

35   ]..

       ]..ι

       ]..

. . . . .

ii

ϛ (ἔτους) Γορδιανοῦ, Τῦβι ιϛ

ὥρᾳ β′ ἡμέρας ἀρχ(ῆς)

40   γένεϲιϲ ϛαβείνου ˮΙϲειτοϲ

ὀνειρετηϲίᾳ   (vac.)

γρ(άψον) τὸ ὄνο(μα) ..... χαρτάριον

ἢ εἰϲ φύλλ[ο]ν .....ϛ καὶ ἐπι.[...]αϲ

δι.ανα..[.]....[.]..τη[..]....[

. . . . .

38 ϛ∫, τυβιῖϛ   39 αρχ′   40 ἴϲειτοϲ   41 l. ὀνειραιτηϲία   42 γ^ρ, ονο̄

'Birth of Apolinarius. Year 2 of Antoninus the catamite, Pachon 22, night before 23, 7th hour. Horoscope, Pisces 6°; Jupiter, Pisces 2° 18′ (340° = Pisces 10°); Moon, Sagittarius 3° (244° = Sagittarius 4°); Saturn, Scorpio . . . (225° = Scorpio 15°).'

'Of Severus his son likewise. Year 6 of Gordian, Phaophi 7, night before 8, 5th hour beginning. Sun and Mercury, Libra (191° & 206° = Libra 11° & 26°); Horoscope, Gemini; Saturn, beginning of Virgo (161° = Virgo 11°); Mars, Scorpio . . . (212° = Scorpio 2°).'

'Birth of De . . . Year 3 of the Philips . . . (night) before 21 . . .'

'Birth of Amm . . . Year 1 of Decius . . . first (hour) of the day. Horoscope, . . .; Venus, . . .; Jupiter, . . .; Saturn, . . .' 38 ff. 'Year 6 of Gordian, Tybi 16, 2nd hour of the day beginning. Birth of Sabinus son of Isis.'

'Request for a dream. Write the name (either on?) a piece of papyrus or on a leaf of . . .'

2 κορύφ(ου). See *LSJ* s.v. κόρυφοϲ III, where it is defined from Theoc. 4. 62 Schol. as an Alexandrian word equivalent to ὁ ὡϲ κόρη οἰφώμενοϲ. Other derivations are given in *Et. M.* 531. 23. The word has remained unrecognized in a previous occurrence in a horoscope on papyrus dated by Elagabalus, see *Studies Presented to F. Ll. Griffiths*, 235 = P. Warren 21. 51 = O. Neugebauer, H. B. Van Hoesen, *Greek Horoscopes*, No. 219 II 1 (p. 56). The plate in P. Warren (No. VII) is not entirely clear. Hunt's description in the note suggests that we should read κορυ) = κορύ(φου); the note in *Greek Horoscopes*, p. 56—κορυ' or κορυο'—might encourage us to read κορυφ = κορύφ(ου), on the assumption that the phi was a cursive one with the roundel wholly to the left of the upright. I rather favour the first, but, whichever version is right, at least the word cannot now be in doubt.

The doubt still persists, however, for III **596** = *Greek Horoscopes*, No. 139 (Plate in C. H. Roberts, *Greek Literary Hands*, 16c). The date is given in *Greek Horoscopes* as β αντωνινου κ[αιϲαροϲ] του κορ[ι]ου and the last word is interpreted as the equivalent of κυρίου. The beginning κο- is clear and from the published plate κορύφου would seem to be a possible reading, but computation for this date does not help to resolve the difficulties which abound in this text and the other on the same sheet, see *Greek Horoscopes*, pp. 45–7, and the presence of Κ[αίcαροc] tends to confirm that κυρίου is intended. Possibly κοιρίου would be an easier phonetic error for κυρίου, cf. Mayser–Schmoll I i p. 90.

The word may have occurred also in P. Tebt. II 414, where a woman writes to her sister πρὸ μὲν πάντων εὔχομαί cε ὑγιαίνιν (l. -ειν) καὶ τὰ παιδία cου κα[ὶ] Πᾶcιν τὸν κόρυφον (5–7), though the editors (7 n.) did not apparently realize this possibility and *LSJ* s.v. II shows a natural tendency to shy away from such a meaning in that context; not so, however, H. Maehler in *GRBS* 15 (1974) 307 n. 3.

2–3 The date is equivalent to 17/18 May, A.D. 219.

4 ἐχθ( ). This notation has been added in a cursive hand and is blotted badly. It therefore looks superficially different from the rest, but seems to be the same hand still. It may represent some part of ἐχθρός, referring to the doctrine of hostile places and stars, see *Greek Horoscopes*, 83–4. If so, it is unusual. Most horoscopes give only data related to astronomical facts, see ibid. p. 162.

5 There is a short rising oblique stroke in the left margin. Also possible is the form ὡροcκο(πεî).

6 The cursive marginal notation]υρμου, which is underlined, is followed by a round blot in a fainter ink. The first surviving letter does not look like ε; not that Ἑρμοῦ would make any obvious sense. Words ending in -υρμός in Kretschmer–Locker, *Rückl. Wb. d. gr. Sprache*, offer no help, though cυρμός can apparently mean the track of a meteor.

8 The traces at the end of the line are raised. Possibly the first is part of the oblique stroke used to abbreviate μοιρ(ῶν) and the second a flourish on a figure such as γ or ϛ.

10–11 The date is equivalent to 4/5 October, A.D. 242.

15 ἀρχὰc Παρθένου. Cf. *Greek Horoscopes*, No. 293 VIII (= XII 1565) 8, Κρόνοc [Δ]ι[δ]ύμοιc ἀρχάc. Computation puts Saturn actually in Taurus 29° = 59°. Gemini begins at 60°.

For the present case the tables for A.D. 242 in B. Tuckerman, *Planetary, Lunar, and Solar Positions A.D. 2 to A.D. 1649*, place Saturn *c.* 160–161°, i.e. midway in Virgo, which covers 150–180°. For such a slow-moving planet this implies a largish error. On the same day in the previous year Saturn was *c.* 149°, which would be very like the parallel case cited above. This date would also suit the data given for the Sun and Mercury, but would not suit Mars in Scorpio. Scorpio is right for A.D. 242, but in 241 Mars was in the beginning of Cancer.

It is not clear whether ἀρχάc implies that there was any real computation behind the data. It might be that the compiler simply found when he looked up the planetary tables (cf. **3299**) for the birth date in question that this was on or very shortly after the date given in the table for the entry of Saturn into Virgo. If this was the method followed, the compiler's eye may have strayed to the column for the previous year at this point.

17 *c.* 12]. ῳ. The trace is a mere dot of ink from the top of a letter. Possible are [Cελήνη Καρκί]νῳ, [Ζεὺc Ὑδρηχ]όῳ, and [Ἀφροδίτη Παρθέ]νῳ. The last is perhaps too long.

19 The year is A.D. 245/6.

20 ν[. This looks like νυκτός, but in 3 and 11 νυκτός falls after the first of the two days concerned, not after the second.

22 The year is A.D. 249/250, a *terminus post quem* for the document, see introd.

24 Cf. 5 and n., 14.

28 Either Ἄρ[ηc or Ἑρ[μῆc could fit the traces; Ἥλιοc and Cελήνη could not.

33 The genitive of a planet name would be odd. Perhaps it was simply γένεcιc] Ἀφροδίτηc, i.e. a woman's name, in which case the entry above was a truncated one like those in 18–20, 38–40.

36 Possibly Ἰχθ]ύcι.

38 The date is equivalent to 11 January, A.D. 243.

41 For the word ὀνειραιτηcία cf. K. Preisendanz, *Papyri Graecae Magicae*, I 329; for similar spells cf. ibid. XII 144–52, VII 359–69, 703–26, and others in the index under ὀνειραιτητόν; one with specifically astrological terminology is VII 795–845. The traces here do not suit the commoner form ὀνειραιτητόν.

42 The ὄνομα would be a magic incantation, probably given below. Very possibly ἢ εἰc should be read, but it has not been verified and the tiny traces cover rather a wide space for only four letters.

43 After φύλλ[ο]ν we need the name of a plant, e.g. δάφνηc, ἐλαίαc, περcέαc, and others in *PGM* Index s.v. φύλλον (Vol. iii p. 198).

3299. PLANETARY TABLES FOR A.D. 217–225

6 1B.8/B(d)   10·5 × 12 cm.   Later 3rd century?

This fragment comes probably from the top of a leaf of a codex, since the recto bears the page number 5 and the verso the page number 6, both placed centrally. The next line on each side consists of the name of an emperor in the genitive, Elagabalus on page 5 and Severus Alexander on page 6. The description of Elagabalus as ἀνοσίου Ἀντωνίνου μικροῦ can be compared with 3298 2 and introd. Then come four columns of figures headed by the numbers of regnal years, one to four in both cases. These are of course conventional designations of the Graeco-Egyptian years beginning on 29 August or 30 August in the years beginning just before Julian leap years. In this system an emperor is assigned the whole of the year in which he acceded as his year 1. Elagabalus acceded in summer A.D. 218, so here the Alexandrian year A.D. 217/8 is called 1 Elagabalus; 4 Elagabalus is A.D. 220/1, his last complete year. He died 11 March, A.D. 222 and therefore lived for a good part of a fifth regnal year, but the Alexandrian year A.D. 221/2 is called here 1 Severus Alexander because he acceded in the course of it.

Luckily similar planetary tables in Greek and demotic Egyptian exist to throw light on the columns of figures below, see O. Neugebauer, H. B. Van Hoesen, *Greek Horoscopes*, pp. 172–3, adding to the list the texts subsequently published by Professor Neugebauer in *CÉ* 47 (1972) 224–6, with ibid. 32 (1957) 269–72; *ZPE* 11 (1973) 101–14.

The tables were to be used to cast horoscopes and they are intended to show in which sign of the zodiac each planet was on any day of the year. Each line of a column contains, in principle, three sets of figures, each of which may consist of either one or two digits. The first gives the month, the second the day, and the third a number representing one of the twelve signs of the zodiac. Where there are two entries for the same month, the figure for the month is omitted from the second entry.

The figures for the Alexandrian months of thirty days range between 1 and 12, α and ιβ, though probably the intercalary days, the Epagomenae, would have been represented by ιγ, see *CÉ* 47 (1972) 225, Text A II 18. The figures for the days run between 1 and 30, α and λ, those for the zodiacal sign range between 1 and 12, α and ιβ, and comparison with modern tables shows that sign 1 is Virgo, the sign in which the sun moved at the beginning of the Graeco-Egyptian year when the Alexandrian reform of the calendar took place, see *CÉ* 47 (1972) 224.

Most entries give the day on which the planet in question moved into the sign indicated from another. In the first entry for each planet, however, its position on the first day of the year is usually given.

The planets are not named. Since the data are given in the conventional order, Saturn, Jupiter, Mars, Venus, Mercury, see *Greek Horoscopes*, p. 164, it was sufficient to separate them by drawing lines across the columns. All above the first line refers to Saturn, all between the first and second lines refers to Jupiter, and so on.

The only feature not found in one or other of the parallel texts is the sensibly convenient arrangement of reserving a separate column for each year.

Since there are no remains of the other half of a double leaf, there is no proof that the fragment comes from a codex, but that is the most likely hypothesis and upon it some calculations can be made.

The parallel tables have data only for the five planets mentioned above and there are traces here of the entry for the last one, Mercury, which should occupy about 12 to 15 lines, in only two columns. Adding these to the *c.* 30 lines surviving and allowing for a bottom margin we may conclude that the page was probably half as tall again or a little more, say in all *c.* 18–20 cm. This is a fairly normal format for a papyrus codex, corresponding to Group 8 in E. G. Turner's classification, see *The Typology of the Early Codex*, 20–1, 24, at least as far as the proportions of height and breadth are concerned, though the dimensions are rather smaller than normal.

Comparing page numbers and the standard layout on both sides we may calculate that the four pages missing at the beginning of the book can have contained the data for sixteen years at the most, less if there was preliminary matter. Therefore the tables cannot have begun earlier than A.D. 201/2 and cannot have extended back into the period covered by the other extant tables on papyrus.

If this manuscript was a codex, its minimum capacity was three double leaves, making twelve pages in all. If the tables continued on the same plan, the last year on page 12 would have been A.D. 248/9. I had thought that, if the tables were intended for ordinary use, it was likely that they covered the extreme span of human life, say eighty or a hundred years. On this basis one might have calculated a likely date for the book at *c.* A.D. 280 to 300. Nothing in the palaeography contradicts this, though it would be uncomfortable to have to bring it very much later than A.D. 300. Tables for this period of time would occupy about twenty-five pages, say seven double leaves. However, Professor Neugebauer is sceptical of the romantic idea that the tables were based on the span of a lifetime. He writes in a letter, 'I have never seen tables adjusted to the length of human life. Much more plausible are planetary periods, e.g. 60 years, common for Saturn, Jupiter, not too bad for Mars.' Tables for sixty years would occupy only fifteen sides in a book of this format, say four double leaves. Of course other matter might well have been incorporated in the same volume.

Table A below gives the Greek numerals for the months of the Alexandrian calendar and their Julian equivalents. A more extensive and more convenient table for turning individual Alexandrian dates into Julian dates is given in P. W. Pestman, *Chronologie égyptienne d'après les textes démotiques*, facing p. 9. Table B gives the Greek numerals for the signs of the zodiac, with the range of degrees assigned to each, by which their positions are defined in B. Tuckerman, *Planetary, Lunar, and Solar Positions A.D. 2 to A.D. 1649.*

F

TABLE A

			Leap Year[1]
α	Thoth	29 Aug.–27 Sept.	30 Aug.–28 Sept.
β	Phaophi	28 Sept.–27 Oct.	29 Sept.–28 Oct.
γ	Hathyr	28 Oct.–26 Nov.	29 Oct.–27 Nov.
δ	Choeac	27 Nov.–26 Dec.	28 Nov.–27 Dec.
ε	Tybi	27 Dec.–25 Jan.	28 Dec.–26 Jan.
ϛ	Mecheir	26 Jan.–24 Feb.	27 Jan.–25 Feb.
ζ	Phamenoth	25 Feb.–26 Mar.	26 Feb.–26 Mar.[2]
η	Pharmuthi	27 Mar.–25 Apr.	
θ	Pachon	26 Apr.–25 May	
ι	Payni	26 May–24 June	
ια	Epeiph	25 June–24 July	
ιβ	Mesore	25 July–23 Aug.	
ιγ	Epagomenae	24 Aug.–28 Aug.	24 Aug.–29 Aug.

TABLE B

α	(Virgo)	150–180°
β	(Libra)	180–210°
γ	(Scorpio)	210–240°
δ	(Sagittarius)	240–270°
ε	(Capricorn)	270–300°
ϛ	(Aquarius)	300–330°
ζ	(Pisces)	330–360°
η	(Aries)	1–30°
θ	(Taurus)	30–60°
ι	(Gemini)	60–90°
ια	(Cancer)	90–120°
ιβ	(Leo)	120–150°

In the translation exclamation marks after the name of a zodiacal sign warn that the entry does not agree with the modern tables of Tuckerman. Many of these disagreements can nevertheless be accepted as the result of differences between the ancient and modern calculations. It is suggested in many of the notes that larger discrepancies derive from errors of copying, but a convincing solution of this type cannot always be found.

Professor Neugebauer has been kind enough to give his expert advice on a typescript and has made valuable corrections at several places. He points out also that the exclamation marks in the translation may give a misleading impression of the quality of the text, which is really in unusually good agreement with modern computation.

[1]   An extra intercalary day (Epagomenae 6) is added in the summer preceding a Julian leap year i.e. in years whose A.D. numbers when divided by four leave a remainder of three.

[2]   Phamenoth 5 is always equivalent to 1 March.

ε

] ἀνοσίου Ἀντωνίνου μικροῦ

]α (ἔτους)				β (ἔτους)				γ (ἔτους)				δ (ἔτους)		
]α	α	β		α	α	γ		α	α	γ		α	α	γ
5]γ	ϛ	γ	**20**	α	α	ϛ	**50**	α	α	ζ		γ	θ	δ
ι	ια	β		ζ	η	ζ		ζ	κδ	η	**75**	α	α	η
ια	ια	γ		α	α	δ		α	α	ιβ		η	ια	θ
α	α	δ	**25**		κθ	ε			η	α		α	α	ϛ
γ	δ	ε		γ	ζ	ϛ		γ	β	β		γ	ζ	ζ
10 ϛ	κη	ϛ		δ	ιε	ζ	**55**	δ	κ	γ		ε	γ	η
α	α	ιβ		ε	κϛ	η		ϛ	β	δ	**80**	ϛ	ιϛ	θ
β	ζ	α		ζ	ζ	θ		ζ	ιϛ	ε		ζ	λ	ι
γ	κϛ	β	**30**	η	κγ	ι		θ	ϛ	ϛ		θ	ιθ	ια
ε	[ι]ζ	γ		ι	θ	ια		ια	γ	ζ		ια	ια	ιβ
15 ζ	ιθ	δ		ια	κζ	ιβ	**60**	ιβ	ιϛ	ϛ		ιβ	κε	α
ι]α	ια	[γ]		α	α	α		α	ϛ	β	**85**	α	α	ιβ
ι]β	ϛ	δ		γ	θ	β			λ	γ			κϛ	α
α	ιβ	α	**35**	δ	ιγ	γ		β	κε	δ		β	κα	β
β	ϛ	β		ε	η	δ		γ	κ	ε		γ	ιε	γ
. . . . .				ϛ	γ	ε	**65**	δ	ιδ	ϛ		δ	ι	δ
					κϛ	ϛ		ε	ιβ	ζ	**90**	ε	δ	ε
				ζ	κβ	ζ		ϛ	θ	η			κθ	ϛ
			40	η	ιζ	η		ζ	κβ	θ		ϛ	ιβ	ζ
				θ	ια	θ		ια	ιζ	ι		ζ	ιε	η
				ι	ε	ι	**70**	ιβ	ια	ια		η	ι	θ
					κθ	ια		α	ą	β	**95**	θ	ε	ι
				ια	κ[	ιβ]		. . . . .					κθ	ια
			45	ιβ	ιη	[α						ι]	κδ	ιβ
				α	α	α						ι]α	ιθ	ą
					κθ	[β						. . . . .		
				. . . . .										

3 αϛ''   20 βϛ''   48 γϛ''   72 δϛ''

ϛ

100 Ἀλεξάνδρου

α (ἔτους)

α	α	δ
α	α	θ
ζ	κθ	ι
α	α	α
β	θ	β
γ	κζ	γ
ε	ε	δ
ϛ	κα	ε
ζ	κθ	ϛ
θ	ζ	ζ
ι	κδ	η
ιβ	κδ	θ
α	α	β
	ϛ	γ
ε	η	δ
ϛ	ια	ε
ζ	ιβ	ϛ
η	ζ	ζ
θ	β	η
	κϛ	θ
ι	κα	ι
ια	ιε	ια
ιβ	ι	ιβ
		]α̣[

. . . . . .

β (ἔτους)

α	α	δ
ε	κ	ε
ια	ια	δ
α	ιβ	ια
γ	κζ	ι
θ	ιη	ια
α	α	θ
	κζ	η
ε	κβ	θ
ζ	ιβ	ι
η	κζ	ια
ι	ιθ	ιβ
ιβ	α	α
α	κβ	β
β	ιϛ	γ
γ	ι	δ
δ	ε	ε
	κθ	ϛ
ε	ιδ	ζ
ϛ	ιθ	η
ζ	ιδ	θ
η	θ	[ι

. . . . .

γ (ἔτους)

α	α	δ
β	ι.	ε
α	α	ια
β	ϛ	ιβ
ε	ϛ	ια
ι	ιθ	ιβ
α	α	α
	ιθ	β
γ	δ	γ
δ	ιε	δ
ε	κζ	ε
ζ	γ	ϛ
η	ιγ	ζ
θ	κ	η
ια	δ	θ
ιβ	λ	ι
α	α	ια
	ια	ιβ
β	θ	α
γ	δ	β
	κθ	γ
δ	κα̣	δ
ε̣	.[.]	ε
		]ϛ
		]ζ
		]η
].		θ

. . . . .

δ (ἔτους)

α	α	ε
α	α	ιβ
γ	ιδ	α
ε	α	ιβ
ια	ιθ	α
α	α	ι
ζ	ε	ια
θ	κζ	ιβ
ια	κ	α
α	α	β
	ιζ	γ
β	ιβ	δ
γ	[.]	ε
δ	ιγ	ϛ
	κε	ε
ζ	α	ϛ
η	[	

. . . . .

150 (col γ), 180 (col δ), 105 (col α), 130 (col β), 155, 160, 165, 170, 175, 135, 140, 145, 110, 115, 120, 125, 185, 190

101 αϛ'' 126 βϛ'' 149 γϛ'' 177 δϛ''

'Page 5.'

'Unholy little Antoninus.'

'Year 1.'

'Saturn	Thoth	1	(29 Aug. 217)	Libra
	Hathyr	6	(2 Nov. 217)	Scorpio
	Payni	11	(5 June 218)	Libra(!)
	Epeiph	11	(5 July 218)	Scorpio
Jupiter	Thoth	1	(29 Aug. 217)	Sagittarius
	Hathyr	4	(31 Oct. 217)	Capricorn(!)
	Mecheir	28	(22 Feb. 218)	Aquarius(!)
Mars	Thoth	1	(29 Aug. 217)	Leo
	Phaophi	7	(4 Oct. 217)	Virgo(!)
	Hathyr	26	(22 Nov. 217)	Libra
	Tybi	17	(12 Jan. 218)	Scorpio(!)
	Phamenoth	19	(15 Mar. 218)	Sagittarius
	Epeiph	11	(5 July 218)	Scorpio(!)
	Mesore	6	(30 July 218)	Sagittarius
Venus	Thoth	12	(9 Sept. 217)	Virgo
	Phaophi	6	(3 Oct. 217)	Libra'

'Year 2.'

'Saturn	Thoth	1	(29 Aug. 218)	Scorpio
Jupiter	Thoth	1	(29 Aug. 218)	Aquarius(!)
	Phamenoth	8	(4 Mar. 219)	Pisces(!)
Mars	Thoth	1	(29 Aug. 218)	Sagittarius
		29	(26 Sept. 218)	Capricorn
	Hathyr	7	(3 Nov. 218)	Aquarius
	Choeac	15	(11 Dec. 218)	Pisces
	Tybi	26	(21 Jan. 219)	Aries(!)
	Phamenoth	7	(3 Mar. 219)	Taurus(!)
	Pharmuthi	23	(18 Apr. 219)	Gemini(!)
	Payni	9	(3 June 219)	Cancer(!)
	Epeiph	27	(21 July 219)	Leo(!)
Venus	Thoth	1	(29 Aug. 218)	Virgo
	Hathyr	9	(5 Nov. 218)	Libra
	Choeac	13	(9 Dec. 218)	Scorpio
	Tybi	8	(3 Jan. 219)	Sagittarius
	Mecheir	3	(28 Jan. 219)	Capricorn
		27	(21 Feb. 219)	Aquarius
	Phamenoth	22	(18 Mar. 219)	Pisces
	Pharmuthi	17	(12 Apr. 219)	Aries
	Pachon	11	(6 May 219)	Taurus
	Payni	5	(30 May 219)	Gemini
		29	(23 June 219)	Cancer
	Epeiph	20?	(14? July 219)	Leo
	Mesore	18	(11 Aug. 219)	Virgo
Mercury	Thoth	1	(29 Aug. 218)	Virgo
		29	(26 Sept. 218)	Libra'

'Year 3.'

'Saturn	Thoth	1	(30 Aug. 219)	Scorpio
Jupiter	Thoth	1	(30 Aug. 219)	Pisces
	Phamenoth	24	(20 Mar. 220)	Aries(!)
Mars	Thoth	1	(30 Aug. 219)	Leo

			8	(6 Sept. 219)	Virgo(!)
		Hathyr	2	(30 Oct. 219)	Libra
55		Choeac	20	(17 Dec. 219)	Scorpio
		Mecheir	2	(28 Jan. 220)	Sagittarius
		Phamenoth	16	(12 Mar. 220)	Capricorn(!)
		Pachon	6	(1 May 220)	Aquarius(!)
		Epeiph	3	(27 June 220)	Pisces(!)
60		Mesore	16	(9 Aug. 220)	Aquarius
	Venus	Thoth	6	(4 Sept. 219)	Libra
			30	(28 Sept. 219)	Scorpio
		Phaophi	25	(23 Oct. 219)	Sagittarius
		Hathyr	20	(17 Nov. 219)	Capricorn
65		Choeac	14	(11 Dec. 219)	Aquarius
		Tybi	12	(8 Jan. 220)	Pisces
		Mecheir	9	(4 Feb. 220)	Aries
		Phamenoth	22	(18 Mar. 220)	Taurus(!)
		Epeiph	17	(11 July 220)	Gemini
70		Mesore	11	(4 Aug. 220)	Cancer
	Mercury	Thoth	1	(30 Aug. 219)	Libra'
	'Year 4.'				
	'Saturn	Thoth	1	(29 Aug. 220)	Scorpio
		Hathyr	9	(5 Nov. 220)	Sagittarius
75	Jupiter	Thoth	1	(29 Aug. 220)	Aries
		Pharmuthi	11	(6 Apr. 221)	Taurus(!)
	Mars	Thoth	1	(29 Aug. 220)	Aquarius
		Hathyr	7	(3 Nov. 220)	Pisces
		Tybi	3	(29 Dec. 220)	Aries
80		Mecheir	16	(10 Feb. 221)	Taurus(!)
		Phamenoth	30	(26 Mar. 221)	Gemini(!)
		Pachon	19	(14 May 221)	Cancer(!)
		Epeiph	11	(5 July 221)	Leo(!)
		Mesore	25	(18 Aug. 221)	Virgo(!)
85	Venus	Thoth	1	(29 Aug. 220)	Leo
			26	(23 Sept. 220)	Virgo
		Phaophi	21	(18 Oct. 220)	Libra
		Hathyr	15	(11 Nov. 220)	Scorpio
		Choeac	10	(6 Dec. 220)	Sagittarius
90		Tybi	4	(30 Dec. 220)	Capricorn
			29	(24 Jan. 221)	Aquarius
		Mecheir	12	(6 Feb. 221)	Pisces(!)
		Phamenoth	15	(11 Mar. 221)	Aries
		Pharmuthi	10	(5 Apr. 221)	Taurus
95		Pachon	5	(30 Apr. 221)	Gemini
			29	(24 May 221)	Cancer
		Payni	24	(18 June 221)	Leo
		Epeiph	19?	(13? July 221)	Virgo'
	'Page 6.'				
100	'Alexander.'				
	'Year 1.'				
	'Saturn	Thoth	1	(29 Aug. 221)	Sagittarius
	Jupiter	Thoth	1	(29 Aug. 221)	Taurus
		Phamenoth	29	(25 Mar. 222)	Gemini(!)

105	Mars	Thoth	1	(29 Aug. 221)	Virgo
		Phaophi	9	(6 Oct. 221)	Libra
		Hathyr	27	(23 Nov. 221)	Scorpio(!)
		Tybi	5	(31 Dec. 221)	Sagittarius(!)
		Mecheir	21	(15 Feb. 222)	Capricorn
110		Phamenoth	29	(25 Mar. 222)	Aquarius
		Pachon	7	(2 May 222)	Pisces(!)
		Payni	24	(18 June 222)	Aries(!)
		Mesore	24	(17 Aug. 222)	Taurus
	Venus	Thoth	1	(29 Aug. 221)	Libra
115			6	(3 Sept. 221)	Scorpio(!)
		Tybi	8	(3 Jan. 222)	Sagittarius(!)
		Mecheir	11	(5 Feb. 222)	Capricorn
		Phamenoth	12	(8 Mar. 222)	Aquarius
		Pharmuthi	7	(2 Apr. 222)	Pisces
120		Pachon	2	(27 Apr. 222)	Aries
			26	(21 May 222)	Taurus
		Payni	21	(15 June 222)	Gemini
		Epeiph	15	(9 July 222)	Cancer
		Mesore	10	(3 Aug. 222)	Leo
125		?	?	?	Virgo'
	'Year 2.'				
	'Saturn	Thoth	1	(29 Aug. 222)	Sagittarius
		Tybi	20	(15 Jan. 223)	Capricorn(!)
		Epeiph	11	(5 July 223)	Sagittarius(!)
130	Jupiter	Thoth	12	(9 Sept. 222)	Cancer(!)
		Hathyr	27	(23 Nov. 222)	Gemini
		Pachon	18	(13 May 223)	Cancer(!)
	Mars	Thoth	1	(29 Aug. 222)	Taurus
			27	(24 Sept. 222)	Aries(!)
135		Tybi	22	(17 Jan. 223)	Taurus
		Phamenoth	12	(8 Mar. 223)	Gemini
		Pharmuthi	27	(22 Apr. 223)	Cancer(!)
		Payni	19	(13 June 223)	Leo(!)
		Mesore	1	(25 July 223)	Virgo(!)
140	Venus	Thoth	22	(19 Sept. 222)	Libra
		Phaophi	16	(13 Oct. 222)	Scorpio
		Hathyr	10	(6 Nov. 222)	Sagittarius
		Choeac	5	(1 Dec. 222)	Capricorn
			?9	(?5 Dec. 222)	Aquarius
145		Tybi	14	(9 Jan. 223)	Pisces(!)
		Mecheir	19	(13 Feb. 223)	Aries
		Phamenoth	14	(10 Mar. 223)	Taurus
		Pharmuthi	9	(4 Apr. 223)	Gemini'
	'Year 3.'				
150	'Saturn	Thoth	1	(30 Aug. 223)	Sagittarius
		Phaophi	18?	(16? Oct. 223)	Capricorn(!)
	Jupiter	Thoth	1	(30 Aug. 223)	Cancer
		Phaophi	6	(4 Oct. 223)	Leo(!)
		Tybi	6	(2 Jan. 224)	Cancer
155		Payni	19	(13 June 224)	Leo
	Mars	Thoth	1	(30 Aug. 223)	Virgo

			19	(17 Sept. 223)	Libra(!)
		Hathyr	4	(1 Nov. 223)	Scorpio(!)
		Choeac	15	(12 Dec. 223)	Sagittarius(!)
160		Tybi	27	(23 Jan. 224)	Capricorn(!)
		Phamenoth	3	(28 Feb. 224)	Aquarius(!)
		Pharmuthi	13	(8 Apr. 224)	Pisces(!)
		Pachon	20	(15 May 224)	Aries(!)
		Epeiph	4	(28 June 224)	Taurus(!)
165		Mesore	30	(23 Aug. 224)	Gemini
	Venus	Thoth	1	(30 Aug. 223)	Cancer
			11	(9 Sept. 223)	Leo
		Phaophi	9	(7 Oct. 223)	Virgo
		Hathyr	4	(1 Nov. 223)	Libra
170			29	(26 Nov. 223)	Scorpio
		Choeac	21?	(18? Dec. 223)	Sagittarius
		Tybi	?	?	Capricorn
		?	?	?	Aquarius
		?	?	?	Pisces
175		?	?	?	Aries
		?	?	?	Taurus'
	'Year 4.'				
	'Saturn	Thoth	1	(29 Aug. 224)	Capricorn
	Jupiter	Thoth	1	(29 Aug. 224)	Leo
180		Hathyr	14	(10 Nov. 224)	Virgo(!)
		Tybi	1	(27 Dec. 224)	Leo(!)
		Epeiph	19	(13 July 225)	Virgo
	Mars	Thoth	1	(29 Aug. 224)	Gemini
		Phamenoth	5	(1 Mar. 225)	Cancer(!)
185		Pachon	27	(22 May 225)	Leo(!)
		Epeiph	20	(14 July 225)	Virgo(!)
	Venus	Thoth	1	(29 Aug. 224)	Libra
			17	(14 Sept. 224)	Scorpio
		Phaophi	12	(9 Oct. 224)	Sagittarius
190		Hathyr	?	(Oct./Nov. 224)	Capricorn
		Choeac	13	(9 Dec. 224)	Aquarius
			25	(21 Dec. 224)	Capricorn(!)
		Phamenoth	1	(25 Feb. 225)	Aquarius
		Pharmuthi	?	(Mar./Apr. 225)	Pisces'

2 ἀνοcίου. See introd. and **3298** 2 n.

μικροῦ. This form, not known before, distinguishes Elagabalus from Caracalla, who was Ἀντωνῖνος μέγας, see P. Bureth, *Les titulatures*, p. 105, cf. XLIII p. 13. I am also grateful to Dr. Coles for discovering and pointing out to me that in the list of emperors XXXI **2551** *verso* instead of Ἀντωνῖνος] ὁ ἕτεροc we should read Ἀντωνῖνο]ς μικρός (i 20).

5]γ. The trace is the right-hand tip of a crossbar which could suit γ, ε, ς, θ. According to Tuckerman Saturn entered Scorpio between 25 and 30 October, Phaophi 28 to Hathyr 3. The least unsatisfactory solution, therefore, is]γ, giving Hathyr 6 = 2 November, A.D. 217, but this is late, especially since, because of the difference in the ancient calculations of longitude, we might expect Scorpio to begin *c.* 206–8° instead of at 210°, see O. Neugebauer and R. A. Parker, *Egyptian Astronomical Texts* iii 226, cf. *Greek Horoscopes*, 171–2. On this basis Scorpio would be entered earlier still, *c.* 5 to 10 October = Phaophi 8–13. It is certainly impossible to read β (= Phaophi) ς = 3 October, and in view of the difficulties in 6–7 we need not try.

6–7 According to Tuckerman Saturn was in retrograde motion inside Scorpio in this period, reaching its lowest point (211. 39) in the period 7–12 July. There are differences here both of extent of motion and of timing.

14 The restoration of iota in [ι]ζ is indicated by Tuckerman's tables. On Tybi 7 = 2 January, A.D. 217 Mars was well within Libra; ten days later it was on the margins of Libra and Scorpio, still in Libra by modern standards but probably in Scorpio by the ancient method of measuring longitude, see 5 n.

16–17 Mars was in retrograde motion at this point, but according to Tuckerman remained in Sagittarius.

18 Usually the first entry for each planet gives its position on Thoth 1, even when the planet enters a new sign during the month, see 24–5, 46–7, 52–3, 85–6, 114–15, 133–4, 156–7, 166–7, 187–8. There are only three other entries like this one: 61, 130, 140.

27–32 All these entries put the planets in the sign above that to which Tuckerman's tables assign them, but they are mostly within the bounds of accuracy to be expected from ancient calculations, see *Greek Horoscopes*, 2, 180–2.

44 κ[ιβ]. Epeiph 20 = 14 July, A.D. 219. It may be that the papyrus had κ[α or κ[β, which would also give a result near enough the expected degree of accuracy.

[Professor Neugebauer observes that for restorations it is best to use the difference-sequences of the text as a whole, not the agreement with Tuckerman, which means very little for individual cases. His calculations and the graphs that he has plotted suggest that the most plausible restoration here would be κ[δ, Epeiph 24 = 18 July.]

47 By 26 September Mercury was well past the middle of Libra, which was entered in the first three or four days of September. If we delete the kappa the date would be 6 September, which would be a satisfactory enough result, but it is hard to ascribe this simply to an error of transcription.

51, 53, 57–9. The entries here put each planet into the sign above that assigned to it by Tuckerman's tables. The errors are at least partly explicable by the different ancient calculation of longitude, cf. 5 n., 27–32 n.

61 See 18 n.

68 This entry is badly wrong, since according to Tuckerman Venus did not enter Taurus till the period 6–11 June = Payni 12–17, which would be written ι ιβ θ, ι ιγ θ etc. There seems to be no likelihood of a straightforward copying error.

[Professor Neugebauer calculates that ι κβ, Payni 22 = 16 June, A.D. 220, would give a sufficiently close result and suggests that the error lies in the figure for the month only.]

92 Venus did not enter Pisces till the period 11–16 February. In view of the good agreement of the neighbouring figures with the modern tables it seems quite likely that the figure for the day has been wrongly copied as ιβ instead of κβ, which would indicate 16 February.

98 The first reading was ια] κβ α. Professor Neugebauer suggested that for the day figure it would be better to read ιθ, and in fact it is better palaeographically to assign the first trace to the top of the alpha of the figure of the month and take the second as the top of iota, though I had taken them together as kappa. After that the remains of a rounded top suit theta quite as well as beta.

104 According to Tuckerman it was at least a month later that Jupiter entered Gemini. If, instead of Phamenoth 29 = 25 March, the date were Pharmuthi 29 = 25 April, Jupiter would be near enough entering Gemini to afford a result satisfactory by ancient methods. It is unlikely that the month number η was mistaken for ζ, but Phamenoth and Pharmuthi are sufficiently similar to cause confusion and the error may have taken place at a stage when the names were still being used, cf. 184 n. For more elaborate tables which give the month names cf. *ZPE* 11 (1973) 101–14.

125 Since there is no line across the column above this entry it still belongs to Venus, which entered Virgo in the period 21–24 August, Mesore 28–Epagomenae 1. If the last date is right it was probably written ιγ α] α[, cf. introd. para. 4.

[Professor Neugebauer calculates that the difference-sequences (cf. 44 n.) suggest that the table would have had here ιγ δ] α[, i.e. Epagomenae 4 = 27 August.]

130 See 18 n.

134 Mars did not descend into Aries till the period 9–14 October = Phaophi 12–17 (β ιβ–β ιζ) . A copying error of κζ for β ιζ does not seem particularly likely.

139 The large error here might be reduced to credible proportions by assuming that the day intended was ια (4 August) instead of α (25 July).

140 See 18 n.

145 The large error might be reduced by assuming that ιδ is an error for κδ (19 January). This would be late, but the preceding two entries and the succeeding two are also slightly late.

151 The damaged figure is perhaps ιη, which would represent 16 October, A.D. 222, on which date Saturn was still in Sagittarius but so close to the boundary that the entry would probably be correct for ancient longitude, cf. 5 n.

157–164 In all these entries modern computation puts the planet still in the sign below the one indicated. The divergences are slight and are probably due to the difference in the ancient longitude, cf. 5 n.

171 κα. Also possible is κδ = 21 December.

172 Venus moved into Capricorn in the period 7–12 January, A.D. 224. Restore a figure between ι[α] and ι[ζ] inclusive.

176 Venus moved into Taurus in the period 16–21 April. The Alexandrian month will be Pharmuthi = η and the day κα–κζ. The trace would suit κ]γ, κ]ε, or κ]ς.

181 The large disparity here could be brought within reasonable bounds by supposing that the day figure α is a mistake for λ = 25 January.

184 To reduce the large discrepancy here we might adopt the same solution as suggested in 104 n. and emend the month numeral from ζ to η on the assumption that Phamenoth was a confusion for Pharmuthi. To emend 1 March to 31 March would reduce the deviation to about the same magnitude as those in the two succeeding entries.

190 Venus entered Capricorn in the period 2–7 November, A.D. 224. Restore a figure between ς (6) and ια (11); to judge from the available space one might eliminate ια (11) as too wide and ι (10) as too narrow and leave ς, ζ, η, θ to choose from, but this type of argument is dubious.

192 If we emend κε to ς ε i.e. Mecheir 5 = 30 January, the entry is correct, but it is hard to think of this as a mere copying error.

[Professor Neugebauer makes the better suggestion that in this case the figure for the month has simply been omitted in error. He points out that ⟨ε⟩ κε, Tybi 25 = 21 January, A.D. 224, would give a sufficiently close result.]

194 η[. Tuckerman's tables indicate 6–11 April, A.D. 225 = Pharmuthi 11–16 = η ια–ις, as the period in which Venus entered Pisces (ζ).

3300. EXTRACT FROM CITY DIRECTORY

48 5B.30/G(3–5)a   5·5 × 20·5 cm.   Later third century

This extract from a list of properties in Oxyrhynchus occupies the back of **3294**, written in A.D. 271/2, and is presumably of about the same date or not much later. The terminology is very like that of P. Osl. III 111, though more information is included there under each house entry. Here the names of owners and occupiers only are given, sometimes with the addition of their occupations. In this it resembles rather the extensive document from Panopolis recently published by Z. Borkowski, *Une description topographique des immeubles à Panopolis.*

ἀρχο(μένων) ἀπὸ οἰκ(ίας) Διογένους
    Διογένης
    Διονύσιος ἀδελ(φός)

1 αρχο̄, οικ   3 αδε̄λ

λιβ(ὸϲ) ἐχο(μένη) Ἡρακλεί[δ]ου οἰκ(ία)

5   αὐτὸϲ Ἡρακλείδηϲ

καμψ(άντων) ἐπὶ νότ(ον) (πρότερον) Αν.[. . .

   Ἀρανάϊϲ καψ[άριοϲ

   Ἀκυλειανόϲ

βορ(ρᾶ) ἐχο(μένη) Θωνίου οἰκ(ία)

10   Θῶνιϲ ἁλιεύϲ

νότ(ου) ἐχο(μένη) Παϲόϊϲ ἁλιεύϲ

νότ(ου) ἐχο(μένη) Πτολεμαίου Ἀμόϊτ(οϲ)

   Φιλέαϲ καὶ Ἰϲίδωροϲ

   Ἀπολλω( ) καὶ Ὡρ[ο]ϲ

15 νότ(ου) ἐχο(μένη) Ἁρποκρ( ) [ο]ἰκοδόμ(οϲ)

νότ(ου) ἐχο(μένη) Ἀφυγχίου ποικιλ(τοῦ)

   αὐτὸϲ Ἀφῦγχιϲ

   Θῶνιϲ ἀδελφ(όϲ)

νότ(ου) ἐχο(μένη) Ἀνεικήτου βαφ(έωϲ)

20   αὐτὸϲ Ἀνείκητοϲ

νότ(ου) ἐχο(μένη) Φιλάμμω(νοϲ) λαχ(ανοπώλου) ἀοίκ(ητοϲ)

νότ(ου) ἐχο(μένη) Ϲαραπιάδοϲ

   Ἡρακλῆϲ

νότ(ου) ἐχο(μένη) Διογ( ) λινοΰφ(ου)

25   Ἄρειοϲ

νότ(ου) ἐχο(μένη) Ἡρακλ( ) α(ὐτὸϲ) Ἡρακλ( )

ν[ό]τ(ου) ἐχο(μένη) Μυ . . . . [.

   Παυϲᾶϲ Ἀχιλ( ) υἱόϲ

   Ἡραΐϲκοϲ ἕτεροϲ

30 καμ(ψάντων) ἐπ' ἀπηλ(ιώτην) Διονυϲίου

   . . . λαϲ τέκτω(ν)

ἀπηλ(ιώτου) ἐχο(μένη) Ἀπολ( ) Κιχόϊϲ

καμ(ψάντων) ἐπὶ βορ(ρᾶν) Ϲαραπιάδοϲ

   Παγᾶϲ

35 βορ(ρᾶ)] ἐχό(μενον) κλειβανῖο(ν)

   . . . .].οϲ[

    .   .   .   .   .

---

4 λιᵝεχο̄, οιᴷ   6 καμψ̄', νοᵀα'   7 αρανᾱϊϲ   9 βορϛεχο̄, οιᴷ   11 νοᵀεχο̄ (and so throughout), παϲόϊϲ   12 αμοιᵀ   14 απολλω̄   15 αρποκρϛ[ο]ικοδοᵘ   16 ποικι^λ   18 αδελφ'   19 βαφ'   21 φιλαμμω̄λαχᶥαοιᴷ   24 διογ'λινουφ'   26 ηρακᾱ‾ηρακ^λ   28 αχῑυϊοϲ   29 ηραϊϲκοϲ   30 καμϛ, απη̄^λ   31 τεκτω̄   32 απη̄εχο̄απο̄^λ   33 καμϛ, βορϛ   35 εχο̄; l. κλιβανεῖον

'Beginning from the house of Diogenes: Diogenes, Dionysius (his) brother.
    Next west: house of Heracleides: Heracleides himself.
Turning to the south: house formerly belonging to An . . . : Aranais, *capsarius*, Aquilianus.
    Next north (*sic*; south?): house of Thonius: Thonis, fisherman.
    Next south: Pasois, fisherman.
    Next south: (house) of Ptolemaeus son of Amois: Phileas and Isidorus, Apollo( ) and Horus.
    Next south: Harpocr( ), builder.
    Next south: (house) of Aphynchius, embroiderer: Aphynchis himself, Thonis (his) brother.
    Next south: (house) of Anicetus, dyer: Anicetus himself.
    Next south: (house) of Philammon, vegetable-seller: uninhabited.
    Next south: (house) of Sarapias: Heracles.
    Next south: (house) of Diog( ), linen-weaver: Areius.
    Next south: (house) of Heracl( ): Heracl( ) himself.
    Next south: (house) of My . . . : Paysas son of Achil( ) (her?) son, Heraiscus, another.
Turning to the east: (house) of Dionysius: . . . las, carpenter.
    Next east: (house) of Apol( ): Cichois.
Turning to the north: (house) of Sarapias: Pagas.
    Next north (?): bakery.'

7 The name Aranais is new. On *capsarii* see P. Giss. 50 introd. In P. Osl. III 111. 233 καψα( ) is taken to be a wrong spelling of καμψά(ντων), but καψα(ρίου), as the occupation of the person whose names precede, may be a preferable expansion of the abbreviation.

9 βορ(ρᾶ) ἐχο(μένη). It is very difficult to construct a diagram to show how this house could be to the north of the one in line 6 and also have on its south side the house in line 11. If this is a mistake for νότ(ου) ἐχο(μένη), a perfectly straightforward plan emerges, viz:

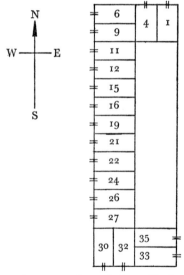

27–9 Neither the reading nor the pattern of sense is clear. If only one inhabitant is listed in 28, the implication is that My . . . is a woman, the owner of the house, which is inhabited by her son Paysas, whose father is Achil( ), and by Heraiscus, another son. This possibility is used in the translation. As an alternative we might translate, 'Paysas, Achil( ) his son, Heraiscus another'. I have not succeeded in matching the traces in 27 to any known name or to a word meaning 'mill'—compare the bakery below (35) and the μυλῶνες in Z. Borkowski, op. cit.

31 Read perhaps *Πάλλας*.

32 Though *Κιχόϊς* does not appear in NB or in D. Foraboschi, *Onomasticon*, it is probably only a variant spelling of *Χιχόϊς*.

34 *Παγᾶς* is not in NB or D. Foraboschi, *Onomasticon*. It probably stands in the same relation to *Παγένης* as *Διογᾶς* to *Διογένης*.

3301–3303. Documents relating to Claudius Cleopatrus, praefectus Aegypti

A new prefect of Egypt, Claudius Cleopatrus, is mentioned in these three very different documents, all considerably damaged. **3303** is undated, the other two have lost the month and day but are dated to a year, **3301** to the consular year A.D. 300 and **3302** to the Egyptian year 29 August 300 to 28 August 301. The next item, **3304**, supplies the earliest date yet known in the prefecture of Clodius Culcianus, 6 June 301, which gives a *terminus ante quem* for **3302** and narrows the possible period to between 29 August 300 and 6 June 301. The last document of the prefecture of Aelius Publius, the predecessor of Cleopatrus, is still IX **1204** which gives 19 August 299 as the date of an event which must fall shortly before the date of the papyrus, which was itself written while Publius was still prefect.

The data may be summarized more simply in a table:

Aelius Publius	Last known just after 19 August 299 (IX **1204**)
Claudius Cleopatrus	Known some time in 300 (**3301**)
	Some time between 29 August 300 and 6 June 301 (**3302**)
	Undated (**3303**)
Clodius Culcianus	First known 6 June 301 (**3304**)

3301. Report of Systatae

35 4B.64/H(1–4)a   16 × 17·5 cm.   A.D. 300

Three systatae, acting as a college, cf. XLIII **3137**, report to the strategus in answer to his inquiry, which was itself prompted by an order of the prefect, that a wanted person's name is not to be found among their records. Since the systates was the chief administrative officer of the tribe, there may be an implication here that there were only three tribes in Oxyrhynchus at this date, though that cannot be taken as sure without confirmatory evidence, cf. XL pp. 6–7, XLIII **3095–8** introd. A change in the number of tribes may have been made at the same time as the introduction of the systatae early in the reign of Diocletian, cf. A. K. Bowman, *Town Councils*, 152 n. 7.

This is the first such report from officers of the tribes and the damage to the ends of the lines deprives us of the exact wording at many places, but one may compare the reports made by property registrars of the results of searches in their records, XXXIII **2665**, M. *Chr.* 196.

The back is blank.

ἐπὶ ὑ[π]άτων τῶν κυρίων ἡμῶν Κωνσταντίου

καὶ Μαξιμιανοῦ τῶν ἐπιφανεστάτων Καισάρων τὸ γ΄.

Αὐρηλίῳ Ζηναγένει cτρατηγῷ Ὀξυρυγχείτου

παρὰ Αὐρηλίων Ὡρίωνος Θέωνος καὶ Χωςίωνος

5   τοῦ καὶ Ἀμυντιανοῦ καὶ Διδύμου τοῦ καὶ Cαραπίωνος

Πύρρου τῶν [τ]ρ[ιῶ]ν cυcτατῶν τῆς [λαμ(πρᾶς) καὶ λαμ(προτάτης) Ὀξ(υρυγχιτῶν)

πόλ(εως).

ἐπιζητοῦντί cο[ι] ἐκ προcτάξεως τοῦ [διαcημοτάτου

ἡμῶν ἡγεμ[ό]νος Κλαυδίου Κλεοπά[τρου   c. 8

εἰ Ἀμμώνιος Cτεφάνου τῶν αὐτόθι [c. 12

10   γνῶcιν αὐτοῦ τὸ τοιοῦτο ἀνενεγκεῖ[ν   c. 11

ἐξετάcει τῶν ἡμετέρων βιβλίων ἕκαcτ[c. 12

φυλῆc γενόμενος τοῦτον οὐδαμοῦ δ[c. 12

φενόμενον .[.]ν οὐθοποτερο[.].[c. 14

καὶ διὰ τοῦτο προcφωνοῦμεν. [

(vac.)

·   ·   ·   ·   ·

13 l. φαινόμενον; ουθ᾽οποτερο[.].[

'Under the consuls our lords Constantius and Maximian, most noble Caesars, (both) for the third time. To Aurelius Zenagenes, strategus of the Oxyrhynchite nome, from Aurelius Horion son of Theon and Aurelius Chosion alias Amyntianus and Aurelius Didymus alias Sarapion son of Pyrrhus, the three of them systatae of [the glorious and most glorious city of the Oxyrhynchites]. In response to your inquiry arising from an order of our [most perfect] prefect Claudius Cleopatrus [commanding (you)], if Ammonius son of Stephanus [is] one of the local populace [immediately] to report such information to his attention, [accordingly] each of us took charge [of] a search of our records [relating to the] tribe [under his control] and not one [of us was able to find] this person appearing anywhere [in the records] and for this reason we make our report.'

3 Ζηναγένει. Cf. XLV **3246** introd. on the name of this strategus.

4 Ὡρίων Θέωνος. See XLIII **3137** 3–4 n. for other references.

4–5 Χωςίωνος τοῦ καὶ Ἀμυντιανοῦ. In view of the comparatively unusual first name he is probably the same as the Chosion who is a systates in XXXIV **2717** 12, 17.

5–6 Διδύμου τοῦ καὶ Cαραπίωνος Πύρρου. Also in **3304** of 6 June, A.D. 301. He may be identical with the systates Aurelius Sarapion in XLIII **3141** 3 of A.D. 300.

7–13 The certain supplement διαcημοτάτου (7) governs the estimates of missing letters in the subsequent lines. The gaps are too long to restore the rest of the wording with certainty. The translation depends on the conjectural restorations given below, which could be varied in many respects but must give the information that a search of the records has been made with a negative result.

ἐπιζητοῦντί cο[ι] ἐκ προcτάξεως τοῦ [διαcημοτάτου

ἡμῶν ἡγεμ[ό]νος Κλαυδίου Κλεοπά[τρου κελευούcης,

εἰ Ἀμμώνιος Cτεφάνου τῶν αὐτόθι [ἐcτίν, εὐθέωc εἰc

10   γνῶcιν αὐτοῦ τὸ τοιοῦτο ἀνενεγκεῖ[ν, κατὰ ταῦτα ἐπὶ

ἐξετάcει τῶν ἡμετέρων βιβλίων ἕκαcτ[ος τῆc ὑφ᾽ ἑαυτὸν

φυλῆς γενόμενος τοῦτον οὐδαμοῦ δ[ιὰ τῶν βιβλίων
φενόμενον κ[ἀ]ν οὐθοπότερο[ς] ἡ[μῶν εὑρεῖν ἐδύνατο
καὶ διὰ τοῦτο προσφωνοῦμεν.

8 On Claudius Cleopatrus see **3301–3303** introd.

13 οὐθοποτερο[.]. This is to be compared with the use of οὐθείς for οὐδείς, cf. Mayser–Schmoll I i 148–9 (33c), and is the equivalent of οὐδοπότερος, cf. E. A. Sophocles, *Lexicon*, and F. Passow, *Handwörterbuch*, s.v. I have not found the form with theta elsewhere. It perhaps ought to be printed as two words, οὔθ' ὁπότερος, since *LSJ* notes οὐδοπότερος s.v. ὁπότερος I 3; cf. P. Flor. III 384. 84 οὐδ' ὁποτέρῳ μέρει.

14 The last letter of προσφωνοῦμεν has a finial which suggests that this is the end of the report, which would in any case be expected to end with this word. The second half of the line was probably blank. Underneath there is a blank margin of *c.* 2·5 cm. with a ragged edge; further down there was probably a date clause giving the month and the day.

3302. Petition to a Prefect

29 4B.56/E(11)a   17 × 27 cm.   A.D. 300/1

A lady petitions the prefect for protection against tax-collectors. Apparently some persons who had tried to keep her out of her inheritance and had been ordered to make restitution were trying now to subject her to liability for taxes on the property for the period in which she had not enjoyed the income. If the addition of ⟨οὐ⟩ to the text in 12 is correct, see n., she was still dispossessed at the time of writing.

The text is much damaged and in addition the statement of the case is so general that we get very little idea of the circumstances.

For the prefect in question see **3301–3303** introd.

The back is blank.

Κλαυδίῳ Κλεοπάτρῳ τῷ διασημ[οτάτῳ ἐπάρχ]ῳ [Αἰγ]ύπτου
παρὰ Αὐρηλίας Cερηνίλλης θυγατρὸς C[υρίωνος τοῦ καὶ Εὐсτο]χίου γυμ(νασιαρχήσαντος)
γεν(ομένου) βουλ(ευτοῦ) τῆς λαμ(πρᾶς)
καὶ λαμ(προτάτης) Ὀξ(υρυγχιτῶν) πόλεως χωρὶς κυρίου χ[ρηματιζούσης τέκνων] δικαίῳ.
ἔ[δ]ει μὴ πρὸς τούτοις τοῖς
ἀπευκτέως παρὰ τῆς τύχης μου συμ.[*c.* 18 letters] ἐπαχθῶς με βιάζεσθαι. ἀλλὰ
5   γὰρ τῆς πρὸς τῶν γονέων κηδαιμονία[ς *c.* 17 letters] ἔτι μὴν καὶ τῶν καταλελιμ-
μένων μοι μάλ{λ}ιστα ὑπ' αὐτοῦ τοῦ πατρὸς ὑπαρχόντων ὑπὸ βιαίων καὶ δυναστῶν παρανό-
μως κρατηθέντων ἐγώ τε ἐντυχείαις ἐχρησάμην περὶ τῆς τούτων ἀποκαταστάσεως
τοῖς πρὸς τῇ ἡγεμονίᾳ γεγονόсι ἀλλὰ μὴν καὶ τῷ σῷ μεγαλείῳ καὶ προστάξεις ἐφύτη-
σαν δι' ἀποφάσεων καὶ ὑπογραφῶν ἀλλὰ μὴν καὶ διαδικασιῶν γεγενημένον ὑπὸ τῶν

2 γυμ𐅵̄'γεν𐅵̄'βουλ̄, λαμ𐅵̄'   3 λαμ𐅵̄''οξ'   4 l. ἀπευκταίως   5 l. κηδεμονίας   5–6 l. κατα-
λελειμμένων   6 ὕπαυτου   8–9 l. ἐφοίτησαν   9 ὑπογραφων; l. γεγενημένων; ὕπο

10 ὑπὸ τῆς ἡγεμονίας δοθέντων κατὰ καιρὸν δικαστῶν ὥςτε μοι καὶ τὴν ἀποκατάςταςιν τού-
τῶν γενέςθαι καὶ εἰςαχθῆναί με εἰς τὴν νομήν. ἀλλ' ἐπιδὴ μᾶλλον ἀνδρεειζόμενοι
περὶ τὸ βιάζεςθαί με οὐ μόνον τῶν [ἡμε]τέρων ὑπαρχόντων ἀφείςτα`ς'θαι ⟨οὐ⟩ βεβού-
λῃντε, ἀλλ' ἔτι ὑποβάλλει με καὶ δι[.....c]υντελεῖν ὑπὲρ αὐτῶν ἀφ' ὧν οὐδὲ τὴ[ν
πρόςοδον ἐκαρπωςάμην κ[*c.* 12   ] τῶν πρακτήρων ειρ[..]η καὶ τ[η-
15 ροῦμαι ςυνεχῶς ἐν τῷ δημ[οςίῳ λογις]τηρίῳ οὐ δίκαια οὐ.[*c.* 10
οὐδὲ ἄξια ἀλλὰ ἀνοίκεια καὶ τῷ[ν νόμων καὶ] τῆς τούτο[ι]ς ἀκολούθως πρυτανευο-
μένης ἡμεῖν ὑπὸ τοῦ ςοῦ μεγαλείου [εἰρήνης. διὸ ἀξιῶ] εἴ ςου δοκεῖ τῇ τύχῃ προςτάξαι
δι' ὑπογραφῆς τὸν ςτρατηγὸν μηδ[ὲν ἄτοπον ἐπιτ]ρέπειν γείνεςθαι κατ' ἐ-
μοῦ ὑπὸ τῶν πρακτήρων ἀλλὰ [*c.* 17   ]υς τοὺς τῇ βίᾳ
20 καρπ[ωςαμέν]ους τὰ ἡμέτερα [*c.* 25   ]α ἀποδεδω-
κ...[......].της παραδ[..]..[*c.* 25   ]υςης ἐπι
γειν..[....].α ἂν διαφέροντα[*c.* 25   ].η δυνη-
θείην ἐ[ν τῇ ἰ]δίᾳ ςυμμένειν ....[*c.* 25   ].τος ἐπὶ
ταύτῃ τ[ῇ ...]..ςίᾳ ὁμολογη[*c.* 23?   δι]ευτύχει.
            (vac.) [
25 ἔτους [ιζ]'' καὶ ιϛϚ'.[
ἴ τις [...]..εἴγνυτο κ...[
κολ[(λήματος).]' τόμ(ου) [

---

10 ὕπο   11 αλ'λ; l. ἐπειδή, ἀνδρεῖζόμενοι   12 ὕπαρχοντων   12–13 l. βεβούληνται
13 αλ'λ, ὕποβαλλει, ὕπερ   17 ὕπο   18 ὕπογραφης   26 l. εἴ τις   27 τομ'

'To Claudius Cleopatrus the most perfect prefect of Egypt, from Aurelia Serenilla daughter of Syrion alias Eustochius ex-gymnasiarch former councillor of the glorious and most glorious city of the Oxyrhynchites, acting without a guardian according to the *ius liberorum*. It was not right that on top of these accidents that have occurred, contrary to my hopes, as a result of my own destiny, (anyone?) should burden me with rough treatment. However, when the care which I received from my parents ... and when the property left to me, especially that left me by my father, was illegally detained by violent and influential persons, I had recourse to appeals for its restitution to the incumbents of the prefecture and finally also to your Highness, and commands were issued, through judgements and subscriptions and even court cases conducted by judges appointed by the prefecture from time to time, that restitution of it should be made to me and I should be installed in possession. But since, gaining confidence in their rough treatment of me, they have not only ⟨not?⟩ consented to vacate my possessions but are still putting my name forward(?) to make various(?) payments in respect of them though I have not enjoyed even the income from them, I have been shut up in the tax-collectors' prison(?) and I am continually kept in custody in the treasury office, suffering(?) treatment that is not just ... not deserved, but incompatible with the laws and the peace granted to us in accordance with them by your Highness. Therefore I request(?), if it please your *genius*, that you give orders by a subscription that the strategus should not allow anything untoward to happen to me at the hands of the tax-collectors but ... those who have enjoyed my property by force ... that I may be enabled to remain where I belong ... Farewell.'

'Year 17 and 16 ...'

'Sheet *n*, roll *n*.'

2 The patronymic is restored from XLII **3139** 2–3.

4 *cυμ.*[. The trace suits β, which suggests *cυμβ*[ᾶcι or *cυμβ*[εβηκόcι. A subject for βιάζεϲθαι may occupy the remaining space, e.g. μηδένα or more probably something alluding specifically to her adversaries.

5 It might be guessed that Serenilla was left an orphan and that her guardians are accused of misusing their powers. The κηδεμονία may refer to measures taken to protect her interests after the deaths of her parents, e.g. τῆϲ . . . κηδαιμονία[ϲ μου καταφρονηθείϲηϲ, 'when the provision made for me by my parents was held in contempt'.

11 ἀνδρεειζόμενοι, l. ἀνδρεῖζ-. This is the second papyrus to testify to the genuineness of the verb ἀνδρεΐζεϲθαι (from ἀνδρεῖοϲ), existing alongside ἀνδρίζεϲθαι (from ἀνήρ), see Men. *Kith.* 76, with the commentary of A. W. Gomme and F. H. Sandbach, p. 415. In the documentary papyri ἀνδρεΐζεϲθαι occurs only here; ἀνδρίζεϲθαι appears in P. Cair. Zen. IV 59579. 5, P. Petrie II 40a. 13, PSI IV 326. 10; 402. 3 and V 512. 29, all of the third century B.C.

12 ⟨οὐ⟩. The addition was suggested by the Press reader. The improvement to the sense and the run of the sentence makes the suggestion irresistible.

13 ὑποβάλλει. Probably this is simply a mistake for the plural. The shade of meaning is not entirely clear. For the translation adopted, 'putting my name forward', cf. WB s.v. ὑποβάλλω (2).

It seems fairly clear that Serenilla is being called upon to pay taxes. Restore perhaps δι[άφορα ϲ]υντελεῖν, 'to make various payments'. Easier would be δη[μόϲια, 'to pay the state taxes', but the trace suits ι better than the first upright of η.

14 ειρ[..]η. The word required may be εἱρκτή, 'prison'. For imprisonment in the πρακτορεῖον see WO I 285, 621–2, cf. G. Chalon, *L'Édit de Tiberius Julius Alexander*, 113–14, R. Taubenschlag, *Op. Min.* ii 715, n. 22. It seems likely that this prison is the same as the one known to exist in the δημόϲιον λογιϲτήριον, see 15 n. The dative εἱρκτῇ looks likeliest, though after it καί seems to have been written over something else, perhaps ν. Restore perhaps κ[ατεκλείϲθην ἐν τῇ] τῶν πρακτήρων εἱρ[κτ]ῇ.

Note that the πρακτῆρεϲ are '*not* to be identified with the earlier πράκτορεϲ', see *Ancient Society* 7 (1976) 305–6 and n. 26. For πράκτωρ see N. Lewis, *Inventory of Compulsory Services*, s.v. To judge from the passages referred to in S. Daris, *Spoglio Lessicale*, s.v. πρακτήρ, this variant is a general term for a tax-collector.

15 δημ[οϲίῳ λογιϲ]τηρίῳ. For this office as the site of a prison see XLIII **3104** 8 n.

16–17 For the restoration of εἰρήνηϲ cf. *LSJ* s.v. πρυτανεύω II 2 & 3. The plural ἡμεῖν may be equivalent to μοι, cf. the use of ἡμέτεροϲ in 12 and 20, or better, as Mr. Parsons suggests, it may mean 'us Egyptians'.

18 ἄτοπον. Cf. e.g. XLIII **3123** 7.

26]..ειγνυτο. The traces are certainly not of μ, rather of].ϲ,].τ, or]π. Nor are they of δ, but possibly (-)εδείκνυτο is here written wrongly as (-)εϲτείγνυτο, cf. XLIII **3113** 20, ὑποδίγνυμι = ὑποδείκνυμι, and Mayser–Schmoll I i p. 147 for τ = δ.

3303. EDICT OF A PREFECT

43 5B.64/K(6–9)b   17 × 7·5 cm.   *c.* A.D. 300–1

 The ends of the lines are so much abraded that little can be made of the text of this edict. All that emerges is the name of the prefect, Claudius Cleopatrus, on whom see **3301–3303** introd., and the fact that he is pronouncing about the supply of boats.

 If the boats were, as one might most naturally assume, for the transport of grain down the Nile to Alexandria after the harvest, the season of the year would probably be summer, say July or August. Since this prefect's predecessor, Aelius Publius, was still in office after 19 August, A.D. 299 (IX **1204**), and his successor, Clodius Culcianus, was in office already by 6 June A.D. 301 (**3304**), the year in question would then be A.D. 300. The argument, however, is far from sure.

The back is blank.

Κλαύδιο[.].ϲ′ Κλεόπατρος ὁ διαϲημότατος ἔπαρχος

Ἐγ[ύ]πτου λέγει. τοὺς τὰ πλοῖα κεκτημένους

τῆϲ χρείαϲ αὐτῶν μὴ ϲφόδρα με........ αἰ[ϲ-

θάνομε διὰ τὸ π[ρ]ὸϲ καιρόν τινα.........

5 ρεϲίαϲ αὐτῶν νομειϲθείϲηϲ α........

τοὺϲ ἐπιτεταγμένουϲ αὐτοῖϲ προϲταχθῆναι

ὑπ' ἐμοῦ παραϲχε[ῖ]ν τινα πλοῖα πρὸϲ καιρὸν

ὑπηρετηϲόμενα καὶ τοῖϲ δεϲπότεϲ .υ....

ἀποδοθηϲόμενα .πει..νυ. ὑπὲρ τοῦ μὴ

10 ...τικον....[..]... τοῦτο τοῖϲ τη....

·   ·   ·   ·   ·

2 l. Αἰγύπτου   3–4 l. αἰϲθάνομαι   5 l. νομιϲθείϲηϲ   7 ϋπεμου   8 l. δεϲπόταιϲ

'Claudius Cleopatrus, the most perfect prefect of Egypt, says:

"I observe that the owners of boats are not (obtaining?) much (share?) in the use of them(?), because for a (short?) time, when their service was considered (essential?), those put in charge of them were commanded by me to provide some boats to serve temporarily and to be returned (forthwith?) to their masters . . ." '

(For the purposes of this highly conjectural translation I have assumed that certain of the unread traces could represent μετέχονταϲ (3), βραχύν, τῆϲ ὑπηρεϲίαϲ (4–5), ἀναγκαίαϲ (5), and εὐθέωϲ (8). These could be right but are not verifiable. The whole sense might be quite different.)

9 Perhaps ἐπεί τε νῦν, introducing another preliminary clause. Another, and perhaps a better, possibility is ἐπεὶ τῄνϙν for ἐπεὶ τοίνϙν, which itself cannot be read.

10 At the end perhaps τῆϲ διᾳ would suit.

3304. AFFIDAVIT

28 4B.58/B(6–8)b+60/C(6–7)a   20 × 25·5 cm.   6 June, A.D. 301

Put together from three fragments found under two inventory numbers, this document mentions the prefect of Egypt Clodius Culcianus and gives a date which is the earliest recorded for him. See **3301–3303** introd. for the effect of this on the list of prefects.

The affidavit was made by a systates of Oxyrhynchus affirming the misdeeds of a fellow citizen. A charge was to be laid in the court of the prefect of Egypt and the affidavit may have been chosen as the formal way of instituting proceedings because the defendant had taken flight, possibly to avoid public service. In W. *Chr.* 402 it seems that the form of an affidavit addressed to the prefect was adopted because the adversary refused to accept a communication. These two cases suggest that the affidavit was used particularly when one party to the dispute could not or would not participate in the ordinary legal procedure. This does not apply, however, to SB X 10288. On the μαρτυροποίημα as an *edictio actionis* see E. Seidl, *Rechtsgeschichte Ägyptens als röm. Provinz*, 116–17.

The back is blank.

ἔτο]υϲ ιζ′ καὶ ιϛϛ τῶν κυρ[ίων ἡμῶν Διοκλητιανοῦ] καὶ Μαξιμιανοῦ Ϲεβαϲτῶ(ν)
καὶ (ἔτουϲ)] ἐνάτου τῶν κυρίων ἡ[μῶν Κωνϲταντίου καὶ Μαξιμι]ανοῦ τῶν ἐπι-
φανεϲτάτων
Και]ϲάρων, Παῦνι ιβ. ὑπατεί[αϲ Ποϲτουμίου Τιτιανοῦ (τὸ β′?) καὶ Οὐιρί]ου
Νεπωτιανοῦ ἐν τῇ λαμ(πρᾷ) καὶ λαμ(προτάτῃ) Ὀξ(υρυγχιτῶν) πόλ(ει).
μαρ]τύρεται Αὐρήλιοϲ Δί[δυμοϲ ὁ καὶ Ϲαραπίων Π]ύρρου ἀπὸ τῆϲ λαμπρᾶϲ
5 καὶ λαμπροτάτηϲ Ὀξυρυγχιτ[ῶν πόλεωϲ ....] ϲυϲτάτηϲ Ἰϲίδωρον
τὸν καὶ Ἀπολλώνιον ἐπικ[*c.* 17 letters] ἀπὸ τῆϲ αὐτῆϲ πόλεωϲ
οὐκ ἀξίωϲ τῆϲ τῶν νόμων [ἐπιϲτρεφείαϲ καὶ τοῦ φ]όβου τοῦ διαϲημοτάτου
ἐ]πάρχου τῆϲ Αἰγύπτου Κλωδ[ίου Κουλκιανοῦ .....] κεναι καὶ ἐπειδὴ
........] . . τὴν παρὰ τῆϲ ἀνδ[*c.* 17 letters] . ἀ[ν]αγκαίωϲ
10 *c.* 12 letters]ωδε τῷ μαρτυρο[ποιήματι *c.* 12 letters]θηκεν. τὸν οὖν
c. 12 letters] οὔτε λόγον . .[*c.* 20 letters]λ . ν πεποιηκέναι
c. 10 letters] . περιγραφῆϲ λ[ειτ]ουργίαϲ ....[.]....[....]. μηδὲ ενφα
c. 4] . αυτω καταϲτήϲαντα, τίνα τρόπον οὐκ οἶδ᾽ [ὅ]πωϲ γεγενῆϲ[θα]ι
πρὸϲ τὴν αὐτοῦ ϲύμβιον Αὐρηλίαν Θερμούθιον καὶ ἐξηπατηκέναι
15 αὐτὴν καὶ ἣν ἔχει ὄνον θήλειαν λευκὴν πῶλον ὡϲ πρὸϲ χρῆϲιν
ἐϲχηκέναι, ταύτην δὲ τῇ τοιαύτῃ ἐπιτιμῆϲι λαβόντα ἀπηλακέναι
καὶ ϲήμερον ἡμέραι τρῖϲ ἐγκρατῆ αὐτῆϲ ὄντα μήτε αὐτὸν πάλιν ἐν-
φανίϲαντα μήτε τὴν ὄνον τῇ οἰκίᾳ τάξει ἀπεκατεϲτακέναι καὶ {.}
ἐπειδὴ τὸ τόλμημα οὐκ ἄλλου ἐϲτὶν ἐπιϲτρεφείου μόνον τῆϲ ἀνδρείαϲ
20 τοῦ διαϲημοτάτου ἐπάρχου Αἰγύπτου Κλωδίου Κουλκιανοῦ τόδε τὸ
μαρτυροποίημα δημοϲίᾳ προὔθηκεν ἵνα πάντεϲ ἰδῶϲι καὶ διὰ τῆϲ
τ]οῦ ϲτατίζοντοϲ β(ενε)φ(ικιαρίου) πίϲτεωϲ μὴ λανθάνῃ τὸ μεγαλεῖον τῆϲ ἡγεμονίαϲ
παρ᾽ ᾗ ἀδίϲτακτόν ἐϲτιν ἐπιϲτῆϲαι πρὸϲ τὴν παράνομον αὐτοῦ ἐπι-
χείρη[ϲ]ιν τὴν δέουϲαν καὶ καθήκουϲαν ἐπιτιμίαν.
25 (m. 2) Αὐρήλιοϲ Δίδυμοϲ ὁ καὶ Ϲαραπίων πεποίημαι τὸ μαρτυροπύημα ὡϲ πρόκ(ειται).

1 ϲεβαϲτω̄   3 λαμϛ, λαμϛοξ′π̄ο̄   5 ϊϲιδωρον   16 l. ἐπιτιμῆϲει, ἀπηλλαχέναι(?)
17 l. τρεῖϲ 18 l. οἰκείᾳ, ἀποκαθεϲτακέναι   21 ϊνα, ϊδωϲι; l. εἰδῶϲι   22 β∕φ   25 l.
μαρτυροποίημα; προκ

'Year 17 and 16 of our lords Diocletian and Maximian Augusti and year nine of our lords Constantius and Maximian the most noble Caesars, Payni 12. In the consulship of Postumius Titianus (for the 2nd time?) and Virius(?) Nepotianus, in the glorious and most glorious city of the Oxyrhynchites. Aurelius Didymus alias Sarapion, son of Pyrrhus, from the glorious and most glorious city of the Oxyrhynchites, . . . systates, witnesses that Isidorus alias Apollonius . . . from the same city has acted in disregard of the punitive process of the laws and of the fear of the most perfect prefect of Egypt Clodius Culcianus and since . . . (13 ff.) in some way, he (Didymus) knows not how, he (Isidorus) got access to his wife Aurelia Thermuthion and deceived her and on the pretext of a loan got the donkey which she owns, a white female foal, but having secured it on this false claim(?) took it away(?) and though he has been in possession of it for three days today has neither appeared again himself nor returned the donkey to its proper place; and since this outrage is subject to no penal authority but that of his Valiance the most perfect prefect of Egypt Clodius Culcianus, he posted this affidavit in public so that all should be informed, so that, by the loyal conduct of the *beneficiarius* stationed here, it should not escape the notice of His Highness of the prefecture, whose undoubted province it is to impose upon this unlawful enterprise the fit and proper punishment.'

(2nd hand) 'I, Aurelius Didymus alias Sarapion, made the affidavit as aforesaid.'

2 ἐνάτου. For the avoidance of theta in dating by regnal years see *ZPE* 24 (1977) 241–3.

3 Cf. PSI IX 1037. 35–6 ὑπατίας Ποστουμίου Τιτιανοῦ [τὸ β′ καὶ Οὐιρίου Νε]πωτιανοῦ″. It is known from *CIL* vi 2143 that Titianus was *consul iterum*, but since τὸ β′ cannot have appeared in XXXVIII **2859** 30, and is restored in PSI IX 1037. 36 and P. Flor. I 3. 23, it is not certain that it has appeared in any of the papyri dated by these consuls. Space seems short enough to justify doubt here.

Οὐιρί]ου. Probably there is no necessity to doubt that the *nomen* of this consul was Virius and that he was related to the Virius Nepotianus who was consul in A.D. 336, but the evidence is slight and there is some confusion about what it is, e.g. in P. Panop. 6. 12–13 n. (*ZPE* 7 (1971) 20–1) and, more seriously, in PLRE I.

First we must consider PSI VII 804. 14–16, because in PLRE I 624–5 it is stated that the consul's full name is recorded there. In the edition the passage runs:

14   ⟨m¹⟩   ] καὶ Οὐιρίου Νεπωτιανοῦ
                ]ν τῶν λαμπροτάτων,
                ] Φαμενὼθ η′.   4 Marzo 301ᵖ.

14 Suppl. [ʼΥπατείας ⟨non è probabile Μετὰ τὴν ὑπατείαν⟩ Φλ. Ποστουμίου Τιτιανοῦ τό β′]. 15 [τοῦ λαμ(προτάτου) ἐπάρχου τοῦ ἱεροῦ πραιτωρίο]υ?

However, the layout and the implausible suggestions for restorations in the notes rouse suspicion that we have here mention of the consuls of A.D. 336 rather than of A.D. 301. In 1970 I was able to inspect the papyrus in the Laurentian Library in Florence and transcribed it as follows:

μετὰ τὴν ὑπατεί]αν Οὐιρίου Νεπωτιανοῦ
καὶ Τεττίου Φακούν] δου τῶν λαμπροτάτων
                ] Φαμενὼθ η′.

The date represents 4 March, A.D. 337.

In *CIL* vi 37118. 12 there appears in a list of eminent persons a Virius Nepotianus who is identified with the consul of A.D. 301. The *nomen* is damaged so that Vibius is palaeographically also possible, see A. Degrassi, *Fasti consolari*, 77 (A.D. 301). It is most unlikely that Vibius is correct, but on the other hand there is no positive proof that this man is the consul of A.D. 301. The evidence for the consul's *nomen* in fact reduces itself to the initial Ο[in P. Flor. I 3. 24 and the final -]ου here, if the traces are correctly assigned to these letters.

However, it remains a very plausible hypothesis that this consul was a namesake of the consul of A.D. 336 and that he is the man mentioned in *CIL* vi 37118. 12.

4 For the systates cf. **3301** 5–6 and n.

5 Before ςυςτάτης supply perhaps something like ὁ τῆς α(ὐτῆς) πόλεως, but one might expect rather ςυςτάτης τῆς α(ὐτῆς) πόλεως, cf. XIV **1627** 5–6. A participle might make a better supplement, if one of a suitable sense could be found.

6 ἐπικ[. Restore perhaps ἐπικ[αλούμενον, to be followed by another alias, or a patronymic, e.g. Ἐπικ[τήτου, which could be followed by τοῦ and the grandfather's name.

7 For the restoration cf. P. Lips. 39. 5–7, ἐχρῆν τοὺς ἅπαξ πειραθέντες (read -ας) ἐπιcτρεφείαc καὶ ἄρχοντος φόβου τοῦ λοιποῦ cωφρονεῖν.

8 One might restore perhaps ἠμελ]ηκέναι, since καταπεφρον]ηκέναι seems too long, but it is more likely that the genitives depend on ἀξίωc, see *LSJ* s.v. ἄξιος III, and that some neutral word, e.g. πεποι]ηκέναι, is required.

9 Probably ἀνδρ[είας αὐτοῦ, alluding to the prefect; cf. 19 and CPR V 7. 9 n. for the use of this title. By way of stopgap one might think of ἐπειδὴ [ἡ τόλμα μέν]ει τὴν παρὰ τῆc ἀνδρ[είας αὐτοῦ διάγνωςι]ν, 'since the outrage is awaiting judicial cognizance from His Valiance'.

10 Probably it was τ]ῷδε τῷ μαρτυρο[ποιήματι, cf. VIII 1114 23–4; by way of stopgap restore e.g. ἀ[ν]αγκαίως [παρέθετο τ]ῷδε τῷ μαρτυρο[ποιήματι, 'he necessarily recorded (it) in this affidavit', followed by ὃ (or καὶ) δημοσίᾳ προὔ]θηκεν, cf. 21.

10–14 From 12 we may perhaps guess that Isidorus had been appointed to some public service and failed to present himself. We might articulate περὶ γραφῆς λ[ειτ]ουργίας, cf. γραφὴ λειτουργῶν, e.g. XXXIV 2714 5–6, but perhaps more likely is περιγραφῆς λ[ειτ]ουργίας, 'loss sustained by the public service'. This may also explain why the affidavit is drawn up by the systates, who was responsible for the appointment of liturgists, cf. P. Mertens, *Les Services de l'état civil*, 30–47, esp. 36–7. On the other hand the ambiguity of αὐτοῦ in 14 leaves it doubtful whether the victim of the confidence trick was the wife of Isidorus or of the systates. If it was Didymus whose wife parted with the donkey, as seems more likely, that is sufficient reason for his action.

16 ἐπιτιμήςι (read -ει). This word appears to be used in an unusual sense. According to *LSJ* s.v. II. 2, it can mean 'rhetorical heightening by the use of a stronger term'. From this it might have come to mean by stages 'exaggeration', 'exaggerated claim', and here 'false claim'.

ἀπηλακέναι stands probably for ἀπηλλαχέναι, cf. Mayser–Schmoll I i 186–91 (simplification of doubled consonants), esp. 187 (λ for λλ), and 144–5 (κ for χ). In the translation this is regarded as transitive, 'took it away', but it may be intransitive, 'having secured it . . . he made off', cf. *LSJ* s.v. ἀπαλλάccω A II.

Possibly, however, it might stand for ἀπεληλακέναι, 'drove it off', since reduplication frequently caused difficulties to writers of late Greek, see B. G. Mandilaras, *The Verb in the Greek Non-literary Papyri*, 200–4.

17 κα]ὶ cήμερον ἡμέραι τρῖc. See Blass–Debrunner, *Grammatik d. neutest. Griechisch*[10], 95–6 (§§ 143–4), for this use of the nominative.

18 The superfluous trace at the end is perhaps a botched ε, the first letter of the next word.

19 ἐπιcτρεφείου. The usual word is ἐπιcτρέφεια and the form here is new. If genuine, it is presumably from an adjective ἐπιcτρέφειοc, whether it is neuter or masculine in this instance. However, the syntax is also suspect. One might expect οὐκ ἄλλου ἐcτὶν ἐπιcτρεφείαc ἢ τῆc ἀνδρείαc, 'is subject to the penal authority of none other than His Valiance'. But there is also the suggestion of contamination with οὐδενόc ἐcτιν ἐπιcτρεφείαc εἰ μὴ μόνον τῆc ἀνδρείαc, 'is subject to the penal authority of none except only His Valiance'.

20 Κλωδίου. It looks as if the writer began to write Κλαυδίου and remembered in the process that Clodius was the correct name.

22 On the βενεφικιάριος cτατίζων see P. Cair. Isid. 63 introd.

3305. COMMUNICATION TO A LOGISTES

48 5B.26/J(1–3)a   10·5 × 5·5 cm.   16 March, A.D. 313

This scrap, containing only the ends of four lines and traces of a fifth from the top of a document addressed to the logistes Ammonianus alias Gerontius, gives us a date for him which is earlier by almost three years than the earliest hitherto known, that in VI **983** (= SB III 6003) 15 (cf. 4) of 21 February, A.D. 316, see 3 n.

The back is blank.

The next item also mentions Ammonianus and very probably dates from the earlier part of his tenure.

ὑπατείας τῶν δεσποτῶν ἡμ]ῶν Γαλερίου Οὐαλερίου Μ[α]ξιμίνου καὶ Φλαυίου

Οὐαλερίου Κωνσταντίνου Αὐτο]κρατόρων Cεβαστῶν τὸ γ̄ Φαμενὼθ κ̄

(*nomen*) Ἀμμωνιανῷ] τῷ καὶ Γεροντίῳ λογιστῇ Ὀξυρυγχίτου

c. 20–25 letters]. τῆς λαμ(προτάτης) πόλεως Ἀλεξανδρέων. ὑπάρχι

5   *c.* 50 letters   ].....[.....

                        .   .   .   .   .

1 φλαυϊου   4 λαμϚ'', ὑπαρχι, l. ὑπάρχει

'In the consulship of our masters Galerius Valerius Maximinus and Flavius Valerius Constantinus Imperatores Augusti for the third time, Phamenoth 20. To Aurelius (or Valerius?) Ammonianus alias Gerontius, logistes of the Oxyrhynchite nome. [From X. . . . from?] the most glorious city of the Alexandrians. There belongs to . . .'

1–2 The date is 16 March, A.D. 313. There is no possibility of restoring μετὰ τὴν ὑπατείαν in place of ὑπατείας and assigning the document to A.D. 314. Maximinus Daia died while retreating before Licinius some time in summer A.D. 313 and was replaced by Licinius in the Egyptian dating formulas between 23 July (XLIII **3144**) and 13 September (P. Cair. Isid. 103, 20), cf. BGU II 409. 13 (25 November), BGU I 349. 14 (26 November). The post-consular dating of A.D. 314, therefore, named the consuls as Constantine and Licinius III, see P. Lond. III 975. 20 (p. 230).

3 For the question of which *nomen* we should supply here, Οὐαλερίῳ or Αὐρηλίῳ, see **3306** 1 n. Dated documents relating to Ammonianus are, in chronological order:

3305	16 March, A.D. 313
VI **983** (= SB III 6003)	21 February, A.D. 316
I **53**	25 February, A.D. 316
VI **896** (= WChr. 48)	1 April, A.D. 316
I **84** (= WChr. 197)	1 November, A.D. 316
XXXIII **2675**	15 January, A.D. 318
PSI V 454	28 January–26 February, A.D. 320

He also appears in **3306**, which is undated. The next logistes, Valerius Dioscurides alias Julianus, is first known in office 30 July, A.D. 321 from VI **900** (= WChr 437). For A.D. 321 as the date of **900** see P. Princ. Roll pp. 32–6. The old date of A.D. 322 is retained in the latest list of logistae (BASP 13 (1976) 38–40), which also omits XXXIII **2675** from the entries for Ammonianus alias Gerontius.

3306. LETTER OF A LOGISTES TO A PRYTANIS

44 5B.61/G(2–3)a   16 × 25 cm.   *c.* A.D. 314

The writer of this document broke off in the middle of the sixth line of text leaving the end of the line and two-thirds of the sheet blank. It is not obvious why he did so. The final word, which remains unread, may have contained some irremediable error, and the *nomen* Aurelius for the logistes may also possibly be an error, though a significant one, see 1 n.

The hand, in which the letters vary greatly in size and are furnished with ugly hooks and flourishes, does not look like an official one, though it is not at all unpractised. The sheet is made of coarse papyrus. These considerations suggest the possibility that the text is writing practice or idle scribbling, in which case it is presumably a private copy of an earlier official document.

The prytanis to whom the letter is addressed is new, see 3 n.

The back is blank.

> ..] Αὐρήλιος Ἀμμωνιανὸς ὁ
> καὶ Γερόντιος λογιστὴς Ὀξυρυγ(χίτου)
> Αὐρηλίῳ Θέωνι ἐνάρχῳ πρυτά-
> νει. ὁ κύριός μου διασημότατος
> 5   καθολικὸς Ἄρριος Διότιμος
> ἐξ ὧν ε.[.]...αι   (vac.)
>   (vac.)

2 οξυρ̅υ̅γ̅

'Aurelius Ammonianus alias Gerontius logistes of the Oxyrhynchite nome to Aurelius Theon prytanis in office. My lord the most perfect *rationalis*, Arrius Diotimus, as a result of the things which ...'

1 It is not clear whether the first word was indented by the space of two to three letters or whether there was something written before it. Certainly letters with even short descenders would have left traces below the tear.

The *nomen* Aurelius is interesting. In all other verifiable cases the logistes is called Valerius. Both of these names are status designations; the Aurelii are private citizens whose status derived originally from the *constitutio Antoniniana* and Valerius is the gentile name of the house of Diocletian, adopted by military and government officers before being replaced by Flavius, the gentile name of the house of Constantine. See in general J. G. Keenan, 'The names Flavius and Aurelius as status designations', in *ZPE* 11 (1973) 33–63, id. 13 (1974) 283–304. He deals with logistae called Valerius in *ZPE* 11 (1973) 44–6, and discusses the identification of the logistes Valerius Dioscurides alias Julianus with the town councillor called Aurelius Dioscurides alias Julianus, concluding, tentatively, that they were the same person and that the name Valerius was a mark of his rank as logistes.[1]

This seems to receive confirmation from XLV 3256 of A.D. 317, where Aurelius Heron alias Sarapion ex-logistes (ἀπὸ λογιστῶν), is virtually certain to be identical with Valerius Heron alias Sarapion, logistes in A.D. 308–9.

Ammonianus as a successor of Heron was entitled to the name Valerius, which he always has elsewhere in the cases where the name can be checked. It may be that Aurelius is an error here—an understandable lapse if he bore that name before he became logistes—but equally it may be that the name Valerius was not conferred at the same time as the office of logistes, in which case he would have remained Aurelius at the beginning of his term of office before the new name was granted. This may be connected with the fact that the logistes (*curator*) was confirmed in office by an imperial letter, see J. H. W. G. Liebeschuetz, *Antioch*, 169 and n. 1. It may have conferred the imperial *nomen* at the same time.

1 Dr. Coles points out that the strategus of A.D. 311, also called Aurelius Dioscurides alias Julianus (XXXIII 2668, P. Merton II 90), is likely to be the same man, since the strategus at this period was chosen from the local councillor class, see *CÉ* 35 (1960) 266.

There is a very similar variation between Aurelius and Flavius in the *nomen* of the logistes Sara-podorus of A.D. 373–4, see **3309–3311** introd., and the same hypothesis has been advanced to explain that case.

Apart from the name of Ammonianus himself, who was in office from A.D. 313 to 320, see **3305** 3 n., our only evidence at the moment, see below 3 n., for the date of this letter comes from the mention of Arrius Diotimus, see 5 n., and his only fixed date is 2 December, A.D. 314. Quite possibly, then, this document does belong to the early part of Ammonianus' service as logistes. Unfortunately the *nomen* is missing in the earliest dated document referring to it and we cannot be sure which of the two should be restored there, see **3305** 3 n.

3 The prytanis Aurelius Theon is new, that is, not in the lists in A. K. Bowman, *Town Councils*, 131–7. Since the office was annual, cf. ibid. 61–5, there is some prospect that new evidence will one day allow this letter to be assigned to an exact year.

5 For this *rationalis* see J. Lallemand, *L'Administration*, 258, PLRE I 261. Only P. Flor. I 54 has a date for him, which is 2 December, A.D. 314, see above 1 n.

3307. Assessment of Gold and Silver

41 5B.86/B(11)a   21 × 27 cm.   Early fourth century

This is an assessment of contributions measured in gold and silver bullion, listing numbers of persons who were liable according to the villages and smaller settlements of the eighth *pagus*. It is written across the fibres, though the back is blank. Possibly some stripping of the fibres of the back had already made it unfit for use in the normal way when the writer took it up.

No date is given, but the document must be subsequent to the creation of the *pagi* in A.D. 307/8, see J. Lallemand, *L'Administration*, 97–8, and a clue may be available from another papyrus from this layer, inv. 41 5B.86/B(3)a, which is addressed to the *prae-positus* of the same *pagus* and dated to A.D. 309. However, **3307** cannot be firmly pinned down to this date. The handwriting would suit any date in the early fourth century.

The last two lines give the total number of persons and two weights of bullion, silver and gold. The weights are conveniently divisible by the number of persons, which strongly implies that each person was liable to contribute fixed weights of 2 grams or scruples (γράμματα) of gold and 1 ounce (= 24 grams) of silver.

If this list does indeed record a flat-rate individual contribution of 2 gr. gold and 1 oz. silver, the symmetry of these figures might suggest that the value of the contribu-tion was theoretically supposed to be half of gold and half of silver at the proportion by weight of 1:12. Such evidence as we have indicates that the ratio of the monetary value of gold and silver fluctuated, see L. C. West and A. C. Johnson, *Currency*, 76–7, 94–5, 108, 138, 185–6, A. H. M. Jones, *The Roman Economy*, 204. A similar and even lower fixed relation between gold and silver occurs in SB III 6086 and XII **1524**, where it is 1:10. In P. Brem. 83 introd. one village total is given as 2 lb. of gold and 25 lb. of silver, i.e. 1:12½, but it is not clear if this relation is maintained throughout. The evidence, in fact, is not enough to confirm that these ratios depend on notions of the values of the two metals. Other considerations may have influenced the fixing of the rates. However, the new fragments of the price edict from Aezani show that an official ratio of 1:12 was in force in A.D. 301, with gold bullion at 72,000 den. (28. 1a) and silver bullion at 6,000 den. (28. 9), cf. M. Giacchero, *Edictum Diocletiani*, 114–15.

The purpose of these contributions is not known. It will shortly be shown that P. Cair. Isid. 89. 11–13—missed by me in *CÉ* 49 (1974) 163–74—firmly links the bullion contributions which were assessed in proportion to the assessment of grain taxes with the compulsory purchases of bullion by the state, see works by R. S. Bagnall forthcoming in *CÉ* 52 (1977), P. Col. VII 138–40 introd. The flat rate contributions of **3307** should, therefore, be unrelated to the imperial bullion purchases. For the taxes which might be collected in bullion see P. Cair. Isid. 69 introd.

```
        κατ' ἄνδρα κήνϲου παγ{ι}αρχίαϲ Τήεωϲ.
               ἔϲτι δέ.

        Τήεωϲ ἄνδ(ρεϲ) ὑποτελ(εῖϲ)      ρκθ
        Παώμεωϲ            ἄνδ(ρεϲ)      ξδ
   5    Παλώϲεωϲ           ἄνδ(ρεϲ)      κγ
        Κεϲμούχεωϲ         ἄνδ(ρεϲ)      ια
        Θώλθεωϲ            ἄνδ(ρεϲ)      δ
        Ϲούεωϲ             ἄνδ(ρεϲ)      ιθ
        Δωϲιθέου           ἄνδ(ρεϲ)      ξε
                    (vac.)
  10    ἐποικιωτῶν ὁμ[οί]ωϲ
        κώμηϲ Παώμεωϲ
        ἐποικίου Μενε....ου, Διονυϲίου ϲτρα(τηγ-)      ἀνήρ      α
        κώμηϲ Δωϲιθέου, ....ίωνοϲ νυνὶ
           τοῦ ἱερωτάτου ταμίου ἐποικ(ίου) π(ρότερον) Δωϲιθέου      β
  15    ἐποικ(ίου) ......ου, Ἀϲκληπιάδου Παυϲῖριϲ ὑποτ(ελὴϲ)      α
        ἐποικ(ίου) Πετροκί, Διδύμου τοῦ κ(αὶ) Εὐδαίμονοϲ      γ
        ἐποικ(ίου) Ϲκ[υτ]αλίτιδοϲ, Ἀϲκληπιάδου      α
        ῾τοῦ α(ὐτοῦ) ἐ[πο]ικ(ίου) Ϲκυταλίτιδοϲ, Λόγγου      α′
        τοῦ α(ὐτοῦ) ἐποικ(ίου), Πτολεμαίου καὶ τῶν κοι(νωνῶν)      ε
  20    ἐποικ(ίου) Ϲαραπᾶ, τοῦ α(ὐτοῦ) καὶ τῶν κοι(νωνῶν)      ε
                    (vac.)
        κώμηϲ Ϲούεωϲ
        ἐποικ(ίου) Ϲτρούθου, Ἀρτεμιδώραϲ      β
```

3 ανδ′ὕποτελ̣   4–9 ανδ′   12 ϲτρα) ανηρ′   14 ἱερωτατου; l. ταμείου; εποικ′π′   15 εποικ′ (also 16–20, 22–4); l. Παυϲίριοϲ; ὑποτ′   16 τουκ   18 α⁻   19–20 α⁻, κοᵗ

ἐποικ(ίου) Ἀλβίνου, Διονυσίου   γ

ἐποικ(ίου) Ψανκερμᾶ   ζ

                                (vac.)

25   γ(ίνονται) ἐπὶ τὸ α(ὐτὸ) ἄνδ(ρες) ὑποτελ(εῖς) τμϛ

      ἀσήμου λί(τραι) κη ὀγ(κίαι) ι, χρυς(οῦ) λί(τραι) β ὀγ(κίαι) δ⁻ γράμ(ματα) κ.

25 γ, α⁻ανδ΄υποτε̄λ   26 λκηογ⁻ιχρυς΄λβογ⁻δ⁻γραμ)κ

'Individual list of an assessment for the pagarchy of Teis, viz:

'Teis	men liable		129
Paomis	men		64
Palosis	men		23
Cesmuchis	men		11
Tholthis	men		4
Suis	men		19
Dositheu	men		65

'Inhabitants of hamlets likewise:

'Village of Paomis:

Hamlet of Mene . . ., (on property of?) Dionysius, (ex-?)strategus	man	1

'Village of Dositheu, (hamlet of?) . . . ion, now belonging to the most sacred
Treasury, once a hamlet belonging to the village of Dositheu(?)   2

Hamlet of . . ., (on property of?) Asclepiades, son of Paysiris	liable	1
Hamlet of Petroki(?), (on property of?) Didymus alias Eudaemon		3
Hamlet of Skytalitis, (on property of?) Asclepiades		1
The same hamlet of Skytalitis, (on property of?) Longus		1
The same hamlet, (on property of?) Ptolemaeus and his partners		5
Hamlet of Sarapas, (on property of?) the same and his partners		5

'Village of Suis

Hamlet of Struthus, (on property of?) Artemidora	2
Hamlet of Albinus, (on property of?) Dionysius	3
Hamlet of Psankerma	7

'Sum total of men liable: 346

      Silver 28 lb. 10 oz.; gold 2 lb. 4 oz. 20 gr.'

1 κατ' ἄνδρα. This term should denote a list with entries under individual names, cf. e.g. XL
2930, **2932**, but it is also used, as here, as a heading to show that the information below is extracted
from such a list, cf. e.g. XL **2928**, **2929**.

κήνϲου. The meaning here appears to be 'assessment'. In the papyri the word is rare and usually
refers to the operations of the *censitores* who conducted land surveys in the late third and early fourth
centuries, see CPR V 4. 7–8 n.

παγ{ι}αρχίας Τήεωϲ. This appears to be an expression synonymous with '8th *pagus*', see especially
XII **1448**, where the place-names offer many parallels to ours, and note the document referred to in
the introduction here. The word παγαρχία is very uncommon before the sixth century, but a parallel
is afforded by a probable use of παγαρχεῖν in C. Theod. VIII 15. 1 (before Constantine's death in May
A.D. 337) to mean 'act as *praepositus pagi*', see M. Gelzer, *Studien z. byz. Verwaltung Ägyptens*, 96 n. 1, cf.
XVII **2110** 4 n. (on παγαρχία in a papyrus of A.D. 370), J. Lallemand, *L'Administration*, 133 n. 4.

12 Μενε . . . . ου. This hamlet is new. It is not Μενεκράτουϲ (XLII **3046** 18), which is in any case
in the territory of the village of Pakerke (eastern toparchy, cf. e.g. X **1285** 89) while this one is assigned
to Paomis (formerly in the Thmoesepho toparchy, cf. e.g. X **1285** 122). Since hamlets often derive
their names from former owners, the attempt has been made to match the traces with personal names
in NB, D. Foraboschi, *Onomasticon*, and W. Pape, *Wb. d. gr. Eigennamen*, but without success.

Διονυσίου στρα(τηγ-). Most of the hamlet names are followed, as here, by another name in the genitive. Perhaps this is the name of the owner of the property where the persons liable to contribute lived. Presumably Dionysius was a strategus or ex-strategus. In this context στρα(τιώτου), or the like, is less probable.

13 ....ίωνος. Perhaps Ϲαπρίωνος would suit the traces.

13–14 Probably κώμης Δωσιθέου should have occupied a separate line, cf. 11, 21. The next word may have been the name of a hamlet or it may be the usual genitive which I have taken as the name of a property owner, see 12 n. The first may be more likely, since 'now belonging to the ... Treasury' answers the presumed purpose of the second.

15 The name of the hamlet looks as if it begins κραρ and ends, after about two more letters, in ου; if so, it is not attested elsewhere.

Παυσῖρις. The ending is presumably genitive, -ις = ιος, as often, see *Class. Phil.* 43 (1948) 243–60, Mayser, *Grammatik*, I ii 21 n. 3. Probably it is the patronymic of Asclepiades, though just possibly Ἀσκληπιάδου is part of the hamlet name.

16 Πετροκί. Here the final stroke looks like iota. In XII **1448** 11 and P. Osl. III 119. 2, 9 it is transcribed Πετροκ( ), the final stroke being interpreted as a mark of abbreviation.

18 Ϲκυταλίτιδος, Λόγγου. Cf. 17. In XII **1448** 12 (*c.* A.D. 318) Ϲκυταλίτιδος Λόγγου was taken as the full name of the hamlet. Here the parallelism and the prefix τοῦ α(ὐτοῦ) ἐ[πο]ικ(ίου) seem to show that Longus was a property owner or a former owner who had given his name to some estate, and that his name denotes only a part of Skytalitis, which occurs without qualification at a later date, XVI **1916** 24, **2025** 28, **2032** 13, **2034** 19, **2035** 30, XVIII **2195** 15 etc., **2207** 31, cf. P. Iand. 51. 6.

This whole line has been added after 19 was written. The total (25) takes account of it.

20 ἐπ. Ϲαραπᾶ. Cf. XII **1448** 13.

22 ἐπ. Ϲτρούθου. Cf. XII **1448** 18.

23 ἐπ. Ἀλβίνου. This hamlet has not been identified elsewhere.

24 ἐπ. Ψανκερμᾶ. Cf. PSI IX 1081. 4, where the note implies that Ψανωρμᾶ (XII **1448** 19) is a misreading of the same. This seems very likely. Unfortunately the original of **1448** is in Baltimore and the authorities of the Johns Hopkins University say that they are unwilling to risk it in the hands of a photographer.

25–6 The calculations which seem to show a flat rate, see introd., are as follows:

$$\text{Gold 2 lb.} \times 288 = 576 \text{ gr.}$$
$$4 \text{ oz.} \times 24 = 96 \text{ gr.}$$
$$20 \text{ gr.} \qquad = \underline{20 \text{ gr.}}$$
$$692 \text{ gr.} \div 346 \text{ men} = 2 \text{ gr. per cap.}$$

$$\text{Silver 28 lb.} \times 12 = 336 \text{ oz.}$$
$$10 \text{ oz.} \qquad = \underline{10 \text{ oz.}}$$
$$346 \text{ oz.} \div 346 \text{ men} = 1 \text{ oz. } (= 24 \text{ gr.}) \text{ per cap.}$$

II. DOCUMENTS OF THE BYZANTINE PERIOD

3308–3311. Documents addressed to the logistes Sarapodorus

Sarapodorus, the logistes of A.D. 373–4, was not known hitherto, that is, he does not occur in the latest list in *BASP* 13 (1976) 38–40. These documents show a variation of his *nomen* between Aurelius and Flavius, which seems to be parallel with the use of both Aurelius and Valerius for the logistes Ammonianus alias Gerontius, see **3306** 1 n. As suggested there, it looks as if logistae acquired the imperial name by a separate grant some time after their entry to the office, though the grant of the name was no doubt connected with the office. Another case described there, that of Valerius, or Aurelius, Heron alias Sarapion, suggests that the *nomen* was not retained after the expiry of the term of service in the imperial administration.

3308. Undertaking on Oath

39 5B.120/B(1)a   fr. 1   8 × 15 cm.   17 January, A.D. 373
              fr. 2 12 × 10·5 cm.

Besides the mention of Sarapodorus, see above, we find here a new *praeses Augustamnicae*, Flavius Eumathius Parthenius, whose appearance allows us to presume that Oxyrhynchus remained in Augustamnica until at least this date, though other evidence had previously led to the conclusion that by A.D. 370 it had passed into Aegyptus, see 7 n.

The document is an undertaking by a stonemason to go somewhere and practise his trade, presumably in performance of a public duty, cf. H. Braunert, *Binnenwanderung*, 314–15, and the literature cited there. The damage makes it uncertain where he was to go. Fr. 1 has the ends of the first fifteen lines, which contained the prescript and the greater part of the body of the text. Fr. 2, slightly wider, has the last four lines, containing the subscription of an amanuensis, virtually complete. As little as one line may be missing between the fragments, but more could quite possibly be lost, see 14–15 n.

The back is blank, so far as it is preserved.

μετὰ τὴν] ὑπατείαν Φλ(αουίου) Δομιτίου Μοδέςτου καὶ
Φλ(αουίου) Ἀρινθέο]υ τῶν λαμ(προτάτων), Τῦβι κβ′.
Αὐρηλίῳ Cα]ραποδώρῳ λογιcτῇ Ὀξυρυγχίτου
παρὰ Αὐρηλ]ίου Γούνθου Ἀμόιτος ἀπὸ κώμης
5   λαο]ξόου. ἀκολούθωc τοῖc προcτα-
χθεῖcιν ὑ]πὸ τῆc ἐξουcίαc τοῦ κυρίου μου τοῦ
λαμπροτάτου] ἡγεμόνοc Φλαουίου Εὐμαθίου

1 φλ′   2 λαμ⟨″   7 φλαουϊου

Παρθενίου ὁ]μολογῶ ὀμνὺς τὸν cεβάcμιον

θεῖον ὅρκον τ]ῶν δεcποτῶν ἡμῶν

10 Οὐαλεντινιανο]ῦ καὶ Οὐάλεντοc καὶ Γρατιανοῦ

τῶν αἰωνίων Αὐγο]ύcτων ἐπὶ τῷ με ἀπαρτῆcαι

    c. 14 letters].....ιc εἰ[c] τὴν ạ.[.].ν[...

    c. 13 letters] τὴν ἐργαcίαν ἐκεῖcαι α..[.

    c. 6 letters ἀποπληρ]ῶcαι καὶ μὴ ἀπολιφθή-

15 cεcθαι ἔcτ' ἂν ἀπο]λυθῶ ἢ ἔνοχοc

    .   .   .   .   .

fr. 2

(m. 2) Ạ[ὐρ(ήλιοc)] Γọ[ῦνθοc ὤμ]οcα τὸν θῖον ὅρκọν

καὶ ἀπαντήcω καὶ τὴν ἐργαcίαν

ἀποπληρῶcαι ὡc πρόκιται. Αὐρήλιọc

Δωρόθεοc Νίλου ἔγραψα ὑπὲρ αὐτοῦ.

13 l. ἐκεῖcε   14 l. ἀπολειφθήcεcθαι   16 l. θεῖον   18 l. ἀποπληρώcω, πρόκειται   19 l. Νείλου

'After the consulship of Flavius Domitius Modestus and Flavius Arintheus, *viri clarissimi*, Tybi 22nd.'

'To Aurelius Sarapodorus, logistes of the Oxyrhynchite nome, from Aurelius Gunthus, son of Amois, from the village of . . ., stonemason. In conformity with the commands issued by the Might of my lord the most glorious *praeses*, Flavius Eumathius Parthenius, I agree, swearing the august, divine oath by our masters Valentinian and Valens and Gratian, the eternal Augusti, that I shall go . . . to . . . and there practise . . . my trade and shall not withdraw until I am released or (may I be) liable (to the penalties of the divine oath) . . .'

(2nd hand) 'I, Aurelius Gunthus, have sworn the divine oath and I shall go and practise my trade, as is aforesaid. I, Aurelius Dorotheus, son of Neilus, wrote on his behalf.'

3 For the restoration of Αὐρηλίῳ see **3309** 3. That document is clearly later than this one because the date clause names the consuls of A.D. 373, whereas this one, of 17 January, still uses the post-consular date by the consuls of A.D. 372. Sarapodorus presumably acquired the *nomen* Flavius later in his term of office, cf. introd. **3308–3311, 3310** 4, **3311** 1.

5 λαο]ξόου. For this form cf. XVI **2041** 1 (λαοξόου, VI/VII A.D.), PSI VIII 955. 17 (λαοξόῳ, VI A.D.). The form most familiar in the papyri is λαξόc. LSJ puts this and other variants under λαοξόοc.

7 λαμπροτάτου. Cf. J. Lallemand, *L'Administration*, 61–2.

The *praeses* has appeared before in P. Med. inv. 165. 7, 10, 13, 14, see *Aegyptus* 56 (1976) 60–64. That document is dated in a consulship of Valentinian and Valens, i.e. A.D. 365, 368, 370, or 373, of which years the last is now seen to be the most likely. The first *cognomen* of the *praeses* was read as Εὐμέτιοc, otherwise unattested. The plate (Tav. V) permits us to read Εὐμάτιοc, though the doubtful vowel is very cursively written. For τ in place of θ see F. T. Gignac, *Grammar*, I 92. The persons concerned in the document come from the Oxyrhynchite and Heracleopolite nomes, from which the editor properly concluded that the *praeses* was governor of Augustamnica. It seems virtually impossible that he was *praeses Thebaidos* because, firstly, we know of Julius Eubulius Julianus in that office in A.D. 372 and of a successor Flavius Eutychius in A.D. 373 (J. Lallemand, op. cit., 252), and secondly because Oxyrhynchus should not fall in the province of the Thebaid. He can only, therefore, be *praeses Augustamnicae*, and on this date, 17 January, A.D. 373, Oxyrhynchus must still fall in Augustamnica in spite of argument to the contrary, see J. Lallemand, op. cit., 54. The fact that in XVII **2110**, of A.D. 370, the prefect of Egypt is said to have arranged official appointments affecting the Oxyrhynchite nome must be taken to show that the prefect retained certain powers in the province of Augustamnica, not that Oxyrhynchus had at that date been transferred from Augustamnica to Aegyptus. Lallemand's conclusions about the relations between prefect and *praeses*, ibid., 59–60, seem too definite.

8 This line suggests the correction of [ὑ]πολόγως ὀμνύω in I 87 (= W. *Chr.* 446). 14–15 to [ὁ]μολογῶ ὀμνύς, and the damaged original can certainly be read in that way. The phrase is very common.

11–12 In I 87 17–19 we find ἀπαντῆcαι ἅμα τοῖc εἰc τοῦτο{ν} ἀποcταλῖ[c]ι [ὁ]φ(φικιαλίοιc), cf. P. Lips. I 45–55, all addressed to *officiales* by guarantors of travelling liturgists, but this cannot be reconciled with the traces in 12. The remains suggest an ending in -(ε)ίταιc, but no word in -ίτηc convincingly parallel with ὀφφικιάλιοc has been found. Something like [ἅμα τοῖc | ἄλλοιc τεχ]νείταιc or τε]χνίταιc, 'along with the other craftsmen', would suit, but has little chance of being right.

12 ạ.[.].ν̣[.... A place-name is probably, though not necessarily, to be expected at some point after εἰ[c] τήν. Neither Ἀλεξάνδρειαν nor the standard epithet, λαμπροτάτην, can be recognized. After ạ there is a descender with the foot hooked to the right; ρ is suggested, but β(?), ι, φ, and ψ(?) are possible, followed by a hole, which may have held a narrow letter or the first part of the letter represented by the first traces after the gap (α, ε, c?). Not Ἀρcινο-, unless mis-spelt Ἀρ[c]εν̣[οι|τῶν πόλιν vel sim.

13 ạ..[.]. Perhaps restore an adverb to go with ἀποπληρῶcαι; ἀμέ[μ]|14πτωc, cf. P. Flor. I 2. 23 and here 14–15 n., might suit, but may not be long enough to fill the space available in 14. Perhaps ἅμα | 14 [ἄλλοιc ... is possible too, cf. 11–12 n.

14–15 Cf. PSI III 162. 14–17 καὶ μὴ ἀπολειφθήcεcθαι ἔcτ' ἂν ἀπολυθῶ εἰc τὸ ἐν μηδενὶ μεμφθῆναι ἢ ἔνοχοc εἴην τῷ ὅρκῳ. This is followed by a sentence naming two guarantors, a regnal year dating clause —not expected in this document, cf. 1–2—and a subscription. It is uncertain how much is missing here between 15 and 16. All that is essential is one line with εἴην τῷ ὅρκῳ, but here too there may have been a clause naming guarantors.

15 Above the second omicron of ἔνοχοc and virtually continuing the line of the descender of the phi of ἀπολιφθή|14[cεcθαι] is an upright which remains unexplained. Probably it is accidental ink.

18 Probably ἀποπληρῶcαι is simply an error caused by a memory of the same form in 14 and should be corrected to ἀποπληρώcω, but both καίs in 17 are uncertainly read, the second being written over something now uncertain, so that there is a possibility that some other construction was used. It is not possible to read ἐπὶ τῷ ἀπαντῆcαι καί ... ἀποπληρῶcαι as in 11–14.

19 One expects ὑπὲρ αὐτοῦ to be followed by μὴ εἰδότος γράμματα or an equivalent. We may suspect that it has been accidentally omitted, but we cannot assume it. On questions of illiteracy and semi-literacy in general see H. C. Youtie, *Scriptiunculae*, ii 611–51.

3309. Application to a Logistes

A 13ᴮ B.5/7(b)   10 × 6 cm.   A.D. 373

This is a mere scrap, with the central parts of the top five lines of a document. The first two lines contain a date clause by the consuls of A.D. 373, the middle one an address to the logistes Sarapodorus, who here has the *nomen* Aurelius, see 3 n. and introd. 3308–3311, and the last two the names of persons applying to him.

The back is blank.

ὑπατείας] τῶν δεσποτῶν ἡμῶν Οὐαλερ[τινιανοῦ
καὶ Οὐ]άλεντος αἰωνίων Αὐγούcτων τὸ δ' [
Αὐρη]λίῳ Cαραποδώρῳ λογιcτῇ Ὀ[ξυρυγχίτου
παρὰ] Αὐρηλίων Θωνίου Παρίων[ο]c καὶ [

5   ....]ο̣υ καὶ Κοπρέωc Θ.̣.[

                    .   .   .   .   .

'In the consulship of our masters Valentinian and Valens, eternal Augusti, for the fourth time (month?, day?). To Aurelius Sarapodorus, logistes of the Oxyrhynchite nome, from Aurelius Thonius, son of Parion, and Aurelius . . ., son of . . ., and Aurelius Copreus, son of Th . . .'

1 Lack of space excludes the restoration of μετὰ τὴν ὑπατείαν. We can also see from **3310** 1–4 that early in A.D. 374 Sarapodorus probably had the *nomen* Flavius, not Aurelius as here.

2 At the end of the line month and day may have been specified, cf. **3308** 2, or the month only, cf. **3310** 3, or neither, cf. e.g. P. Lips. 85. 3; 86. 3.

In the early part of this year the dating clause refers to the consuls of the previous year, cf. **3308** 1–2. Unfortunately there are not many complete dating clauses of A.D. 373 and they do not allow any close dating of the change from the post-consular form. To judge from a search of WB III p. 76, WB Suppl. p. 355 and the indexes of SB VI–XI, the latest date in this form is **3308** 1–2 of 17 January, A.D. 373, and the earliest by the consuls of the year is in P. Mert. I 37. 1–2 of 3rd September.

3 Αὐρη]λίῳ. Lambda is certain. See introd. **3308–3311** for the significance of the alternation of Aurelius and Flavius.

4–5 The translation assumes that there was an entire name at the end of 4 and a patronymic at the beginning of 5 ending in]ου. Another possibility is that a longer name was divided between the lines and followed by an alias, τ]οῦ καὶ Κοπρέως, in which case the translation should read, '. . . and (from) Aurelius . . . alias Copreus, son of Th . . .'

5 Θε.[would suit well; the final traces perhaps favour Θερο[rather than Θεω[.

3310. APPLICATION TO A LOGISTES

40 5B.112/2(1–3)a   12·5 × 8 cm.   26 January–
24 February A.D. 374?

Very serious damage has reduced this document to three tattered fragments, the largest and the only one transcribed here containing the first four lines virtually complete, significant remains of the next four, and mere traces of four more before the text breaks off. The other two scraps are joined by only a single horizontal fibre of the front and the remains of writing are too damaged for any useful transcript to be offered. The back, as far as it is preserved, is blank.

The information of value which the fragment offers is the latest date (if it is rightly read, see 3 n.) for the logistes Sarapodorus and the *nomen* Flavius, see introd. **3308–3311**.

μετὰ τὴν ὑπατcίαν τῶν δεcπ[ο]τῶν ἡμῶν

Οὐαλεντινιανοῦ κα[ὶ] Οὐά[λεντος τ]ῶν αἰωνίων

Αὐγούcτων τὸ δ, [Μεχ]είρ.   (vac.)

Φλαουίῳ Cαραποδώρ[ῳ λ]ο[γ]ιcτῇ Ὀξυρυγχείτου

5   παρὰ Αὐρηλίου Πα..... Χωοῦτος ἀπὸ τῆς αὐτῆς

πόλεως. κεκτημε... οἰκοπεδ[.]. ον.[.].

ἐν τῇ αὐτῇ πόλει ἀκολούθως τῇ γεγερημένῃ εἰς

ἐμὲ πράcει, ἀλλ' ἐμοῦ διὰ τὴν παλεώτητα το.[.].[

8 l. παλαιότητα

```
          ...].[.]....................οικοδομ...
10        ....................]....λ....ϲονκ...
          ....................].... καταφρονο..
          ....................]....[.]........[...
                .    .    .    .    .
```

3 The remains of the foot of the iteration figure suit δ. If we were to read γ, which is only just possible and very far from likely, the year would be A.D. 371; β, which is palaeographically possible, would indicate A.D. 369. The theory of the use of the imperial *nomen* advanced for the case of Ammonianus alias Gerontius, see **3306** 1 n., **3308–3311** introd, is that it was granted to logistae in connection with their office but separately from it and at a later date. If that theory is correct, the fact that in **3309**, dated to A.D. 373 by the same consuls for the fourth time, the *nomen* of the logistes is given as Aurelius, would compel the conclusion that **3310**, giving it as Flavius (4), is the later document, which means that we should read δ here and convert the date to 26 January–24 February, A.D. 374.

6 The traces at the end suggests οἰκοπέδ[ο]ν ὄντ[ο]ϲ, which is hard to place in a good grammatical context. The first word might be κέκτημε (= κέκτημαι, cf. παλεώτητα, 8), but it is hardly possible to find space for an object, such as μέροϲ, after it; or the first word might be κεκτημένοϲ *vel sim.*, which should take the accusative also, but οἰκόπεδον ὄν and οἰκόπεδα ὄντα do not suit the traces. If used as a substantive meaning 'owner', κεκτημένοϲ might possibly be followed by a genitive, but no convincing sentence structure has yet been suggested. It may be suspected that κεκτημένοϲ οἰκοπέδ[ο]ν ὄντ[ο]ϲ did stand here in spite of the loose grammar.

3311. PETITION TO A LOGISTES

40 5B.116/A(1–2)a   25·5 × 27·5 cm.   *c.* A.D. 373–4

An approximate date can be given to this document because of the appearance of the logistes Sarapodorus, see **3308–3310**. It should be later than **3308** and **3309** because he here has the *nomen* Flavius, see introd. **3308–3311**.

The two sisters who submitted the petition, Cyrilla and Martha, wished to recover the estate of a cousin on their father's side, Gemellus, who 'on the point of death allowed (?) the property left behind by him (to come?) under the control of' his maternal uncle, Ammonius (4–5). The text is doubtful here and it is not clear whether Ammonius became the full legal owner of the property or not. According to the women's narrative Ammonius died without leaving a will or naming heirs, but a certain Ammon was holding on to the estate unlawfully. They asked that he should be summoned and forced to make restitution to them.

Ammon is said not to be the heir (11), but probably this means only that he was not, according to the women, heir to the estate of Gemellus. Very likely he was next of kin and heir to Ammonius all right, but the textually doubtful and perhaps deliberately vague form of words in 4–5 was probably meant to imply that Ammonius was never the full legal owner of the estate of Gemellus. I am grateful to the University Press reader for suggesting this view of the case to me.

The family relationships are as follows:

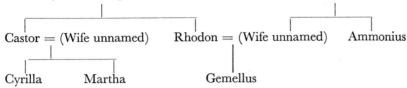

All but Cyrilla and Martha were dead at the time of writing.

The document is blank on the back and virtually complete, though it has suffered some damage, especially to the lower left corner. The piece of papyrus seems to have been cut from near the beginning of a roll, because besides a normal join near the ends of the lines there is a join on the left and at that point the left-hand sheet shows vertical fibres. This suggests that it was the so-called *protocollon*, which was normally attached in this way to form a cover and guard sheet for the roll, see E. G. Turner, *Greek Papyri*, 5. The writing runs along the fibres of the second and third sheets except that in two places the crossbars of two letters have just strayed on to the *protocollon* (2, 9).

Φλαο[υίῳ] Cαραποδώρῳ (vac.) λογιϲτῇ (vac.) Ὀξυρυγχίτου
παρὰ Αὐρ[ηλίω]ν Κυρίλλαϲ καὶ Μάρθαϲ ἀμφοτέρων ἐκ πατρὸς Κάϲτοροϲ ἀπὸ τῆϲ αὐτῆϲ
πόλεωϲ. [Γέ]μελλοϲ υἱόϲ ἐϲτιν ῾Ρόδωνοϲ ὄντοϲ θείου ἡμῶν πρὸϲ πατρόϲ,
ὃϲ μέλλων τελευτᾶν τὰ καταλειφθέντα ὑπ’ αὐτοῦ πράγματα ειϲ. ϲεν ὑπὸ τὴν
5 ἐξουϲίαν Ἀμμωνίου τινόϲ, ἀποτακτικοῦ, κατὰ μητέρα θείου αὐτοῦ τυγχάνοντοϲ,
παρακελε[υ]όμενοϲ μὴ δι’ ὄχλου ἡμᾶϲ αὐτῷ γίγνεϲθαι. ϲυμβέβηκεν δὲ τὸν αὐτὸν
Ἀμμώνιον ἀποτακτικὸν ὄντα οὐ μετ’ οὐ πολὺ ἐκ τῶν ἀνθρώπων ἀπελθεῖν.
τὰ δὲ τοῦ προειρημένου ῾Γεμέλλου᾽ πράγματα ἡμῖν ἀνῆκεν ταῖϲ ἐκ τοῦ πατρικοῦ γένουϲ
τυγχανούϲαιϲ. ἐπεὶ οὖν οὔτε βουλημάτιον ὁ Ἀμμώνιοϲ ϲυνεϲτήϲατο
10 οὔτε [ἀ]πέδειξεν κληρονόμουϲ, ἀποτακτικὸϲ δὲ ὢν ἐτελεύτα τὸν βίον,
ἀλλ’ Ἄμμων τιϲ ταῦτα τὰ μὴ ἀνήκοντα αὐτῷ πράγματα μὴ ὢν κληρονόμοϲ
κατέχει πρὸϲ βίαν, διὰ τοῦτο ἀξιοῦμεν τὴν ϲὴν ἐμμέλιαν ὥϲτε κελεῦϲαι τὸν
αὐτὸν Ἄμμωνα παραϲτῆναι καὶ καταναγκαϲθῆναι, μὴ ὄντα υἱὸν τοῦ Ἀμμωνίου
μηδὲ κληρον]όμο[ν] ἀποδοῦναι ἡμῖν τὰ τοῦ Γεμέλλου πράγματα ταῖϲ οὔϲαιϲ
15 ἐκ τοῦ πατρι]κοῦ αὐτοῦ γένουϲ ἵνα δυνηθῶμεν ἐκ τῆϲ ϲῆϲ βοηθείαϲ μηδεμίαν
περιγραφὴν ὑπομ]ένειν. (vac.)
(m. 2) Αὐρήλιαι Κυ]ρίλλα καὶ Μάρθα ἐπιδεδώκαμεν. Αὐρήλιοϲ Θεόδωροϲ Θωνίου
ἔγραψα ὑπὲρ αὐ]τῶν γράμματα μὴ εἰδειῶν.

2]ν corr. from ϲ?; ἀπό corr. from something now uncertain 3 υῑοϲ 4 ῡπ, ὑπο
11 αλλ’ 12 l. ἐμμέλειαν 13 υῑον 15 ῑνα 18 l. εἰδυιῶν

H

'To Flavius Sarapodorus, logistes of the Oxyrhynchite nome, from Aurelia Cyrilla and Aurelia Martha, both daughters of Castor, from the same city. Gemellus is a son of Rhodon, our uncle on our father's side. On the point of death he allowed(?) the property left behind by him (to come?) under the control of a certain Ammonius, a monk, who happened to be his uncle on his mother's side, exhorting us not to cause him any trouble. It came about that the said Ammonius, who happened to be a monk, not long after departed from among mankind. The property of the aforementioned Gemellus reverted to us, since we are of his father's family. Since, then, Ammonius neither drew up a will nor designated heirs, and lived his life to the end as a monk, but a certain Ammon is detaining by force this property that does not belong to him, not being the heir, for this reason we beg your Providence to order the said Ammon to make an appearance in court and to be compelled, since he is not a son of Ammonius or an heir, to restore to us the property of Gemellus, since we are of his father's family, so that as a result of your assistance we may be able to avoid suffering any loss.'

(2nd hand) 'We, Aurelia Cyrilla and Aurelia Martha, submitted the petition. I, Aurelius Theodorus, son of Thonius, wrote on their behalf since they do not know letters.'

4 εις.cεν. Just possibly ϝ should be read in place of ς; the next letter was very small, probably α rather than ο, which is usually larger in this hand. The best solution seems to be to understand the word as εἴαcεν, transcribing it εἴ{ς}αcεν.

5 ἀποτακτικοῦ. The most detailed study of this word is by E. Wipszycka in *Le Monde grec* (*Hommages à C. Préaux*), 632–4; the evidence appears at first sight to support the conclusion that the term applies to coenobitic monks as distinct from hermits. The editor of XLIV 3203 took the opposite view, see ibid. 6 n., and it is noteworthy that the central figure of the small archive in P. Herm. Rees 7–10 is described as ἀποτακτικόc in 9. 2, but as ἀναχωρητής (*vel sim.*) in 7. 21 and 10. 2. The translations 'recluse, hermit' are given in G. W. H. Lampe, *A Patristic Greek Lexicon*, s.v. I remain very uncertain of the exact meaning of the word. It may even not have had any very precise technical connotation, or if it had, the technical meaning may not have been strictly observed in practice.

[The Press reader has also suggested that the odd expression in 4, the failure of Ammonius to make a will, and the undertaking of the sisters not to make trouble for him may imply that an ἀποτακτικόc was in strict theory not allowed to own property. This attractive suggestion recalls the hypothesis that the word actually means 'a monk who has renounced property', put forward in an unpublished dissertation which I have not been able to consult, namely M. Krause, *Das Apa Apollon Kloster in Bawit* (diss. Leipzig 1958), 213–14. This meaning is rejected by Wipszycka, op. cit., 634, because the documents undoubtedly show ἀποτακτικοί administering their own property, e.g. XLIV 3203. Perhaps we should envisage the possibility that practice did not conform with theory, but it is hard to make any judgement on the present evidence.]

7 The expression οὐ μετ' οὐ πολύ, containing a pleonastic cumulation of the negative, and meaning 'soon, shortly after, not long afterwards', *vel sim.*, has appeared at least twice before in the papyri, BGU II 614. 14, MChr. 96 ii 9 (= Archiv 1 (1900–1) 300 line 9 = P. Bour. 20. 27—in which version simply οὐ μετὰ πολύ is printed). In both places the first οὐ is bracketed as an unintentional repetition by the writer, but it has been pointed out that it should be retained, see BL I 56 (from BGU III index p. 3), Archiv 1 (1900–1) 311, and especially O. Gradenwitz, *Einführung in die Papyruskunde*, 40 n. 1. See also G. W. H. Lampe, *A Patristic Greek Lexicon*, s.v. οὐ (6).

10 οὔτε [ἀ]πέδειξεν. The reading, not entirely sure, may be supported by reference to P. Ryl. II 153. 15–17, κληρονόμον . . . ἀποδείκνυμι(αποδιγνυμι pap.) τὸν ἀφήλικά μου υἱόν.

12 For the official use of ἐμμέλεια cf. CPR V 12. 5 n.

14 μηδὲ κληρον]όμο[ν]. This restoration seems very probable, cf. 11, but something else, e.g. κατὰ τοὺς ν]όμο[υc], is conceivable.

15–16 For the conjectural restoration μηδεμίαν [περιγραφὴν ὑπομ]ένειν cf. MChr. 96 ii 18 ἵνα μή . . . δοκοίη περιγραφήν τινα ὑπομένειν.

III. PRIVATE LETTERS

3312. PRIVATE LETTER

34 4B.74/F(1–3)d   10·2 × 17·5 cm.   Second century

Suddenly, among the routine final greetings of this fragment of a private letter, the recipient is offered a piece of news which is very relevant to the now fashionable studies of imperial slaves and freedmen: 'Herminus went off to Rome and became a freedman of Caesar in order to take up official appointments.' As so often in private letters we get only a tantalizing glimpse of an interesting process.

The handwriting probably belongs to the middle of the second century. In many ways it resembles P. Lond. II 178 (a) and particularly (b) of A.D. 145 (pp. 207–8; Plates II No. 52), and it is somewhat like P. Mert. II 73 of A.D. 164.

      ·   ·   ·   ·   ·

     c. 12 letters].[*c.* 8 letters

     c. 10 letters]..υιο.[2–4

     ...] τὰ ἀβάϲκαντα ‘αὐτ'οῦ τέ-

     κνα καὶ Ἰϲιδώραν τὴν

5   ἀδελφήν ϲου καὶ Ἀθηναΐδα.

     καὶ γράψον μοι ἀϲπαλῶϲ

     περὶ Διονυϲαρίου ὅτι πόϲων

     μηνῶν ἐϲτιν. ἀϲπάζετ[αί

     ϲε Γαΐ⟨α⟩ καὶ τὰ τέκνα αὐτ[ῆϲ

10   καὶ ὁ ϲύμβιοϲ. γίνωϲ⟨κε⟩ οὖ[ν

     ὅτι Ἑρμῖνοϲ ἀπῆλθεν ἰϲ Ῥώμ[ην

     καὶ ἀπελεύθεροϲ ἐγένετ[ο

     Καίϲαροϲ ἵνα ὀπίκιω λάβ[ῃ.

     ἀϲπάζου πάντας τοὺϲ

15   ϲοὺϲ κατ' ὄνομα καὶ οἱ ⟨ἐ⟩μοὶ

     πάντεϲ ϲε ἀϲπάζονται.

        ἐρρῶϲθαί ϲε εὔχομαι.

Back (downwards)].ου Ὀξυρυγχ( )

(at foot, upside down in relation to the front, m. 2) ..ιϲτη.

6 l. ἀϲφαλῶϲ   11 l. εἰϲ   13 l. ὀφφίκια

'. . . (I greet your son and?) his children—may the evil eye not touch them—and Isidora your sister and Athenais; and write to me without fail about Dionysarion, how many months old she is. Gaia greets you and so do her children and her husband. You should know, then, that Herminus went off to Rome and became a freedman of Caesar in order to take up official appointments. Greet all your people by name. All mine greet you too. I pray for your health.'

2 The context implies that ἀcπάζομαι or ὁ δεῖνα ἀcπάζεται precedes something like τ]ὸν υἱόν [cου |³ καὶ] τὰ ἀβάcκαντα ʽαὐτ'οῦ τέ |⁴κνα.

6 ἀcπαλῶc. For π in place of φ see Mayser–Schmoll I i pp. 145–6. Cf. 13 n.

9 Γαί⟨α⟩. This solution to the difficulty is suggested by the more obvious omission of letters in 10 (γίνωc⟨κε⟩ οὖ[ν) and 15–16 (οἱ ⟨ἐ⟩μοὶ πάντεc).

11–13 The straightforward background to assume is that Herminus was a *servus Caesaris* who had saved enough money to buy his freedom, cf. G. Boulvert, *Domestique et fonctionnaire sous le Haut-Empire romain*, 98–100. The traces of infiltration from outside the ranks of the *servi Caesaris* are rare and doubtful, see G. Boulvert, op. cit., 113, P. R. C. Weaver, *Familia Caesaris*, 36, H. Chantraine, *Freigelassene u. Sklaven*, 81–2. For the material advantages of the freedman's career see G. Boulvert, op. cit., 114–18.

13 ὀπίκια = ὀφίκια = ὀφφίκια. For π = φ cf. 6 n.; for simplification of double consonants in general see Mayser–Schmoll I i 186–191, but this one is not listed. The passages cited in S. Daris, *Il lessico latino*, s.v. ὀφφίκιον do not give another example of its use to mean 'official appointment', though this is a normal sense of the Latin word. In the papyri it is used most frequently of the bureaux of high-ranking officials.

15 οἱ⟨ἐ⟩μοί. Mr. Parsons suggests that we should perhaps write οἱ 'μοί and regard it as a legitimate use of aphaeresis, cf. Mayser–Schmoll I i 135 (§ 29. 4a), F. T. Gignac, *Grammar*, I 319–20.

19 Not κίcτην; possibly πιcτήν, with a rather broad pi; possibly ἐπιcτη. (unfinished?). I can detect no relevance to the letter.

3313. PRIVATE LETTER

48 5B.25/H(1)a   18 × 31 cm.   Second century

Apollonius and Sarapias, the senders of this agreeable letter, express their pleasure at the news of the forthcoming wedding of a young man who is presumably (see 4 n.) the son or stepson of Dionysia, the recipient. They regret that for business and health reasons they cannot attend, and then, in the most interesting section of the letter, they explain what arrangements they have made to supply flowers for the wedding.

Dionysia had ordered a large quantity of roses and 2,000 narcissi. Roses were not yet plentiful at the time. Only 1,000 could be found and, to make up for this, 4,000 narcissi were sent instead of 2,000.

In the next section Apollonius and Sarapias apparently refuse payment, saying that they love the children as if they were their own. They send greetings to the members of Dionysia's family and end the letter proper with a further assurance that they had done all they could to find as many roses as were wanted.

There follows a farewell formula probably in the hand of one of the senders. It is a practised and rapid cursive very different from the body of the letter, which is carefully written in a good upright professional-looking documentary hand. On the back is the address, written downwards along the fibres in a larger version of the first hand.

The document should probably be assigned to the second century. The main hand resembles that of the famous Gnomon of the Idios Logos, see R. Seider, *Paläographie d. gr. Papyri*, I Taf. 22, or BGU V Taf. 1, or W. Schubart, *Griechische Paläographie*, Abb. 36. This was probably written down between A.D. 149 and 160, see BGU V p. 4, though it may possibly be somewhat later, see XLII **3014** introd. The use of the term διαλογιϲμός makes it unlikely that **3313** could date from much later than A.D. 200, see 7 n.

Professor Turner would prefer to compare the hands of II **270** (Pl. VIII) of A.D. 94 and XXXI **2611** (Pl. X) of A.D. 193, which provide convenient *termini*, but he agrees with the suggested dating.

Ἀπολ[λώνι]οϲ καὶ Ϲαραπιὰϲ Διονυϲίᾳ
       (vac.)   χαίρειν.
χαρ[ᾶϲ ἡμ]ᾶϲ ἐπλήρωϲαϲ εὐαγγελιϲαμένη
τὸν γ[άμον] τοῦ κρατίϲτου Ϲαραπίωνοϲ καὶ εὐθέωϲ
5 ἂν ἤλθ[ομε]ν διακονήϲοντεϲ αὐτῷ ὡϲ ἐν εὐκταιοτάτῃ
ἡμῖν ἡμ[έ]ρᾳ καὶ ϲυνευφρανθηϲόμενοι, ἀλλὰ διὰ τὸν
δι[αλο]γιϲμὸν καὶ ὅτι ἀναλαμβάνομεν ἀπὸ νωθρείαϲ
οὐκ ἠδυνήθημεν ἐλθεῖν. ῥόδα πολλὰ οὔπω γέγο-
νεν ἐνθάδε, ἀλλὰ ϲπανίζει, καὶ ἐκ πάντων
10 τῶν κτημάτων καὶ παρὰ πάντων τῶν ϲτεφανη-
πλόκων μόλιϲ ἠδυνήθημεν ϲυνλέξαι ἃ ἐπέμ-
ψαμέν ϲοι διὰ Ϲαραπᾶ χείλια, τρυγηθέντων καὶ
ὧν ἔδει αὔριον τρυγηθῆναι. νάρκιϲϲον ὅϲην ἤθε-
λεϲ εἴχομ`εν´, ὅθεν ἀντὶ ὧν ἔγραψαϲ διϲχειλίων
15 τετρακιϲχειλίαν ἐπέμψα`μεν´. οὐ βουλόμε`θα´ δέ ϲε
οὕτωϲ κ[ατ]αγεινώϲκειν ἡμῶν ὡϲ μεικρολόγων
ὥϲτε καταγελῶϲαν γράψαι πεπομφέναι τὴν
τιμήν, ὁπότε καὶ ἡμεῖϲ ἔχομεν τὰ παιδία
ὡϲ ἴδια τέκνα καὶ πλέον τῶν ἡμῶν τιμῶμεν
20 καὶ ἀγαπῶμεν αὐτὰ καὶ οὕτωϲ χαίρομεν ἴϲα
ϲοι καὶ [τ]ῷ πατρὶ αὐτῶν. περὶ ὧν ἄλλων θέλειϲ
γρ[ά]ψο[ν ἡμ]ῖν. ἄϲπαϲα[ι] Ἀλέξανδρον τὸν
κράτιϲτον καὶ τοὺϲ ἀβαϲκάντουϲ `αὐτοῦ´ Ϲαραπίωνα
καὶ Θέωνα καὶ Ἀριϲτόκλειαν καὶ τὰ τέκνα

7 νωθρείαϲ, ε inserted in paler ink   14 εἴχομ`εν´, μ corr. from ν     15 βουλόμε`θα´, ϛ corr.
from αι   19 ἴδια   20 ἴϲα

25   Ἀριστοκλείας. μαρτυρήςει coι Cαραπᾶc περὶ τῶν ῥόδων ὅτι πάντα πεποίηκα εἰς τὸ
ὅcα ἤθελεc πέμψαι coι, ἀλλὰ οὐχ εὕρομεν.

(m. 2) ἐρρῶcθαί ce εὐχόμεθα, κυρία.

Back (m. 1) Διονυcίᾳ γυναικὶ (vac.) Ἀλεξάνδρου.

27 εὕρομεν altered from εὗρον

'Apollonius and Sarapias to Dionysia, greeting. You filled us with joy by announcing the good news of the wedding of the excellent Sarapion and we would have come immediately to serve him on a day greatly longed for by us and to share his joy, but because of the circuit sessions and because we are recovering from illness we could not come.'

'There are not many roses here yet; on the contrary they are in short supply, and from all the estates and from all the garland-weavers we could hardly get together the thousand that we sent you with Sarapas, even by picking the ones that ought to have been picked tomorrow. We had as much narcissus as you wanted, so instead of the 2,000 you wrote we sent 4,000.'

'We wish you did not despise us as misers so far as to laugh at us and write that you have sent the money, when we too regard the young people as our own children and esteem and love them more than our own, and so are as happy as you and their father.'

'Write to us about anything else you want. Give our greetings to the excellent Alexander, and to Sarapion and Theon—may the evil eye not touch them!—and to Aristoclea and to Aristoclea's children.'

'Sarapas will tell you about the roses—that I have made every effort to send you as many as you wanted, but we could not find them.'

(2nd hand) 'We pray for your health, lady.'

Back. (1st hand) 'To Dionysia, wife of Alexander.'

4 κρατίcτου. Cf. 22–3, where the same word describes the father. The usage in these places is probably to be compared with that in P. Brem. 65. 10 and P. Giss. 26. 4, where the word is applied to the well-known Apollonius, strategus of Apollonopolis Heptacomias *c.* A.D. 113–120, and appears to be simply a term of respect. Cf. W. Bauer, *Wb. zum NT*, s.v. (2).

It might possibly be equivalent to Latin *egregius*, originally used of high equestrian officials but progressively debased till it could be acquired by the Egyptian middle classes, cf. O. Hornickel, *Ehren- u. Rangprädikate*, 19–22; an especially interesting case occurs in IX **1204** 13–16 (A.D. 299). The present document is too early for this to be likely.

For *egregius* as a military title see *BASP* 13 (1976) 5–6.

Cαραπίωνοc. The bridegroom is apparently the same as the son of Alexander greeted in 23. Dionysia is the wife of an Alexander, no doubt the same one (29). The use of αὐτοῦ, rather than coῦ or ὑμῶν, in 23 perhaps suggests that Dionysia was the second wife and not actually the mother of the children of Alexander named in that sentence. This stemma will show what is envisaged, though it is conjectural to some extent:

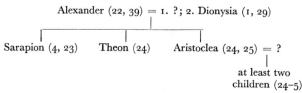

Alexander (22, 39) = 1. ?; 2. Dionysia (1, 29)

| Sarapion (4, 23) | Theon (24) | Aristoclea (24, 25) = ? |

at least two
children (24–5)

7 δι[αλο]γιcμόν. This refers to the periodic review of the financial and judicial affairs of each nome by the Roman governor, lately studied by G. Foti Talamanca, *Ricerche sul processo nell'Egitto*

romano, 1 : *L'Organizzazione del 'Conventus' del 'Praefectus Aegypti'*. See pp. 165–7 for the decline and cessation of the use of the word in this sense by about the end of the second century.

Presumably Apollonius expected to be called to appear in court.

8–9 A papyrus of the reign of Antoninus Pius (SPP XXII 183. 76) attests that the festival called Rhodophoria began in the region of Socnopaeu Nesus on Mecheir 12 = 6 February, cf. H. C. Youtie, *Scriptiunculae* i 529. This was presumably a date by which a good supply of early roses could be expected. We may deduce that our letter was written near this time of year, possibly a little earlier, since the writer says that roses were not yet plentiful.

Theophrastus (*Hist. Plant.* vi 8, 5) says that roses and other flowers were even as much as two months earlier in Egypt than in Greece. Martial (vi 80) praises Domitian's winter roses by saying that they were better than Egyptian ones.

12 Sarapas is evidently the bearer of the letter as well as the escort of the flowers, see 25–7.

13–15 The rose bloomed later than the narcissus and was the latest of the spring flowers according to Theophrastus, *Hist. Plant.* vi 8, 2.

14 εἴχομ'εν'. Cf. 15 and 27 for other corrections of the first person singular to the plural. No doubt one of the parties drafted or dictated the letter on behalf of both. In 26 a singular verb has escaped correction.

3314. LETTER OF JUDAS

36 4B.95/E(1)a   14·5 × 21·5 cm.   Fourth century

The plight of the writer, who lay injured and helpless after a riding accident, makes this letter more interesting than most. He was stranded in the Egyptian Babylon, about one hundred and twenty miles north of his home in Oxyrhynchus, after failing to find a passage on a boat. This is the letter he wrote to his father and his wife, asking the latter to come with her brother to look after him.

We might conclude from the names mentioned—Joses, Maria, Judas, and Isaac—that the letter originates from a Jewish family and circle, even though the writing indicates that it dates from the fourth century, when Christians began to use biblical names. Judas, because of the notoriety of Judas Iscariot, appears at first sight particularly improbable as a Christian name, cf. *CPJ* iii 501 introd., but Eusebius mentions a chronographer called Judas, living in the early third century, in words that make it virtually certain that he was a Christian (*H.E.* vi 7).

Moreover, in his mention of a 'cup of water' the writer may be alluding to the gospel of Mark 9 :41, see 10–11 n.

κυρίῳ μου πατρὶ Ἰωσῆ καὶ τῇ συμβίῳ μου
        Μαρίᾳ   Ἰούδας.
προηγουμένως εὔχομαι τῇ θίᾳ προνοίᾳ
περὶ τῆς ὑμῶν ὁλοκληρίας ἵνα καὶ ὑγιαίνοντας
5   ὑμᾶς ἀπολάβω. πᾶν οὖν ποίησον, κυρία μου
ἀδελφή, πέμψον μοι τὸν ἀδελφόν σου, ἐπιδὴ εἰς

ιωςη   3 l. θείᾳ   6 l. ἐπειδή

νόcον περιέπεca ἀπὸ πτώματος ἵππου.

μέλλοντός μου γὰρ cτραφῆναι εἰς ἄλλο μέρος,

οὐ δύναμαι ἀφ᾽ ἐμαυτοῦ, εἰ μὴ ἄλλοι δύο ἄνθρωποι

10 ἀντιcτρέψωcίν με καὶ μέχρις ποτηρίου

ὕδατ[ο]c οὐκ ἔχω τὸν ἐπιδιδοῦντά μοι.

βοήθηcον οὖν, κυρία μου ἀδελφή. cπουδαῖόν coι

γενέcθω ὅπωc τὸ τάχος πέμψῃς μοι, ὡς

προεῖπον, τὸν ἀδελφόν coυ. εἰς τὰς τοιαύτας

15 γὰρ ἀνάγκας εὑρίcκονται οἱ ἴδιοι τοῦ ἀνθρώπου.

ἵνα οὖν καὶ coὶ παραβοηθήcῃς μοι τῷ ὄντι

ἐπὶ ξένης καὶ ἐν νόcῳ ὄντι. καὶ πλοῖον

ἐπεζήτηca ἐνβῆναι καὶ οὐχ εὗρον τὸν

ἐπιζητοῦντά μοι. ἐν τῇ γὰρ Βαβυλῶνεί εἰμει.

20 προcαγορεύω τὴν θυγατέρα μου καὶ πάν-

τας τοὺς φιλοῦντας ἡμᾶς κατ᾽ ὄνομα.

(vac.)

καὶ ἐὰν χρίαν ἔχῃς κέρματος, λάβε παρὰ

Ἰcὰκ τὸν κολοβόν, τὸν ἔνγιcτά coι μένον[τ]α.

(vac.)

(m. 2) ἐρρῶcθαι ὑμᾶς εὔχομαι

25   πολλοῖς χρόνοις.

Back ἀπόδος cυμ.... ± 50 letters

16 l. cύ   18 l. ἐμβῆναι   19 l. Βαβυλῶνί εἰμι   22 l. χρείαν   23 l. τοῦ κολοβοῦ, τοῦ
ἔγγιcτά coι μένοντος

'To my lord father, Joses, and to my wife, Maria, Judas. To begin with I pray to the divine providence for the full health of you (both), that I find you well. Make every effort, my lady sister, send
me your brother, since I have fallen into sickness as the result of a riding accident. For when I want
to turn on to my other side, I cannot do it by myself, unless two other persons turn me over, and I have
no one to give me so much as a cup of water. So help me, my lady sister. Let it be your earnest en-
deavour to send your brother to me quickly, as I said before. For in emergencies of this kind a man's
true friends are discovered. So please come yourself as well and help me, since I am truly in a strange
place and sick. I searched for a ship to board, but I could not find anyone to search on my behalf.
For I am in Babylon. I greet my daughter and all who love us by name.'
'And if you have need of cash, get it from Isaac, the cripple, who lodges very close to you.'
(2nd hand) 'I pray for the health of you both for many years.'
Address. 'Deliver . . .'

3 θίᾳ προνοίᾳ. The divine providence appears in Christian contexts but is not specifically Christian, see M. Naldini, *Cristianesimo*, p. 14. For a Jewish example see Philo, *In Flaccum* 125; other very
similar phrases are listed in the index to Cohn's edition of Philo, s.v. πρόνοια.

6 ἀδελφή. No blood relationship is implied by his addressing his wife in this way, see S. Witkowski, *Epist. priv. gr.* 35. 1 n., H. Zilliacus, *Zur Sprache gr. Familienbriefe*, p. 31.

7 ἀπὸ πτώματος ἵππου. I have rendered this ambiguous phrase by 'as the result of a riding accident'. However, if he had meant 'when my horse fell' rather than 'when I fell off my horse', he would probably have put it more specifically. Possibly the expression deliberately avoids the direct admission that he fell off.

10–11 ποτηρίου ὕδατος. This is reminiscent of N.T. Mark 9:41, ὃς γὰρ ἂν ποτίσῃ ὑμᾶς ποτήριον ὕδατος ἐν ὀνόματι ὅτι Χριστοῦ ἐστε, ἀμὴν λέγω ὑμῖν ὅτι οὐ μὴ ἀπολέσῃ τὸν μισθὸν αὐτοῦ, cf. Matthew 10:42, καὶ ὃς ἐὰν ποτίσῃ ἕνα τῶν μικρῶν τούτων ποτήριον ψυχροῦ (ὕδατος ψυχροῦ some mss.) μόνον εἰς ὄνομα μαθητοῦ, ἀμὴν λέγω ὑμῖν, οὐ μὴ ἀπολέσῃ τὸν μισθὸν αὐτοῦ. Still, the resemblance is not sufficiently extensive to be treated as an undoubted quotation. Professor Turner has pointed out to me that the undoubted allusion to these passages in P. Abinn. 19. 8–10 is very nearly certain to be Christian, cf. P. Abinn. introd. p. 31.

For the grammar compare P. Tebt. I 56. 7–8, οὐκ ἔχομεν ἕως τῆς τροφῆς τῶν κτηνῶν ἡμῶν, P. Lond. I 77. 73, οὐκ ἔχω ἕως ἑνὸς τριμησίου, cf. Mayser II, 2 pp. 360–1, 525.

ἐπιδιδοῦντα = ἐπιδιδόντα. Cf. P. Mich. VIII 515. 2, 4 n., s.v. διδῶ.

16 See R. C. Horn, *Use of the Subjunctive*, 120–1, for other papyrus examples of commands expressed by ἵνα and ὅπως; cf. J. H. Moulton–N. Turner, *A Grammar of New Testament Greek* iii 94–5, T. Kalén, *Selbständige Finalsätze*.

19 The implication of γάρ is not perfectly clear. Babylon was the main military base in Egypt and directly on the Nile. It is hard to imagine that the difficulties of finding a boat would be greater there than elsewhere. Mr. Parsons makes the plausible suggestion that γάρ looks back to ἐπὶ ξένης (17).

22–3 παρὰ τόν κτλ. Since this letter is otherwise pretty correct, I suggest that the writer had in mind an expression such as 'go to Isaac and get it'; cf. P. Mich. VIII 476. 27, ὕπαγε παρὰ Κουρείλλαν καὶ δέξαι. As the text stands we must correct the accusatives to the genitive.

23 κολοβόν. This might mean 'crippled' or 'short' and there is also an ethnic Κολοβός, see Pape–Benseler, *Gr. Eigenn.*, s.v.

ἔγγιστα. Possibly this means 'who lodges with you'. For ἔγγιστα meaning 'chez', see D. Tabachovitz, *Études sur le grec de la basse époque*, 62–3.

24–5 The second hand is apparently Judas' own, while the body of the letter, including what amounts to a postscript, 22–3, is in the hand of a scribe.

26 The address ran the whole length of the papyrus but the surface has been stripped and the remains are too scanty to be intelligibly represented by means of the Leiden system. After ἀπόδος the next word may be συμμάχῳ, 'letter carrier', cf. P. Cair. Isid. 80. 4 n.; it is not συμβίῳ or either of the appropriate names, see 1, or any usual formula. Probably the address was complicated because Judas was isolated. Instead of catching a friend going in the right direction, the usual private postman in ancient Egypt, he had to find a stranger, who was perhaps to hand the letter on to some official messenger who would have to have detailed instructions.

IV. SUB-LITERARY TEXT

3315. Greek–Latin Glossary

36 4B.92/E(a)   4 × 11·5 cm.   First/second century

This scrap with parts of fourteen lines of Latin written in Greek letters comes from a glossary of the type described in the introduction to XXXIII **2660**. It contains parts of two sections, one on the signs of the zodiac, the other on winds. Very similar sections appear in some of the glossaries published in *CGL* Vol. iii, but in none of those do these two sections occur so close together. Nothing remains of the Greek equivalents.

The letters of the hand are upright informal capitals, clearly but not very evenly formed, with some unobtrusive serifs. It may be compared with C. H. Roberts, *Greek Literary Hands*, 10 a, b, c, and should probably be assigned to the first century, possibly to the early second.

On the back in cursive writing running across the fibres and standing upside down in relation to the writing on the front is ἔτους[or ἔτους .[.

$$
\begin{array}{ll}
& \cdot \quad\quad \cdot \quad\quad \cdot \quad\quad \cdot \\
& Cκορπιω .\ \ [\\
& Cαγιτταριους\ [\\
& Καπρικορνο[υς \\
& Ακουαριους\ [\\
5 & Πιcκης \\
& δη\ ουεντειc\ [\\
& ουεντους \\
& Ακουιλω \\
& Αυcτερ \\
10 & Αφρεικους \\
& Φαουωνιους \\
& Ουολτουρνους \\
& Cεπτεμτριω \\
& Cουβcωλανου[c \\
& \cdot \quad\quad \cdot \quad\quad \cdot \quad\quad \cdot \quad\quad \cdot
\end{array}
$$

'... Scorpio, Sagittarius, Capricornus, Aquarius, Pisces. De ventis: ventus, Aquilo, Auster, Africus, Favonius, Volturnus, Septemtrio, Subsolanus, ...'

1 *Cκορπιω .*. An extra nu would be a likely mistake for a Greek writer, but the final trace appears to be the foot of a single upright. Probably it was an intrusive iota. The previous line must have read *Λιβρα* or *Λειβρα* and could not have left any traces so low as this one. The order of the signs of the zodiac is the regular and natural one, cf. e.g. Neugebauer and Van Hoesen, *Greek Horoscopes*, p. 1.

13 *Cεπτεμτριω*. The second tau has been corrected from beta, an understandable lapse caused by a memory of 'September'. Lists of month names also appear in these glossaries. The mu has been left uncorrected and this orthography may be regarded as permissible; see Lewis & Short, s.v. septentriones.

INDEXES

Square brackets indicate that a word is wholly or substantially restored by conjecture or from other sources, round brackets that it is expanded from an abbreviation or a symbol. An asterisk denotes a word not recorded in LSJ or suppl. The article is not indexed.

I. EMPERORS AND REGNAL YEARS

AUGUSTUS

θεὸς Καῖσαρ (Year 34) **3276** 16 **3283** 15.

GAIUS

Γάϊος Καῖσαρ Cεβαστὸς Γερμανικός (Year lost) **3267** 4–5.

NERO

Νέρων Καῖσαρ Cεβαστὸς Γερμανικὸς Αὐτοκράτωρ (Year 8) **3272** introd. 2–3.
Νέρων (Years 3 and 4) [**3279** 19].

VESPASIAN

θεὸς Οὐεσπασιανός (Year 5) **3276** 10 **3277** 8 (**3278** 14) **3279** 13 **3282** 14 (**3283** 10).

DOMITIAN

Δομιτιανός (Year 11) **3283** 16.

TRAJAN

Αὐτοκράτωρ Καῖσαρ Νέρουας Τραϊανὸς Cεβαστὸς Γερμανικὸς Δακικός (Year lost) **3275** 37–9, 41–3
Τραϊανὸς Καῖσαρ ὁ κύριος (Year 3) **3274** 19, [46].
. . . Τραϊανός . . . (Year lost) **3274** 26.
θεὸς Τραϊανός (Year 1) **3276** 17.

HADRIAN

θεὸς Ἁδριανός (Year 12) **3282** 10.

ANTONINUS PIUS

Αὐτοκράτωρ Καῖσαρ Τίτος Αἴλιος Ἁδριανὸς Ἀντωνῖνος (Year 13) **3285** introd.
Ἀντωνῖνος Καῖσαρ ὁ κύριος (Year 12) **3276** 8 **3277** 7 **3278** 10 **3279** 10 **3283** 8 [**3284** 8].

ELAGABALUS

ἀνόσιος Ἀντωνῖνος μικρός (Years 1–4) **3299** 2.
Ἀντωνεῖνος ὁ κόρυφ(ος) (Year 2) **3298** 2.

SEVERUS ALEXANDER

Ἀλέξανδρος (Years 1–4) **3299** 100.

GORDIAN III

Γορδιανός (Year 6) **3298** 10, 38.

PHILIPPI

Φίλιπποι (Year 3) **3298** 19.

Decius

Δέκιος (Year 1) **3298** 22.

Gallus and Volusianus

Αὐτοκράτορες Καίσαρες Γάϊος Οὐίβιος Τρεβωνιανὸς Γάλλος καὶ Γάϊος Οὐίβιος . . . (Year 3) **3288** 12–14.

Valerian, Gallienus, and (Saloninus?)

Αὐτοκράτορες Καίσαρες Πούπλιος Λικίννιος Οὐαλεριανὸς καὶ Πούπλιος Λικίννιος Γαλλιηνὸς Γερμανικοὶ Μέγιστοι Εὐσεβεῖς Εὐτυχεῖς καὶ Πούπλιος . . . (Year 6) **3289** 19–22.

Gallienus

Αὐτοκράτωρ Καῖσαρ Πούπλιος Λικίννιος Γαλλιηνὸς Γερμανικὸς Μέγιστος Εὐσεβὴς Εὐτυχὴς Σεβαστός (Year lost) **3293** 23–6.

Aurelian and Vaballathus

Αὐτοκράτωρ Καῖσαρ Λούκιος Δομίττιος Αὐρηλιανὸς Εὐσεβὴς Εὐτυχὴς καὶ Ἰούλιος Αὐρήλιος Σεπτίμιος Οὐαβάλαθος Ἀθηνόδωρος ὁ λαμπρότατος . . . (Year 2 and 5) **3294** 14–19.

Diocletian

Αὐτοκράτωρ Καῖσαρ Γάϊος Οὐαλέριος Διοκλητιανὸς Εὐσεβὴς Εὐτυχὴς Σεβαστός (Year 1) **3295** 20–1.

Diocletian and Maximian

Αὐτοκράτωρ Καῖσαρ Γάϊος Αὐρήλιος Οὐαλέριος Διοκλητιανὸς καὶ Αὐτοκράτωρ Καῖσαρ Μᾶρκος Αὐρήλιος Οὐαλέριος Μαξιμιανὸς Γερμανικοὶ Μέγιστοι Εὐσεβεῖς Εὐτυχεῖς Σεβαστοί (Year 7 and 6) **3296** 17–19.

Diocletian and Maximian Augusti, Constantius and Galerius Caesars

οἱ κύριοι ἡμῶν Διοκλητιανὸς καὶ Μαξιμιανὸς Σεβαστοὶ καὶ οἱ κύριοι ἡμῶν Κωνστάντιος καὶ Μαξιμιανὸς οἱ ἐπιφανέστατοι Καίσαρες (Year 17 and 16 and 9) **3304** 1–3.

Galerius and Licinius Augusti, Maximinus and Constantine Caesars

ἐπὶ τῶν δεσποτῶν ἡμῶν Γαλερίου Οὐαλερίου Μαξιμιανοῦ καὶ Οὐαλερίου Λικιννιανοῦ Λικινίου τῶν ἀνικήτων Σεβαστῶν καὶ τῶν δεσποτῶν ἡμῶν Μαξιμίνου καὶ Κωνσταντίνου τῶν ἐπιφανεστάτων Καισάρων υἱῶν τῶν βασιλέων (Year lost?) **3270** 24–8.

Valentinian, Valens, and Gratian

οἱ δεσπόται ἡμῶν Οὐαλεντινιανὸς καὶ Οὐάλενς καὶ Γρατιανὸς οἱ αἰώνιοι Αὔγουστοι (no year) **3308** 9–11·

II. CONSULS

A.D. 300 ἐπὶ ὑπάτων τῶν κυρίων ἡμῶν Κωνσταντίου καὶ Μαξιμιανοῦ τῶν ἐπιφανεστάτων Καισάρων τὸ γ′ **3301** 1–2.

A.D. 301 ὑπατεί[ας Ποστουμίου Τιτιανοῦ (τὸ β′?) καὶ Οὐιρί]ου Νεπωτιανοῦ **3304** 3.

A.D. 309 ὑπατείας τῶν δεσποτῶν ἡμῶν Οὐαλερίου Λικιννιανοῦ Λικινίου Σεβαστοῦ καὶ Φλαυίου Οὐαλερίου Κωνσταντίνου υἱοῦ βασιλέων **3270** 1–3.

A.D. 313 ὑπατείας τῶν δεσποτῶν ἡμῶν Γαλερίου Οὐαλερίου Μαξιμίνου καὶ Φλαυίου Οὐαλερίου Κωνσταντίνου Αὐτοκρατόρων Σεβαστῶν τὸ γ′ **3305** 1–2.

A.D. 373 μετὰ τὴν ὑπατείαν Φλ(αουίου) Δομιτίου Μοδέστου καὶ Φλ(αουίου) Ἀρινθέου τῶν λαμ(προτάτων) **3308** 1–2.

— ὑπατείας τῶν δεσποτῶν ἡμῶν Οὐαλεντινιανοῦ καὶ Οὐάλεντος τῶν αἰωνίων Αὐγούστων τὸ δ′ **3309** 1–2.

A.D. 374 μετὰ τὴν ὑπατείαν τῶν δεσποτῶν ἡμῶν Οὐαλεντινιανοῦ καὶ Οὐάλεντος τῶν αἰωνίων Αὐγούστων τὸ δ′ **3310** 1–3.

III. MONTHS

IV. PERSONAL NAMES

Δομίττιος *see* Index I s.v. Aurelian and Vaballathus.

Δωρόθεος, Aur., alias Nilus 3308 19.

Ἑρμῖνος, *Caesaris libertus* 3312 11.

Εὐβίων, s. of Ptollion 3276 15.

Εὐδαίμων, Aur., s. of M. Aurelius Eudaemon, gd.-s. of Heracleides, m. Aurelia Nice alias Taias 3295 13.

Εὐδαίμων, Didymus alias 3307 16.

Εὐδαίμων, M. Aurelius, s. of Heracleides, gd.-s. of Dioscorus, m. Tayris, f. of Aur. Eudaemon 3295 5, 23.

Εὐδαίμων, slave of M. Antonius Spendon φορολόγος 3273 2.

Εὐμάθιος: Flavius Eumathius Parthenius, *praeses Augustamnicae* 3308 7.

Εὐστόχιος, Syrion alias, ex-gymnasiarch, late councillor of Oxyrhynchus, f. of Aurelia Serenilla [3302 2].

Ζηναγένης, Aur., strategus 3301 3.

Ζωῖλος 3269 14.

Ἡραΐσκος, s.(?) of Achil( ), b.(?) of Paysas 3300 29.

Ἡρακλ( ) 3300 26, 26.

Ἡρακλείδης 3300 4, 5.

Ἡρακλείδης, Aur., councillor of Alexandria 3287 2.

Ἡρακλείδης, f. of Demetria alias Asclatarium, gd.-f. of Sarapion 3282 4.

Ἡρακλείδης, f. of M. Aurelius Eudaemon, s. of Dioscorus, h. of Tayris 3295 6.

Ἡρακλῆς 3300 23.

Ἡρᾶς, d. of Amois, m. of Ammonius, w. of Πετ[.....]ς (gen.) 3276 7.

Ἡρᾶς, f. of Pnepheros, s. of Pnepheros, h. of Thatres 3280 2.

Ἡρώδης 3296 10.

Θ..[, f. of Aur. Copreus 3309 5.

Θαῆσις, d. of Didymus, m. of Paysiris, w. of Theon 3283 7.

Θαῆσις, m. of Amois, w. of Terentius, d. of Ptolemaeus 3278 9.

Θαῆσις, m. of Terentius, w. of Diogenes, d. of Poseidonius 3278 3.

Θατρῆς, m. of Aur. Pamunis, w. of Thonis 3292 4.

Θατρῆς, m. of Pnepheros, w. of Heras 3280 3.

Θεμόθις(?) *see* Index V(c) s.v. Θεμόθεως(?), διῶρυξ Θ.

Θεόδωρος, Aur., s. of Thonius 3311 17.

Θερμούθιον, Aurelia 3304 14.

Θέων 3313 24.

Θέων, Aur., 3287 13.

Θέων, Aur., exegetes, councillor, s. of Sarapion ex-exegetes, gd.-s. of Sarapion, b. of Aur. Theoninus alias Sarapion and of Ammonius 3289 3.

Θέων, Aur., prytanis in office 3306 3.

Θέων, Aur., s. of Sarapion, prytanis in office 3293 8.

Θέων, f. of . . . τρία 3274 3, 32.

Θέων, f. of Aur. Horion systates 3301 4.

Θέων, f. of Aur. Theon 3295 3.

Θέων, f. of Lucilla alias Theonis 3296 4.

Θέων, f. of Theon, s. of Theon, h. of Diogenus, gd.-f. of Paysiris, gd.-s. of Ammonius, gt.-gd.-s. of Theon, gt.-gt.-gd.-s. of Ammonius 3283 2, 15.

Θέων, gd.-f. of Theon, f. of Theon, gt.-gd.-f. of Paysiris, s. of Ammonius, gd.-s. of Theon, gt.-gd.-s. of Ammonius 3283 2, 12.

Θέων, patron of Plution 3275 47.

Θέων, s. of Ammonius, f. of Ammonius, gd.-f. of Theon, gt.-gd.-f. of Theon, gt.-gt.-gd.-f. of Theon, gt.-gt.-gt.-gd.-f. of Paysiris 3283 14.

Θέων, s. of Theon, gd.-s. of Theon, m. Diogenus, f. of Paysiris, h. of Thaesis, gt.-gd.-s. of Ammonius, gt.-gt.-gd.-s. of Theon, gt.-gt.-gt.-gd.-s. of Ammonius 3283 2.

Θεωνῖνος, Aur., alias Sarapion, ex-chief priest, exegetes, councillor, s. of Sarapion ex-exegetes, gd.-s. of Sarapion, b. of Aur. Theon and of Ammonius 3289 2.

Θεωνίς, Aurelia Lucilla alias, d. of Theon 3296 4, [22].

Θοῆρις *see* Index V(c) s.v. Δρόμου Θοήριδος; VI(a).

Θώνιος 3300 9.

Θώνιος, Aur., s. of Parion 3309 4.

Θώνιος, f. of Aur. Theodorus 3311 17.

Θῶνις, b. of Aphynchis/Aphynchius ποικιλτής 3300 18.

Θῶνις, f. of Aur. Pamunis, m. Thatres 3292 4.

Θῶνις, fisherman 3300 10.

Ἰούδας, h. of Maria 3314 2.

Ἰουλιανός: M. Aedinius Julianus, *praef. Aeg.* 3286 12.

Ἰούλιος *see* Index I s.v. Aurelian and Vaballathus.

Ἰσάκ 3314 23.

Ἴσεις, m. of Sabinus 3298 40.

Ἰσιδώρα 3312 4.

Ἰσιδώρα, Alexandrian, d. of Apollonius, adopted by Dionysius alias . . . onius, m. of Claudius Potamon and Claudius Apoll( ) 3271 3.

Ἰσίδωρος 3300 13.

Οὐαλεριανός see Index I s.v. Valerian, Gallienus, and (Saloninus?).

Οὐαλέριος see Index I s.vv. Diocletian; Diocletian and Maximian; Galerius and Licinius Augusti, Maximinus and Constantine Caesars; II (A.D. 309; A.D. 313).

Οὐεργίλιος: Cn. Vergilius Capito, *praef. Aeg.* 3271 1.

Οὐεςπαςιανός see Index I s.v. Vespasian.

Οὐίβιος see Index I s.v. Gallus and Volusianus.

Οὐίριος see Index II (A.D. 301).

Πα-, Aur., strategus 3293 1.

Πα..... (gen.), Aur., s. of Chous 3310 5.

Παγᾶς 3300 34.

Πάλλας(?), carpenter 3300 31.

Παμμένης see Index V(c) s.v. Παμμένους Παραδείςου.

Παμοῦνις, Aur., s. of Thonis, m. Thatres 3292 3.

Πανεςνεῦς, s. of Horus, priest 3275 3, 44.

Πανεχώτης, f. of [.....]ρις, gd.-f. of Sarapion 3279 9.

Παρθένιος: Flavius Eumathius Parthenius, *praeses* Augustamnicae [3308 8].

Παρίων, f. of Aur. Thonius 3309 4.

Πασόϊς, fisherman 3300 11.

Πατερμοῦθις, f. of Belles 3273 7.

Παυλεῖνος: Curtius Paulinus, tribune 3279 20.

Παυςᾶς, s.(?) of Achil( ), b.(?) of Heraiscus 3300 28.

Παυςῖρις 3307 15.

Παυςῖρις, s. of Theon, gd.-s. of Theon, m. Thaesis, gt.-gd.-s. of Theon, gt.-gt.-gd.-s. of Ammonius, gt.-gt.-gt.-gd.-s. of Theon, gt.-gt.-gt.-gt.-gd.-s. of Ammonius 3283 7.

Παυςιρίων, s. of . . . , gd.-s. of Aperos, m. Didyme 3279 2.

Πετεῦρις, gd.-f. of Petcyris(?), f. of Apollonius 3276 2.

Πετεῦρις(?), s. of Apollonius, gd.-s. of Peteyris, f. of Ammonius, gt.-gd.-s. of Eubion, gt.-gt. gd.-s. of Ptollion 3276 2, [20?].

Πετοςῖρις 3277 3.

Πλουτίων, freedman of Theon 3275 46.

Πνεφερῶς, gd.-f. of Pnepheros, f. of Heras 3280 2.

Πνεφερῶς, s. of Heras, gd.-s. of Pnepheros, m. Thatres 3280 2.

Ποςειδώνιος, f. of Thaesis 3278 3.

Ποςτούμιος see Index II (A.D. 301).

Ποτάμων: Claudius Potamon, s. of Isidora d. of Apollonius 3271 2.

Πούπλιος see Index I s.vv. Valerian, Gallienus, and (Saloninus?); Gallienus.

Πρειφέρνιος see Πριφέρνιος.

Πριφέρνιος: A. Prifernius Augurinus, *idiologus* 3274 1, 29 3275 10 (πρει- pap.).

Πτολ[3277 12 (cf. 2?).

Πτολεμαῖος 3307 19.

Πτολεμαῖος, Aur., alias Nemesianus, strategus 3292 1.

Πτολεμαῖος, f. of Δι[c. 10], s. of P . . . 3277 2, (12?).

Πτολεμαῖος, f. of Thaesis 3278 9.

Πτολεμαῖος, s. of Amois 3300 12.

Πτολλᾶς, Aur. 3287 5.

Πτολλίων 3274 24.

Πτολλίων, f. of Eubion, gd.-f. of Peteyris, gt.-gd.-f. of Apollonius, gt.-gt.-gd.-f. of Peteyris(?), gt.-gt.-gt.-gd.-f. of Ammonius 3276 15.

Πύρρος(?), f. of . . . m. of Peteyris 3276 3.

Πύρρος, f. of Aur. Didymus alias Sarapion systates 3301 6 [3304 4].

Ῥόδων, f. of Gemellus 3311 3.

Cαβεῖνος, s. of Isis 3298 40.

Cανκυίνιος: Q. Sanquinius . . . inius Maximus, epistrategus 3273 1.

Cαραπάμμων, Aur., hyperetes [3293 22].

Cαραπᾶς 3313 12, 25.

Cαραπᾶς, s. of Athenaeus, gd.-s. of Sarapion 3268 5.

Cαραπιάς 3300 22, 33 3313 1.

Cαραπίων 3291 1 3313 4, 23.

Cαραπίων, Aur., s. of Aphynchis 3270 4.

Cαραπίων, Aur., strategus 3289 1 3290 5.

Cαραπίων, Aur. Didymus alias, s. of Pyrrhus, systates 3301 5 3304 [4], 25.

Cαραπίων, Aur. Theoninus alias, ex-chief-priest, exegetes, councillor, s. of Sarapion ex-exegetes, gd.-s. of Sarapion, b. of Aur. Theon and of Ammonius 3289 2.

Cαραπίων, ex-exegetes, s. of Sarapion, f. of Aur. Theoninus alias Sarapion, Aur. Theon, and Ammonius 3289 5.

Cαραπίων, f. of Arsinoe, gd.-f. of Dionysius 3281 3.

Cαραπίων, f. of Aur. Theon prytanis in office 3293 9.

Cαραπίων, f. of Sarapion ex-exegetes, gd.-f. of Aur. Theoninus alias Sarapion, Aur. Theon, and Ammonius 3289 6.

Cαραπίων, gd.-f. of Sarapas, f. of Athenaeus 3268 6.

Cαραπίων, gd.-f. of Sarapion, f. of Harpocration, s. of Harpocration 3282 3, 12.

Cαραπίων, s. of Harpocration, gd.-s. of Sarapion, m. Demetria alias Asclatarium 3282 2.

Cαραπίων, s. of Paysirion, m. [.....]ρις 3279 8.

Cαραπίων, Serenus alias, royal scribe 3284 4, 6.

V. GEOGRAPHICAL

(a) COUNTRIES, NOMES, TOPARCHIES, CITIES, ETC.

Ὀξυρυγχιτῶν πόλις, ἡ λαμπρά **3294** (2), 5
Ὀξυρυγχιτῶν πόλις, ἡ λαμπρὰ καὶ λαμπροτάτη
3270 4 (**3295** 1–2) [**3296** 3, 4–5?] **3297** 2–3
[(**3301** 6)] (**3302** 2–3) (**3304** 3, 5).
Ὀξυρύγχων πόλις **3274** (5), 34 [**3275** 19] **3276** 3

[**3277** 3] **3278** 4 **3279** 3 (**3280** 3) **3281** 3
(**3282** 4) **3283** 3.
παγαρχία Τήεως **3307** 1 (παγιαρχ- pap.).
Ῥωμαῖος [**3295** 18].
Ῥώμη [**3312** 11].

(b) Villages, etc.

Ἀλβίνου (ἐποίκιον) **3307** 23.
Δωσιθέου **3307** 9, 13, 14.
Θῶλθις **3307** 7.
Κεσμοῦχις **3307** 6.
Μενε....ου (ἐποίκιον) **3307** 12.
Νεσμῖμις **3292** 5, 10.
Παλῶσις **3307** 5.
Παῶμις **3307** 4, 11.
Πέλα **3269** 3.
Πετροκί (ἐποίκιον) **3307** 16.
Cαραπᾶ (ἐποίκιον) **3307** 20.

Cενοκῶμις **3275** 4.
Cκυταλίτιδος (ἐποίκιον) **3307** 17, 18.
Coῦις **3307** 8, 21.
Cτρούθου (ἐποίκιον) **3307** 22.
Τακόνα **3273** 9.
Ταλαώ **3272** introd. 1.
Τῆις **3307** 1, 3 *see also* Index V(a) s.v. παγαρχία
  Τήεως.
Φοβόου, -ώου **3268** 11 **3287** 6.
Ψανκερμᾶ (ἐποίκιον) **3307** 24.

(c) Miscellaneous

Ἀδύμου (κλῆρος) **3288** 1.
Ἄνω Παρεμβολῆς (amphodon) **3276** 1, 21 **3277** 1,
  [5] **3278** 8
γ̄ (district of Alexandria) **3271** 6?
Δεκάτης (amphodon) **3282** 8.
Δρόμου Γυμνασίου (amphodon) **3272** 4 **3276** 14.
Δρόμου Θοήριδος (amphodon) **3272** 3.
Ἡρακλέους τόπων (amphodon) **3272** 6.
Θεμόθεως(?), διῶρυξ Θ. **3268** 9.
Ἱππέων Παρεμβολῆς (amphodon) **3279** 7 **3283** 6
  3295 9, 28.

Κυν.[**3291** 3?
Λυκίων Παρεμβολῆς (amphodon) **3272** 2.
Ματρίνου, θύραι Μ. **3270** 10, 13, [21], 24.
Μητρῴου (amphodon) **3272** 5.
Παμμένους Παραδείσου **3283** 13, 18.
Πλατείας (amphodon) **3272** 7.
Cενεμςεέ, (περίχωμα) **3270** 23.
Τανύρεως, θύραι Τ. **3269** 3 **3270** 10, [12].
....εως (κλῆρος) **3287** 9.

VI. RELIGION AND ASTROLOGY

(a) Religion

Ἄμμων **3275** 5 **3292** 7.
ἀνόσιος *see* Index I s.v. Elagabalus.
ἀποτακτικός **3311** 5, 7, 10.
ἀρχιερατεύειν **3289** 3.
Ἡρακλῆς *see* Index V(c) s.v. Ἡρακλέους τόπων.
θεῖος **3308** [9], 16 (θι- pap.) **3314** 3 (θι- pap.).
θεός **3275** 5 **3276** 10 **3277** 8 **3278** 14 **3279** 13
  3282 10, 14 **3283** 10, 15 **3292** 8 *see also* Index I
  s.vv. Augustus, Vespasian, Trajan, Hadrian.
Θοῆρις **3275** 28 *see also* Index V(c) s.v. Δρόμου
  Θοήριδος.

ἱερεύς **3275** 5, 28 [**3292** 6].
ἱερόν **3275** 6, 15 **3292** 9.
ἱερός **3272** introd. 2 **3288** 11 **3307** 14.
μέγιστος **3275** 5 **3292** 8.
Μητρῷον *see* Index V(c) s.v. Μητρῴου.
ὅρκος **3275** 40, 46 **3295** 19, 24 **3308** [9], 16.
πρόνοια, ἡ θεία **3314** 3.
προφήτης **3292** 6.
σεβάσμιος **3308** 8.
συνιερεύς **3275** 8, 18.
σύνναος **3292** 8.

(b) Astrology (see also Index XII)

VII. OFFICIAL AND MILITARY TERMS AND TITLES

VIII. PROFESSIONS, TRADES, AND OCCUPATIONS

IX. MEASURES

(a) Weights and Measures

(b) Money

X. TAXES

XI. GENERAL INDEX OF WORDS

ἀφῆλιξ 3295 17.
ἀφιστάναι 3302 12.

βασιλεύς 3270 3, 28.
βασιλικός see Index VII s.v. βασιλικὸς γραμματεύς.
βαφεύς see Index VIII.
βεβαιοῦν [3270 17].
βενεφικιάριος see Index VII.
βία 3302 19 3311 12.
βιάζεσθαι 3302 4, 12.
βίαιος 3302 6.
βιβλίδιον 3289 15 (βιβλειδ- pap.).
βιβλίον 3289 13 3301 11.
βίος 3311 10.
βοήθεια 3311 15.
βοηθεῖν 3314 12.
βορρᾶς (3300 9, 33, [35]).
βούλεσθαι 3285 14 3295 7 3302 12 3313 15.
βουλευτής see Index VII.
βουλή see Index VII.
βουλημάτιον 3311 9.

γ̄ see Index V(c).
γάμος [3313 4].
γάρ 3302 5 3314 8, 15, 19.
γειν- see γιν-.
(-)γειν- 3302 32.
γένεσις 3298 1, 18, 21, 40.
γενναῖος see Index VII.
γένος [3276 6] [3277 4] 3278 7 [3279 6] [3281 6] 3283 5 3284 6 3311 8, 15.
γεωργεῖν 3288 2.
γίγνεσθαι 3311 6 see also γίνεσθαι.
(-)γιν- 3302 32 (γειν- pap.).
γίνεσθαι 3275 29, 32 3276 10, 11 3277 [8], 10 3278 13 3279 [12], 15, 22 3282 13, 16 3283 7, 10, (11), 17 3286 7 (3287 10) 3289 12, 14 3292 10 3295 10 3301 12 3302 (2), 8, 9, 11, 18 3304 13 (3307 25) 3310 7 3312 12 3313 8 3314 13; cf. 3311 6 (γίγνεσθαι).
γινώσκειν 3289 12 3296 9 3312 10.
γνῶσις 3301 10?
γονεύς 3282 7 3302 5.
γράμμα 3275 49 3295 27 3296 14 3311 18 see also Index IX(a).
γραμματεύς see Index VII s.v. βασιλικὸς γραμματεύς; VIII.
γράφειν 3275 9, 47 3285 12, 27, 31 3290 13 3295 26 (3298 42) 3308 19 [3311 18] 3312 6 3313 14, 17, 22.
γραφή (3276 16) 3279 23 3283 15, 18 3295 16.
γυμνασιαρχεῖν see Index VII.
γυμνασιαρχία see Index VII.

γυμνασίαρχος see Index VII.
γυμνάσιον see Index V(c) s.v. Δρόμου Γυμνασίου; VII s.v. and s.v. δωδεκάδραχμος.
γυνή 3295 11 3313 29.

δανειστής 3274 15, [43].
δέ 3267 10, 12 3270 18 3271 4?, 4 3273 9 3275 16, 33 [3276 17] 3283 17 3285 2, 3, [11], [14], 18, [22], 24, 25, 28, 29, 32, [35], 38, 43 3288 2, 3 3289 9 3294 13 3296 8 3304 16 3307 2 3311 6, 8, 10 3313 15.
(-)δεικνύναι 3302 26?
δεῖν 3284 5 3285 26, [31?] 3293 11 3302 3 3304 24 3313 13.
δεκατέσσαρες 3270 14.
δεσπότης 3303 8 [3305 1] 3308 9 3309 1 3310 1 see also Index I s.vv. Galerius and Licinius Augusti, Maximinus and Constantine Caesars; Valentinian, Valens, and Gratian; II (A.D. 309; A.D. 313; A.D. 373; A.D. 374).
δηλοῦν 3274 14, [41] 3276 10 3277 8 3278 13 3279 12 3282 12 3283 9 3284 7 3293 10.
δημοσίᾳ 3304 [10?], 21.
δημόσιος [3302 15] see also Index X.
διά 3269 11, 14? 3270 11 3271 1 3274 [4], 32 3286 2 3287 2 3290 3 3293 6, 8 3295 2, 15 3296 10, [20] 3301 [12?], 14 3302 9, 18 3303 4 3304 21 3310 8 3311 6, 12 3313 6, 12.
διαδικασία 3302 9.
διαθήκη 3289 11.
διακονεῖν 3313 5.
διακόσιοι [3268 13?].
διακρίνειν [3285 30].
διαλαλεῖν 3296 10.
διαλογισμός see Index VII.
διαπέμπειν 3291 4.
διάσημος see Index VII.
διατιθέναι 3274 13.
διατρίβειν 3285 26 (διατρειβ- pap.).
διαφέρειν 3293 19 3297 11 3302 22.
διδόναι 3287 11 3294 9 3302 10.
διευτυχεῖν [3302 24].
δίκαιον 3302 3.
δίκαιος 3302 15.
δικαστής 3285 5, 20, [25], 35 3302 10.
διό 3295 14 [3302 17?].
διοικεῖν see Index VII s.v. φυλαρχία.
διοικητής see Index VII.
δισχίλιοι 3313 14.
διῶρυξ 3268 9.
δοκεῖν 3274 11, [39] 3285 [9?] 3302 17.
δραχμή see Index IX(b).
δρόμος see Index V(c) s.vv. Δρόμου Γυμνασίου, Δ. Θοήριδος.

δύνασθαι 3288 9 3302 22 3311 15 3313 8, 11
　3314 9.
δυνάστης 3302 6.
δύο 3271 1 3314 9.
δωδεκάδραχμος see Index VII.

ἐάν 3285 [11], [14], [18], [22], 24, [25], [28], [32],
　[35], [38], 40, 43 3314 22.
ἐᾶν 3311 4?
ἑαυτοῦ 3285 29, 30, 33, 39 3289 7 see also αὑτοῦ.
ἔγγιστα 3314 23 (ενγ- pap.).
ἐγγράφειν 3273 5 3294 10.
ἐγκρατής 3304 17.
ἐγχεῖν 3285 35.
ἐγώ 3270 1, 10, 18, 21, 24, [26] 3274 [10], 11, 15,
　[17], 38, 39, [42], [44] 3275 18 3276 6, [14],
　[17] 3277 5 3278 8, (15) 3279 8, 17, [21] 3282
　12 3283 6, 12, 15, 17, 19 3284 5 3286 9 3288 8
　3289 8, 9, 10, 17 3290 3, 10 3291 3 3293 5
　3295 8, 10, 10 3296 8, 11, [20] 3301 1, 8
　3302 4, 4, 6, 7, 10, 11, 12, 13, 17, 18 3303 7
　3304 [1], [2] [3305 1] 3308 6, 9, 11 3309 1
　3310 1, 8, 8 3311 3, 6, 8, 14 3312 6 3313 [3], 6,
　16, 18, 19, [22] 3314 1, 1, 5, 6, 8, 10, 11, 12, 13,
　16, 19, 20, 21.
ἔδαφος 3287 9.
ἐθέλειν see θέλειν.
ἔθιμος 3295 18.
εἰ 3276 6 (ἤ) 3277 4 (ἤ) 3278 6 (ἤ) 3279 6 (ἤ)
　3280 5 (ἤ) [3281 6] 3282 6 3283 5 3285 [5?]
　3289 16 3301 9 3302 17, 26 (ι pap.) 3314 9.
εἶ (μήν) 3285 46.
εἰδέναι 3275 49 [3293 17] 3295 26 3304 13, 21
　3311 18.
εἶδος 3279 19.
εἴκοσι 3296 16.
εἶναι 3269 14 3270 9 3271 6 3273 9 3274 18, [45]
　3275 6, 32, 40 3276 6, [16] [3277 4] 3278 6
　3279 6 3280 5 [3281 6] 3282 7 3283 5, 14
　3284 5, 8 3285 2, 4, 6, 19, 25, 29, [29?] 3289
　16 3292 9, [14] 3293 14 3294 13 3295 13
　3296 15 3304 17, 19, 23 3307 2 3311 3, 3, 7,
　10, 11, 13, 14 3312 8 3314 16, 17, 19.
εἰρήνη [3302 17].
εἱρκτή [3302 14?].
εἰς 3273 3, [6] 3276 5, 7, 17 [3277 4, 6] 3278 6, 10
　3279 6, [9, 11] [3280 5] 3281 5 3282 6, 9
　3283 5 [3284 8] 3285 35, 39 3286 9 3287 7
　3290 8, 11 3294 8 3296 7 3298 3, 11, 20, 43
　3302 11 3308 12 3310 7 3312 11 (ιc pap.)
　3313 26 3314 6, 8, 14.
εἷς 3274 [18], [45] 3296 17.
εἰσάγειν 3302 11.
εἰσδιδόναι 3273 3.

εἰσφέρειν 3288 11.
εἰχθυνηρά see Index X s.v. ἰχθυνηρά.
εἰχθῦς see ἰχθῦς.
ἐκ 3269 11 3274 6, 35 3275 24, 31 3276 5, [13]
　3277 [4], 11 3278 6 3279 6 3280 5 3281 6
　3282 6 3283 5 3284 6 3290 9 3295 10 3296 6
　3301 7 3306 6 3311 2, 7, 8, [15], 15 3313 9.
ἕκαστος 3288 6 3289 7 3294 12 [3301 11?].
ἑκάτερος 3267 7, [9].
ἐκβαίνειν 3268 8.
ἐκεῖσε 3308 13.
ἐκκαλεῖν 3296 11.
ἔκκλητος 3296 15, 24? (ἐκλ[= ἐκ⟨κ⟩λ[ητ-?).
ἑκουσίως 3268 6 3270 8.
ἐλθεῖν 3313 5, 8.
ἐμαυτοῦ 3282 11 3314 9.
ἐμβαίνειν 3314 18 (ενβ- pap.).
ἐμμέλεια see Index VII.
ἐμός 3312 15 (οιμοι = οἰ ⟨ἐ⟩μοί pap.).
ἐμφα[3304 12 (ενφα[pap.).
ἐμφανίζειν 3304 17 (ενφα- pap.).
ἐν 3269 6 3270 21, 22 3271 6 3273 3 3275 6, [19]
　3276 16 3279 18, 19, 22 3283 14, 18 3285 15,
　25, 25, 40, 40 3286 8 3289 12, 16 3292 [9], 10
　3295 17 3297 8 3302 15, [23] 3304 3 3310 7
　3313 5 3314 17, 19.
ἔναρχος see Index VII.
ἔνατος 3304 2.
ενγ- see ἐγγ-.
ἐνθάδε 3284 5 3313 9.
ἐνιστάναι 3269 2 3276 8 [3277 6] 3278 10 3279 10
　3283 8 3286 7 3294 7 3295 2, 14 3296 5, 7.
ἔνοχος 3275 39 3308 15.
ἐντυχία 3302 7 (-εια pap.).
ἐνφανίζειν see ἐμφανίζειν.
ἐξαίφνης [3292 15].
ἐξακόσιοι 3296 16.
ἐξαπατᾶν 3304 14.
ἐξεῖναι 3267 13.
ἐξετάζειν 3284 7.
ἐξέτασις 3301 11.
ἐξηγητεύειν see Index VII.
ἐξηγητής see Index VII.
ἐξουσία 3308 6 3311 5.
ἐπαγόμεναι see Index III.
ἔπαρχος see Index VII.
ἐπαχθῶς 3302 4.
ἐπεί 3292 10 3302 21? 3303 9? 3311 9.
ἐπειδή 3296 5 3302 11 (επιδη pap.) 3304 8, 19
　3314 6 (επιδη pap.).
ἐπελθεῖν 3292 12.
ἐπερωτᾶν 3270 20 3285 5 [3296 23].
ἐπί 3267 5 3269 4, 13 3270 24 3274 8, 36 3275 36
　[3276 14] [3277 5] 3278 7 3279 7, 18 3282 8

3283 6, 12, 16 **3285** 27 **3289** 8, 9 **3292** 13 **3295** 8 **3300** 6, 30, 33 **3301** 1 **3302** 21?, 23 **3307** 25 **3308** 11 **3314** 17.

ἐπιγιν- **3302** 21?

ἐπιδεικνύναι **3285** 6, 9, 11, [11?], [18?], 20, 20, 26 **3289** 15.

ἐπιδέχεςθαι **3268** 7 **3270** 8.

ἐπιδιδόναι **3273** 15 **3274** 16, 44 **3295** 14, 23 **3296** 21 **3311** 17 **3314** 11 (ἐπιδιδουντα pap.).

ἐπιδοχή **3270** 18, [20].

ἐπιζητεῖν **3301** 7 **3314** 18, 19.

ἐπικ[**3304** 6.

ἐπικαλεῖν **3286** 11.

ἐπικρίνειν [**3275** 35] **3276** 13 **3278** 14 [**3279** 16, 20] **3282** 13 **3283** 12, 16.

ἐπίκριςις see Index VII.

ἐπιςκοπεῖν **3285** 34.

ἐπίςταλμα **3284** 7.

ἐπιςτέλλειν **3287** 6 **3290** 7 **3293** 6, 20 [**3297** 12].

ἐπιςτολή **3275** 12 (**3291** 3?) **3296** 6, 8.

ἐπιςτολιμαῖος **3296** 14.

ἐπιςτράτηγος see Index VII.

ἐπιςτρέφεια **3304** [7], 19? (-φειου pap.).

*ἐπιςτρέφειος **3304** 19?

ἐπιτάςςειν **3303** 6.

ἐπιτηρητής see Index VII.

ἐπιτίμηςις **3304** 16.

ἐπιτιμία **3304** 24.

ἐπιτρέπειν [**3302** 18].

ἐπίτροπος (guardian?) **3296** 6 see also Index VII (procurator).

ἐπιφανής see Index I s.vv. Diocletian and Maximian Augusti, Constantius and Galerius Caesars; Galerius and Licinius Augusti, Maximinus and Constantine Caesars; II (A.D. 300).

ἐπιφέρειν **3276** 14 **3283** 13 [**3293** 22] **3296** 6.

ἐπιχείρηςις **3304** 23.

ἐπιχωρεῖν **3285** [9?], 16.

ἐποίκιον **3307** 12, (14–20), (22–24) see also Index V(b) passim.

ἐποικιώτης **3307** 10.

ἑπτακόςιοι **3287** 10.

ἐργαςία **3308** 13, 17.

ἐργατεία **3267** 6.

ἕςτε [**3308** 15].

ἕτερος **3273** 7 **3289** 10 **3300** 29.

ἔτι **3275** 16 **3289** 5 **3302** 5, 13.

ἔτος **3267** 4 **3272** introd. 4 **3274** [19] **3275** 13, [40?] [**3282** 9] **3302** 25 [**3304** 1] **3315** introd. (ἔτος) **3269** 2 **3274** 46 [**3275** 40?] **3276** 8, 10, 16, 17 [**3277** 7, 8] **3278** 10, 13 **3279** 10, 13, 19, 19 **3282** 14 **3283** 8, 10, 14, 16 [(**3284** 8)] **3287** 12 **3288** 12 **3289** 19 [**3293** 23] **3294** 7, 7, 14, 17 **3295** 2, 14, 14, 20 **3296** 17, 18 **3298** 2, 10, 19,

22, 38 **3299** 3, 20, 48, 72, 101, 126, 149, 177 [(**3304** 2)].

εὐαγγελίζεςθαι **3313** 3.

εὐεργέτης **3274** 14, 42.

εὐθετεῖν **3273** 6.

εὐθέως **3291** 1, 4 **3313** 4.

εὐκταῖος **3313** 5.

εὔπορος **3273** 6.

εὑρίςκειν **3285** 40 **3291** 1 **3313** 27 **3314** 15, 18.

Εὐςεβής see Index I s.vv. Valerian, Gallienus, and (Saloninus?); Gallienus; Aurelian and Vaballathus; Diocletian; Diocletian and Maximian.

Εὐτυχής see Index I s.vv. Valerian, Gallienus, and (Saloninus?); Gallienus; Aurelian and Vaballathus; Diocletian; Diocletian and Maximian.

εὔχεςθαι **3293** 21 (**3297** 13) **3312** 17 **3313** 28 **3314** 3, 24.

ἐφιςτάναι **3304** 23.

ἔχειν **3267** 9 **3269** 6 (**3270** 33?) **3284** 7 **3300** 4, 9, 11, 12, 15, 16, 19, 21, 22, 24, 26, 27, 32 (all ἐχο(μένη)), 35 (ἐχό(μενον)) **3304** 15, 16 **3313** 14, 18 **3314** 11, 22.

εχθ( ) **3298** 4?

ἔχθεςις (**3270** 32?).

ἕως **3285** 37 [**3293** 13] **3297** 7.

ἤ **3270** 11 [**3275** 39] **3285** [7?] **3298** 43 **3308** 15.

ἡγεμονία see Index VII.

ἡγεμών see Index VII.

ἡμέρα **3286** 8 [**3296** 5] **3297** 8, 9 **3298** [23], 39 **3304** 17 **3313** 6.

ἡμέτερος **3289** 5 **3301** 11 **3302** [12], 20.

ἡμίςεια **3274** 12, 14, [40].

ἥμιςυς **3267** 10 (**3275** 26?, 26?, 27?).

ἡςςᾶν **3285** 14.

ἤτοι **3295** 11.

θεῖος (divine) see Index VI(a).

θεῖος (uncle) **3311** 3, 5.

θέλειν **3313** 13 (ἤθελες), 21, 27 (ἤθελες).

θεός see Index I s.vv. Augustus, Vespasian, Trajan, Hadrian; VI(a).

θῆλυς **3304** 15.

θῖος see Index VI(a) s.v. θεῖος.

θυγατήρ **3296** 4 **3302** 2 **3314** 20.

θύρα **3268** 11 **3269** 3, 6 **3270** 10, 11, 12, 21, [23] (all lock-gates) **3285** [39], 41, 42 (all doors).

ἰ see εἰ.

ἰδία [**3302** 23].

ἴδιος **3285** 41 **3288** 7 **3289** 8 **3313** 19 **3314** 15 see also Index VII s.v. ἴδιος λόγος.

ἰδιόςπορος (**3287** 8).

ἱερεύς see Index VI(a).

XII. LATIN

PLATE I

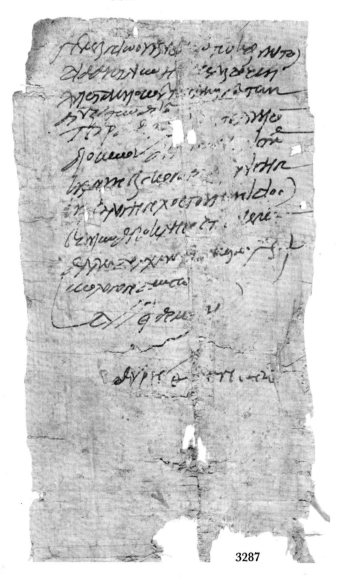

3267

3269

3297

3287

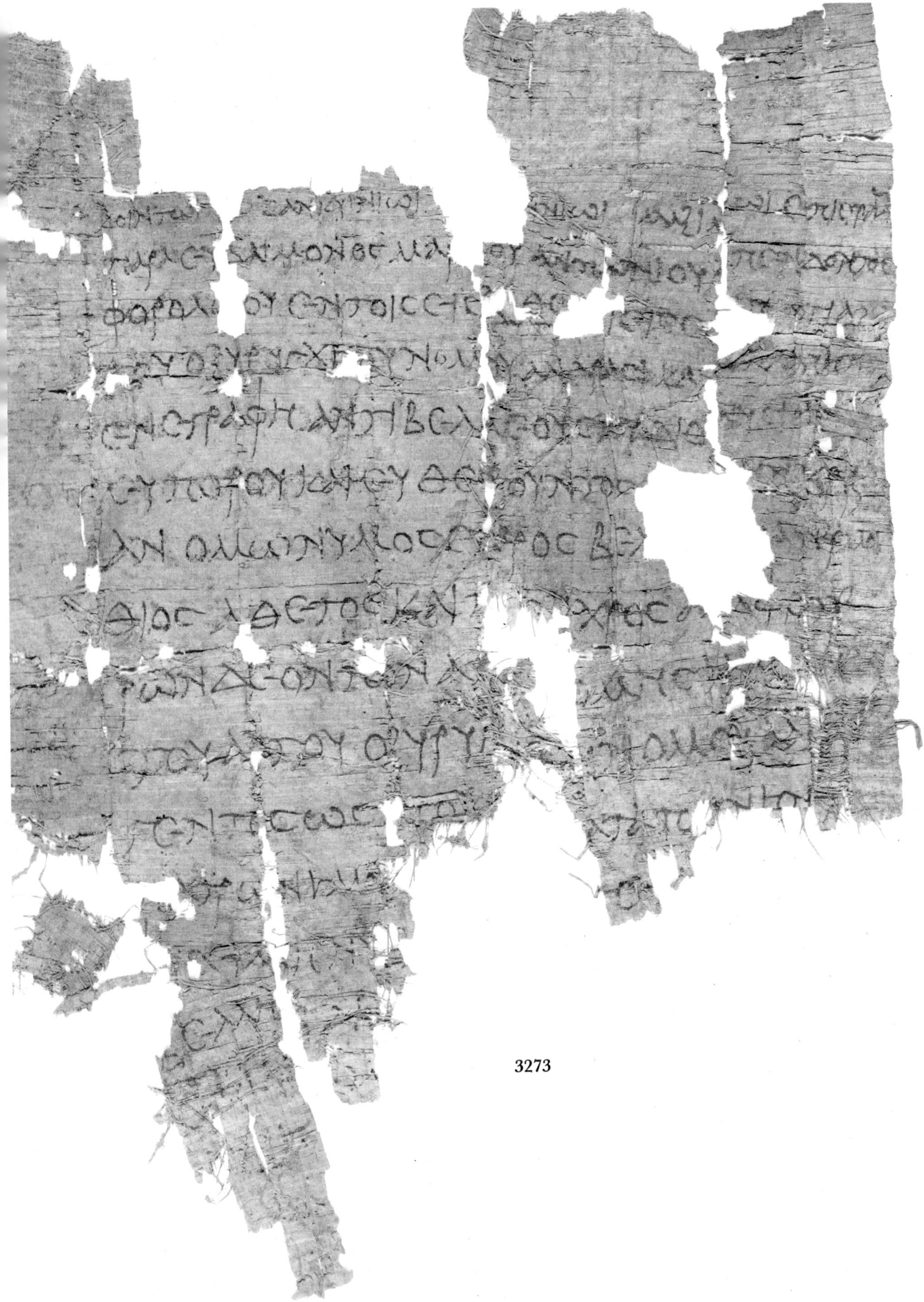

PLATE II

3273

PLATE III

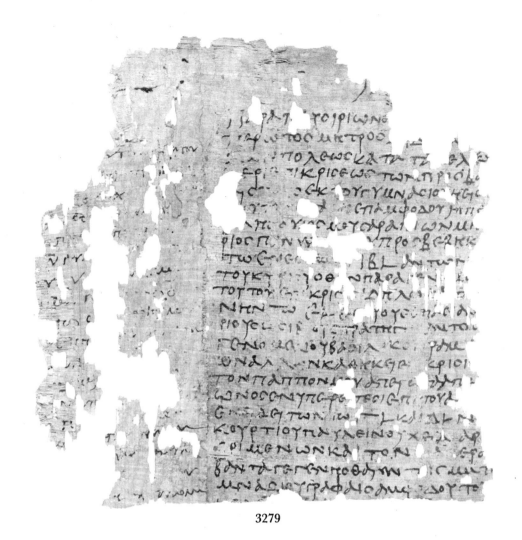

3279

3271

3286

PLATE IV

3285, fr. 1

3285, fr. 2

3288

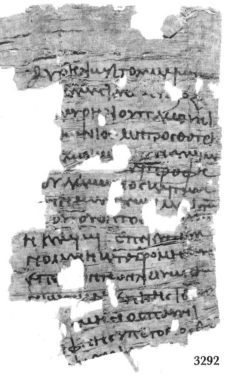

3292

PLATE V

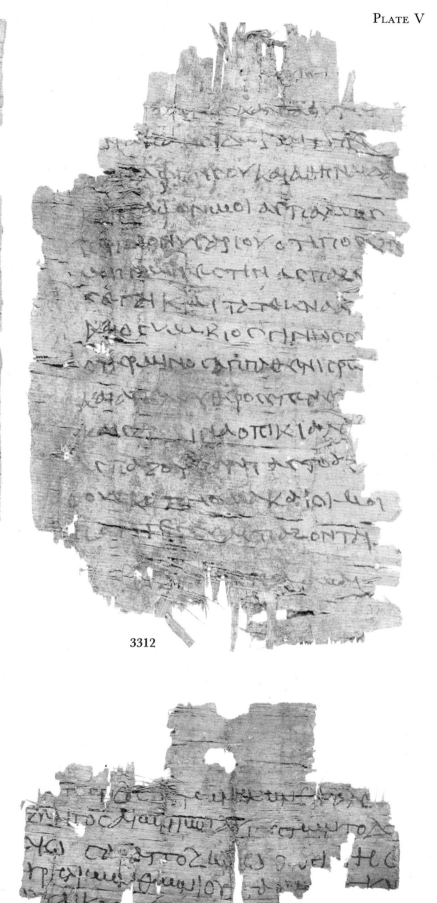

3312

3300

3309

PLATE VI

ο ε...ωσαρατιας διανοια

ΧΗΡΕΙ

...ΠΝΙρωεδ...ε...ΓΓΕ...
...ΟΥΚΡΑΤΙΣΤΟΥΣΑΡΑΤΙΩΝΟΣΕΚ...ΕΙΟΥ...
...ΔΙΑΚΟΝΗ...ΤΕΣΑΥΤΟ...ΩΣΕ...ΚΤΑΔΙ...
...ΛΕΥΝΕΥΦΡΑΝΘΗΣΟΜΕΝΟ...ΛΔΙΔΙΟΝ
...ΟΝΚΑΙ...ΕΝΛΑΛΑΙΛΑΜΒΑΝΟΜΕΝΑΠΟΤΩΝΩΡΙΩΝ
...ΙΣΗ...ΕΝΕΛΘΕΙΝΡΟΔΑΤΟΛΛ...ΟΥ...ΩΣΓΕΤΟ
ΝΕ...Η...ΛΛΑΣΤΩΝΙ...ΕΙΚΑΙΕΚΤΩΝΤΩΝ
...ΚΑΙΠΑΡΑΤΤΑΝΤΩΝΤΩΝΟΣΤΕΦΑΝΗ
...ΜΔΥΝΗΘΩΜΕΝΟΥΝΛΕ...ΔΕΤΕΙΜ
...ΡΑΤΑΧΕΙΝΔΤΡΙΗΘΕΝΤΩΝΚΑΙ
...ΤΗ...ΘΗΝΑ...ΝΑΡΚΥΣΣΟΝΟΣΗΝΗΘΕ
...ΙΤΙΩΝΕΓΡΑΤΑΣΥΣΧΕΙΜΩΝ
...ΟΥΕΣΤΙΟΜΕΙΔΕΣ...
...ΕΙΣΚΕΙΝΗΜΩΝΩΣΑΛΕΙΚΡΟΛΟΓΩΝ
...ΛΩ...ΑΝΤΡΑΤΔΙΤΕΤΟΛΦΕΝΔΙΠΗ
ΤΗ...ΗΝΟΤΙΣΟΤΕΚ...ΗΛΜΗΣΕΧΟ...ΕΝΤΑΤΑΙΔ...
...ΤΛΕΟΝΤΩΝΝΕΚ...ΟΥΝΤΙΑΙΩΝΕΝ
...ΜΕΝ...ΤΚΑΛΟΥΤΩΣΧΑΙΡΟΜΕΝΙΣΔ
...ΤΡΙΑΣΤΩΝΤΕΡΙΩΝΔΛΛΩΝΕ...
...ΛΠΤΙΑΣ...ΛΛΕΞΩΝΔΡΟΝΤΟΝ
...ΛΝ...ΟΤΣΑΡΑΤΙΩΝΔ
...ΕΔΑΝΙΚΡΙΤΑΤΕΚΝΔ
...ΕΑΡΤΗΡΗΟΥΣΟΙΡΑΡΑΤΑΣΤΙΣ
...ΤΑΡΕΤΣ ΗΚΛΕΙΣΤΟ
...ΝΛΟΥΧΕΙΡΟΜΕΝ

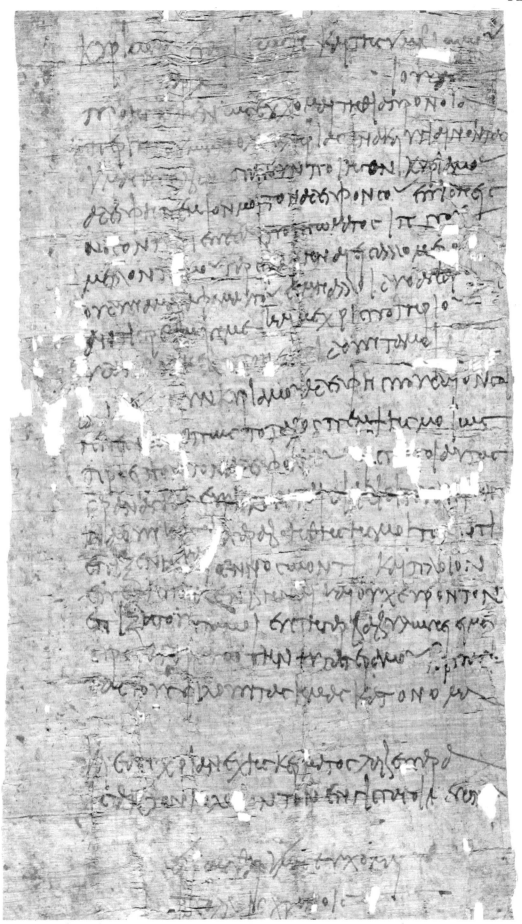

PLATE VII

PLATE VIII

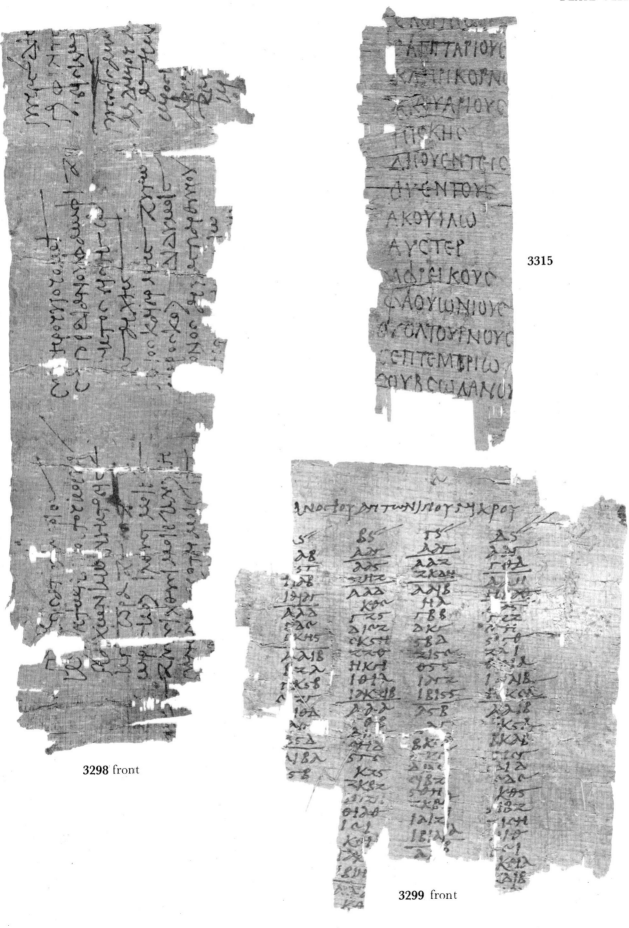

3298 front

3315

3299 front

2007.06.22   (9.15)